T0271334

The RMB Exchange Rate

Past, Current, and Future

The RMB Exchange Rate
Past, Current, and Future

Yin-Wong Cheung

City University of Hong Kong, Hong Kong

Kenneth K Chow

Hong Kong Institute for Monetary Research, Hong Kong

Fengming Qin

Shandong University, China

NEW JERSEY · LONDON · SINGAPORE · BEIJING · SHANGHAI · HONG KONG · TAIPEI · CHENNAI · TOKYO

Published by

World Scientific Publishing Co. Pte. Ltd.

5 Toh Tuck Link, Singapore 596224

USA office: 27 Warren Street, Suite 401-402, Hackensack, NJ 07601

UK office: 57 Shelton Street, Covent Garden, London WC2H 9HE

Library of Congress Cataloging-in-Publication Data
Names: Cheung, Yin-Wong, author. | Chow, Kenneth K., author. | Qin, Fengming, author.
Title: The RMB exchange rate : past, current, and future / Yin-Wong Cheung (City University of
    Hong Kong, Hong Kong), Kenneth K Chow (Hong Kong Institute for Monetary Research,
    Hong Kong), Fengming Qin (Shandong University, China).
Description: New Jersey : World Scientific, 2016. | Includes index.
Identifiers: LCCN 2016026892 | ISBN 9789814675499 (hbk : alk. paper)
Subjects: LCSH: Renminbi. | Foreign exchange--China. | China--Economic policy--2000–
Classification: LCC HG3978 .C449 2016 | DDC 332.4/50951--dc23
LC record available at https://lccn.loc.gov/2016026892

British Library Cataloguing-in-Publication Data
A catalogue record for this book is available from the British Library.

Copyright © 2017 by World Scientific Publishing Co. Pte. Ltd.

All rights reserved. This book, or parts thereof, may not be reproduced in any form or by any means, electronic or mechanical, including photocopying, recording or any information storage and retrieval system now known or to be invented, without written permission from the publisher.

For photocopying of material in this volume, please pay a copying fee through the Copyright Clearance Center, Inc., 222 Rosewood Drive, Danvers, MA 01923, USA. In this case permission to photocopy is not required from the publisher.

Desk Editors: Dr. Sree Meenakshi Sajani/Dong Lixi

Typeset by Stallion Press
Email: enquiries@stallionpress.com

Printed in Singapore

Contents

Preface

The re-entering of China to the global stage has shifted gravity towards East Asia. The economic reform initiative masterminded by the legendary Deng Xiaoping has put the Chinese economy on a strong growth trajectory. The reform efforts are quite uneven across sectors — the progress in financial sectors has noticeably lagged behind the production and trade sector. The uneven development pattern, however, does not prevent China from transforming its inefficient and autarkic economy into the largest trading nation and, by purchasing power parity measures, the largest economy in the world in about three decades.

It is perhaps not a surprise for China to promote the global acceptance of its currency, the renminbi (RMB), by leveraging its growing economic strength and influence in the international trade. When China hinted its desire to seek the overseas use of the RMB after the global financial crisis, skeptics abound about the prospects of the RMB's global role. China's underdeveloped financial markets and stringent capital controls are obvious hindrances for its currency to become a global currency. The prospect is also undermined by the fact that China's financial reform has been progressed in fits and starts.

Nonetheless, a few optimists point to China's economic prowess and do not consider an international RMB a hyperbole. Indeed, the global use of the RMB is gaining traction despite its penetration of the international financial market has concentrated in the area of cross-border trade settlements. And, the RMB's growing influence on the global economy is well illustrated by strong market responses to China's change in its RMB central parity formation mechanism in August 2015.

China's policy making emphasizes independence, gradualism, and controllability. In preparing this monograph, we recognized these features are embedded in the history of China's exchange rate policy. Thus, after an overall view of China's recent economic performance, we provide a succinct recount of the evolution of China's exchange rate policy in the last few decades. Then we focus on the issues surrounding the arguments about RMB valuation and the arrival of RMB to the global financial market. Of course, the selection of the topics reflects our own tastes and experiences. We do not pretend to give an encyclopedic treatment on China's exchange rate policy and the RMB. We hope, however, the reader gets some clear-headed analysis of issues behind debate about the Chinese currency.

We are indebted to our coauthors for sharing their valuable knowledge via our previous collaborative works, our colleagues for their insightful and constructive comments and suggestions, the hospitality of institutions that provided a nice environment for us to work on parts of the manuscript, and individuals who helped us collect some data and prepared some graphs. Their valuable inputs are indispensable for the completion of the manuscript. Of course, we are responsible for any remaining deficiencies. We also would like to thank colleagues at World Scientific who patiently and professionally guided us through the publication process.

Cheung gratefully acknowledges the Hung Hing Ying and Leung Hau Ling Charitable Foundation for their generous support.

About the Authors

**Yin-Wong Cheung** is the Hung Hing Ying Chair Professor of International Economics, Department of Economics and Finance, City University of Hong Kong. Concurrently, Cheung is the Professor Emeritus of the Economics Department at the University of California, Santa Cruz, and a Chair Professor of the Shandong University. He obtained his Bachelor, Master, and PhD degrees, respectively, from the University of Hong Kong, the University of Essex, and the University of Pennsylvania. His areas of research include econometrics, applied econometrics, exchange rate dynamics, asset pricing, output fluctuation, and economic issues of Asian Economies.

**Kenneth K Chow** obtained his Bachelor and M Phil Degrees in Economics from the Chinese University of Hong Kong, and Master of Statistics from the University of Hong Kong. He is an Assistant Manager of the Hong Kong Institute for Monetary Research (HKIMR), which is a research arm of the Hong Kong Monetary Authority (HKMA). He is currently conducting macroeconomic research relating to Hong Kong capital flows, financial stability of Hong Kong, the RMB internationalization, and the Chinese monetary policy.

Fengming Qin obtained her Bachelor and Master degrees in Economics from Shandong University, and PhD from Xiamen University of P. R. China. Currently she is the Professor of International Economics, in Department of Finance, Shandong University. Her major research interests are international trade and finance, comparative financial system, and regional economic and finance integration.

Chapter 1

Introduction

When Deng Xiaoping, the then paramount leader of China launched economic reforms in 1978, the world did not pay much attention, and took it as another campaign by the Communist Party. However, the significance and benefit of the reform initiative unfolded as China has kept up its efforts to implement economic reforms. The interplay of startling economic performance and deepening reform efforts in the subsequent years have reminded people what the French leader Napoleon Bonaparte said almost two centuries ago: "Let China sleep, for when the Dragon awakes, she will shake the world."[1]

For a period of over one hundred years that spanned from the late Qing dynasty to the early stage of the People's Republic of China, China experienced a dormant phase in economic growth. During this period, China was inflicted with domestic conflicts, civil wars, and foreign aggressions including the Japanese invasion. Before the 1978 reform program, China was an economically backward country with limited ties with the rest of the world. Deng's program of *Gaige Kaifang* (改革開放), which literally means "reforms and opening up," set the stage for China to reenter the global community. The policy slogan highlights the two basic elements of the policy shift — enhance the efficiency of the economy and connect it to the global market.

---

[1] Napoleon's aphorism was cited in various ways. For instance, when Xi Jinping referred to it in 2014 in France, "lion" is used instead of "dragon."

1

A notable premise of Deng's *Gaige Kaifang* program is to enhance economic efficiency under the communist paradigm, and the goal is to transform the system to a form of socialism with Chinese characteristics. It is an ambitious agenda with no historical precedence. Despite the ebb and flow, China has made impressive advances in lifting the standard of living of its populace. For instance, between 1979 to 2014, the Chinese real economy grew 26-fold in local currency terms and 45-fold when the measurement is done with the notion of purchasing power parity (PPP). The blistering growth has propelled China to the league of the largest economies in the world. Mirroring its brisk growth, China's real output per capita increased 18 times in local currency terms and 48 times in PPP terms. The performance numbers are quite impressive for a populous country like China.

On the "opening up" front, China has also made some astonishing achievements. With its continuous opening up efforts, China has evolved from an almost autarkic economy to a major trading nation in the world. The open-door policy under the reform initiative has altered China's self-reliance and isolation stance. By 2009, China eclipsed Germany to become the largest exporting country in the world. In another three years, China overtook the US and became the largest trading nation, a title that the US had held on for over six decades. These records were set against the backdrop of the Chinese trade being just 7% of that of the US back in 1979. In addition, China has become a major player in the global capital market — she is among the league of top foreign direct investment recipients and providers.

Besides the trade arena, China has been strengthening its roles in the international monetary system since the turn of the 21st century. Specifically, China has stepped up its efforts to promote the international use of its currency, the renminbi (RMB). With its increasing economic strength and trade network, the global financial system is anxiously awaiting the emergence of the Chinese currency. There are different interpretations of China's concerted action to promote the cross-border use of the RMB. One possible motivation is that the policy is part of the overall financial liberalization program with the side-effect of reducing China's reliance on the US-centric global financial system.

China has been quite active in establishing the infrastructure — first in Hong Kong followed by other financial centers around the world — for deploying the RMB in the global monetary system. Leveraging on its extensive trade network, China started with encouraging the use of the RMB to settle cross-border trade. The effort has paid off quite well. Back in January 2012, the RMB was the 20th most used world payments currency by value (SWIFT, 2013). By 2015, it became the fifth most commonly used currency (SWIFT, 2015a). The stellar trade settlement performance affirms that the currency RMB is progressing steadily to dominate China trade in the near future and to become a global currency. The role of the RMB in the global financial system was vindicated by the International Monetary Fund's (IMF) decision in November 2015 to admit the Chinese currency to its special drawing rights currency basket.

China's ascent as the world's economic power may be unexpected but is definitely felt. For instance, with its massive trade activity, China's exports, especially its exports of manufactures, put substantial pressures on the competing industries in the importing countries. The huge run up of commodity prices around the turn of the 21st century and the subsequent price volatility were commonly attributed to China's fluctuating demand for natural resources and raw materials along its growth cycle. As China is increasingly integrated with the world, the global economy is becoming increasingly susceptible to developments in China's financial sector. A recent case in point was the widespread global responses to the turmoil in the Chinese equity market and the change in the RMB fixing mechanism.

The implications of China's phenomenal rise are not confined to economics alone as economic matters are closely related to, say, political matters. While the intention of introducing market forces to the planned economy is quite transparent, China's communist background does not help to dispel concerns about possible hidden agenda behind its expansion and about the making of a regional or global hegemony. At the same time, to protect its growing economic interests overseas, China is getting assertive in matters concerning international order.

In the last three decades or so, China actively participated in various international organizations and played the role of a responsible stakeholder. Circumstantial evidence, however, suggests that China's development has outgrown, at least, some existing international organizations, which were mostly formed under the influences of incumbent powers, especially the US. At the same time, the traditional powers have not been totally receptive to China's emerging roles in the international arena. For instance, the US policy of "rebalancing" toward Asia is widely seen as a policy of reining in and confining China's influence in the region. At the same time, China did not hesitate to establish international organizations on its own terms. The success of launching the Asian Infrastructure Investment Bank in 2015 is a well-cited example of the Chinese effort. Over time, China is likely to assert far-reaching influences on the landscapes of international economic order and geopolitics.

Against this backdrop, the book attempts to provide a succinct and up-to-date, albeit selective, account of China's exchange rate policy. China's economic success has put its public policies in the limelight. The stake of ignoring China increases when the Chinese economy grows remorselessly. As the largest trading nation and the second largest economy, China has become a systemic important economy in the world.

The RMB's exchange rate is the price at which the Chinese economy is linked to the rest of the world. It was under close scrutiny when China's trade surplus surged in the early 2000s and reached a high of 10% of gross domestic product (GDP) in 2007. As China's trade surplus expands, complaints abound about China's predatory foreign exchange policy. Specifically, China is accused of artificially depressing the value of the RMB to gain unfair advantages in the global market. Such a policy afforded China huge trade surplus and ballooned its holding of foreign exchange reserves, and, at the same time, led to severe global imbalances and triggered global financial crisis. Since then, debates on the RMB have come up in different forms and from different perspectives.

Since 2010, the focus has gradually shifted from the valuation to the internationalization of the RMB. When China revealed its initiative to develop the role of the RMB in settling cross-border transactions in the late 2000s, skeptics pointed to China's severe capital control policy and questioned the effectiveness of the initiative. Despite some gloomy skeptics, the outcome of the RMB internationalization strategy is clear. Retrospectively speaking, given China's success in reforming its trading sector, its shift to financial market reform is not surprising. The promotion of the overseas use of the RMB is part of the concerted effort to liberalize China's financial markets.

There are differing views on the role of the RMB and its prospects in the global monetary system. Nevertheless, China's efforts in reforming financial markets and liberalizing the exchange rate are recognized by IMF when it anointed the RMB the fifth currency of its special drawing rights currency basket. If China is plotting a "RMB zone" to challenge the US-centric financial system, which has dominated the international monetary system after the World War II, the special drawing rights status offers some ammunition.

To set the stage for discussing China's exchange rate policy, Chapter 2 overviews a few select economic triumphs that China has accomplished after launching its reform in 1978. The focus is not on explaining the causal links between reform measures and economic performance. For our purposes, we highlight China's increasing importance in the global market by offering quantitative measures of its growth experiences in its economy, international trade activity, and foreign direct investment flows.

China's efforts in uplifting its economy have deep implications not only for itself, but for the global economy. The rapid rise of China has changed international economic balance, the international order, and geopolitics. Undoubtedly, China's role in the international community has grown together with its economic strength. In Chapter 2, we note that China has gradually evolved from a passive to an active stakeholder of the existing international order. Further, it is willing to establish its multilateral organizations to carry out its own economic development agenda.

Before discussing the recent issues on valuation and internationalization of the RMB, Chapter 3 provides a brief history of China's foreign exchange policy. We do not give a detailed account of China's policy making and its changes since the currency was introduced back in 1948. We, however, attempt to succinctly point out the main policy characteristics in selected historical periods. Not surprisingly, the formulation of China's exchange rate policy reflects the political philosophy and agenda prevailing in these historical periods. A possibly oversimplified characterization is that, in setting the exchange rate policy, the weight of economic factors has been gaining over time at the expense of political considerations during the post-1978 reform era.

Further, similar to reform measures introduced in other sectors of the economy, the evolution of exchange rate policy has displayed one or a combination of these Chinese policy characteristics, namely, independence, controllability and practicability, and gradualism. Recognizing these policy elements helps to interpret China's policy on its currency, the renminbi, including its recent initiatives to promote the international use of its currency, and to revamp the exchange rate formation mechanism.

Chapter 4 is devoted to the debate on whether the RMB is overvalued or not. The RMB valuation is a contentious international issue triggered by China's escalating trade surplus and foreign exchange reserve holding in the 2000s. Exchange rates are prices that affect flows of goods, services, and capital across national borders; as a consequence, they affect domestic and overseas economic activities. Despite their importance, a style fact of exchange rate economics is that we do not have a commonly agreed model to explain exchange rate behavior consistently across currencies and over time.

Instead of arguing whether the RMB is misaligned (over- or undervalued), the chapter employs basic economic reasoning to assess some basic currency valuation issues. If one accounts for uncertainties associated with modeling and empirical estimation, the evidence on RMB misalignment has to be interpreted with great caution. In essence, there is a high level of impreciseness attached to RMB misalignment estimates found in most studies. Despite the complaint against RMB undervaluation has subsided since the IMF asserted the currency is no longer undervalued in May 2015, the discussion in this chapter raises the awareness against drawing conclusions on exchange rate misalignment without referring to the high level of uncertainty surrounding a misalignment estimate.

Since the 2008 global financial crisis, China has intensified its efforts to promote the global role of the RMB. Just over the last few years, the world has witnessed a rapid increase in the use of the RMB in, say, cross-border trade settlement. While China's capital control policy and premature domestic financial markets invite skeptics, it is hard to underestimate the potential impacts of RMB internationalization on the international monetary architecture, geopolitics, and geoeconomics. Chapters 5 and 6 recount various aspects of the use of the RMB in the global system. First, we provide some background information of a global currency, and the policy shift to internationalize the RMB. Second, we outline and discuss the main promotional policies including the introduction of offshore RMB trading that facilitate the cross-border use of the currency. Then, we evaluate the current status of the offshore RMB market and the level of international use of the RMB, and assess the future prospect of the RMB to be a global currency.

Some concluding remarks are offered in Chapter 7.

Chapter 2
The Chinese Economy

While the middle kingdom may not have the oldest continuous civilization, it has its glorious days in the history. In addition to China's ancient contributions to science,[1] it was a dominating economic powerhouse in the premodern times. For instance, Maddison (1998) estimates that China had per capita GDP higher than Europe before 1280, and accounted for 23.2% to 32.4% of world output from years 1700 to 1820. China was connected to the rest of the world via both ground and marine trading routes, and was one of the major global trading centers. During the *de facto* silver standard era of the 16th and 17th centuries, China incurred huge trade surpluses and accumulated one-fourth to one-half of total world production of silver at that time.[2] Note that silver was the settlement currency of international trade during the silver standard period.

These glorious days only aggravate China's resentment toward the political and economic humiliations that inflicted China in the 19th and 20th centuries. The fall of the historical giant was attributed to both domestic and foreign factors. Despite the blame on corrupt Qing dynasty, the imperialist repression and exploitation of foreign powers are conceived to be devastating forces that brought the Chinese economy to a halt, if not a collapse.

---

[1] See, for example, Joseph Needham's series of books (1954–2004) on China's achievements in science and technology. A concise description is found in, for example, Merson (1990).

[2] See Sakakibara and Yamakawa (2003a, 2003b) and the references cited there.

Against this backdrop, the communist People's Republic of China established in October 1949 had curtailed its political and economic links with most countries in the capitalist world. In the 1950s, its relationship with the Soviet Union also cooled off due to ideological disputes. During its first three decades, the communist China was quite isolated from the main global economy stage; it was proud of being "self-reliant" in building its economic and political structures.

The policy of isolation or self-reliance took a big turn when the US lifted trade embargo and China joined the United Nations in 1971. In the 1978 National Party Congress, China officially acknowledged its policy directive of reforms. Literally, the policy directive is dubbed "改革開放" (*Gaige Kaifang*), which literally means "reforms and opening up."[3] The change in policy stance has critically defined the tone of China's economic reforms in the subsequent decades and transformed China's political and economic relationships with the rest of the world.

2.1 The Post-1978 Era

The year 1978 is a watershed in the modern history of China's economic development. Before the reform, the Chinese economy was stuck at a low level of per capita GDP and was among the league of low-income countries. For instance, its real per capita GDP ranking was at the low level of 115 in 1970.[4]

The reform initiative has created opportunities. In the pursuit of economic reforms to build a modern country, China has experienced a tremendous growth momentum. Since 1978, China has been gradually transited from a planned economy toward a market-oriented one, and from an agricultural economy to an industrial one. More importantly,

---

[3] Specifically, the reform agenda advocated in the Third Plenum of the 11th National Congress of the Communist Party of China (December 22, 1978) was summarized by the so-called four modernizations — the modernization of agriculture, industry, science and technology, and the military — that aim to build a modern China with the so-called socialism with Chinese characteristics. See, for example, Rosen (1999) and OECD (2005) for accounts of the open door policy and its implications.

[4] Based on World Bank data available via the website http://knoema.com/WBWDIGDF 2015Aug/world-development-indicators-wdi-august-2015.

China has evolved from a virtually closed economy to a major player in the global market. Its accession to the World Trade Organization (WTO) in 2001 reaffirmed China's determination to join the international trade club and integrate with the rest of the world.

In 35 years between 1979 and 2014, China established itself as the world's factory, occupied a significant position of the global production chain, built an extensive trade network, and grew from a very minor player to the largest trade country in the world. China's growing trade prowess has benefitted from its populous workforce and the huge influx of foreign direct investment.[5] The rapid expansion of production has pushed up demand for raw materials and created opportunities for countries exporting natural resources. At the same time, the surge in China's exports has created stiff competition in the global export market, especially in the manufacturing sector. The ballooning Chinese manufacturing industry, indeed, is blamed for hollowing out the manufacturing sectors in the other countries.[6]

During the 1997–98 Asian financial crisis, Asian countries, including Thailand and Malaysia, sharply devalued their currencies to spur their weakened exports and economic growth. China at that time maintained its stable currency policy and did not succumb to competitive devaluation. The policy commitment is viewed as a sign of China's willingness and ability to contribute to the stability of the regional and global economy. It is asserted that the stable RMB exchange rate helped to rein in the contagion crisis effect. After the crisis, China has continued its efforts to reform its economy.

China's phenomenal growth in trade and its economy attract both praises and criticisms. For instance, China is commended for improving the living standards of its vast populace and supporting regional growth. In addition to hollowing out and pulverizing the manufacturing sector of other economies, China is accused of manipulating the RMB exchange rate to gain unfair advantages in the global market. The exchange rate

---

[5] It is noted, however, the population of ages between 15 and 64 started to fall in 2012, indicating that China's demographic dividend is diminishing.

[6] See, for example, Cabinet Office, Government of Japan (2002, Chapter 3), Hu *et al.* (2002), and Pritchard (2001).

manipulation leads to a number of global issues including "deflation" in the global market, and the severe global imbalance that triggered the 2007–08 global financial crisis. Arguably, China's exchange rate policy is one of the most debated policy issues in the global community around the turn of the 21st century. We discuss the RMB exchange rate policy in the next few chapters.

After growing remorselessly for three decades, China's export-cum-investment-led economic strategy is facing a number of challenges. For instance, compared with a low starting point in the 1980s, China has to overcome a strong headwind to further expand its already large market share overseas. In the meanwhile, China has to face competition from other upcoming low production cost countries in, for example, Southeast Asia and Africa.

Since the 21st century, Southeast Asian countries including Bangladesh, Cambodia, and Vietnam have become viable alternatives to China for foreign direct investment, especially in low-end manufacturing industries. At the same time, the African continent has become a serious contender for foreign direct investment from China and the rest of the world. Countries such as Rwanda and Ethiopia are keen to tout an edge in cheap labor, against the backdrop of rising wages and worker shortages in China. Anecdotal evidence suggests that the monthly wage in Africa is just about US$50 and is likely to stay at a very competitive level in the coming decades. The figure compares quite favorably with, say, the minimum monthly wage of RMB1,808 (around US$295) in Shenzhen, China. Of course, two natural alternatives for China to sustain its economic performance are (a) to move up the quality ladder and (b) to switch to a consumption-led model.[7]

Following impressive strides in upgrading its economy through expanding trade, China has pushed on with its reform efforts on revamping financial markets in the 21st century. Financial liberalization can be viewed as the second leg of the overall economic reform. In the first phase, China has been developing and expanding its production capacity, exporting manufactures, and integrating with the rest of the world. In the second phase, China is strengthening its financial infrastructure, exporting capital,

---

[7] See, for example, Benkovskis and Wörz (2015), Dorrucci *et al.* (2013), Fu *et al.* (2012), and Pula and Santabárbara (2011) on quality improvement and consumption-led growth.

and integrating with the global monetary system. A well-functioning financial sector improves resource allocation and enhances economic efficiency. The liberalization of the financial sector, which is relatively underdeveloped in China, can provide an additional growth engine.

In the rest of the chapter, we discuss the basic economic conditions in China. The RMB exchange rate policy — an important component of China's financial liberalization policy — will be discussed in the subsequent chapters.

2.2 Blistering Growth

Since the inception of the economic reform era, China has been on a quite phenomenal growth trajectory.[8] Figure 2.1 shows China's real GDP in local currency from 1979 to 2014. Similar data of four Asian economies (Hong Kong, Taiwan, Korea, and Singapore) and two advanced economies (Japan and US) are included. To facilitate comparison, the data are

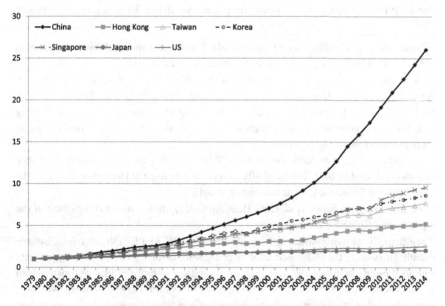

Figure 2.1   Real GDP in Local Currency (1979 = 1)

[8] An earlier recap of China's economic performance is provided in Cheung, Chinn and Fujii (2007a)

normalized to 1 in 1979. Clearly, the Chinese economy outperformed all the other economies. The gaps between China's real GDP and those of other economies appear to be widened in the 21st century.

Indeed, in the three-and-half decades from 1979 to 2014, the Chinese economy, in local currency real terms, grew 26-fold, and delivered an average annual growth rate of 9% (Table 2.1, Panel A).[9] The growth was over 10% for the period 1991–2014, and was close to 10% in the 21st century.[10] These growth numbers dwarf those of the vibrant Asian economies, which have an average growth rate between 5% and 7%, and of the two advanced economies that fetched average growth rates below 3%. The phenomenal growth is sometimes dubbed the China "economic miracle," which is compared with the strong growth experiences of, say, Japan in the post–World War II period and the four little dragons in the 1970s to early 1990s.[11]

The growth comparison is even more striking when data adjusted for purchasing power parities (PPPs) are used. Panel B of Table 2.1 presents the GDPs and their growth rates derived from PPP-based data provided by the World Bank.[12] Specifically, when the size of the economy is measured on the PPP basis, the Chinese economy grew 45-fold in 35 years, and overtook

---

[9] Cheremukhin *et al.* (2015) based on a standard two-sector model showed that, during 1953–1978, China's GDP grew at a respectable annual rate of 5.6%.

[10] There are concerns about the reliability of the official growth data; see, for example, Fernald *et al.* (2015), Henderson *et al.* (2012), Holz (2004), Klein and Ozmucur (2003), Koch-Weser (2013), Rawski (2001, 2002), and Wang and Meng (2001). Even Keqiang Li, before he became the Premier, was cited of saying local GDP data were "man-made and therefore unreliable," *The Economist* (2015a).

China in December 2005 revised its GDP upward after the first National Economic Census conducted in 2004. The latest official revision was done in December 2014 after the third National Economic Census conducted in 2013.

[11] See, for example, Cheung *et al.* (2007a). Smith (2015) offers a recent comparison of the Japanese and Chinese economies.

[12] See http://data.worldbank.org/indicator/NY.GDP.PCAP.PP.CD/countries?display= default. In essence, the PPP-based GDP data are internationally comparable output data compiled using internationally comparable price indices — called PPPs — estimated from surveys conducted by the International Comparisons Program. The PPP between two countries is defined as "the rate at which the currency of one country needs to be converted into that of a second country to ensure that a given amount of the first country's currency will purchase the same volume of goods and services in the second country as it does in the first," International Comparison Program (2004). See, also, World Bank (2008a, 2008b, 2015).

Table 2.1   Real Gross Domestic Product

	China	Hong Kong	Taiwan	Korea	Singapore	Japan	Unites States
A. Real GDP (local currency, million)							
1979	2,105,040	412,286	2,014,890	165,887,200	39,813	262,430,031	6,466,200
1991	6,017,120	919,811	5,193,846	462,954,800	98,308	438,590,224	8,948,400
2002	17,563,600	1,310,705	9,559,334	921,759,000	189,283	477,914,900	12,908,800
2014	54,791,461	2,144,645	15,492,144	1,426,540,300	380,585	527,227,400	16,085,600
Growth Rate (% p.a.)							
79–14	9.73	5.08	6.13	6.48	6.82	2.14	2.67
91–14	10.06	3.88	5.05	5.29	6.17	0.93	2.48
02–14	9.89	4.04	4.26	4.00	5.93	0.81	1.86
B. GDP (PPP $, million)							
1979	386,284	28,681	57,512	93,084	12,152	945,531	2,545,449
1991	1,231,239	108,624	229,527	367,525	74,503	2,518,990	6,174,050
2002	4,427,492	190,779	520,677	901,907	176,804	3,382,971	10,977,525
2014	17,617,321	397,507	1074,525	1,778,823	452,686	4,750,771	17,418,925
Growth Rate (% p.a.)							
79–14	12.78	7.92	8.83	9.53	9.51	4.78	5.68
91–14	12.32	6.01	7.20	7.45	8.34	2.99	4.57
02–14	12.11	6.13	6.35	6.09	8.06	2.83	3.90

Note: Real GDP in local currencies and PPP-based GDP in selected years and their average annual growth rates over the 1979–2014, 1991–2014, and 2002–2014 periods are reported.
Source: CEIC, and IMF World Economic Outlook Database, World Bank.

the US to become the largest economy in 2014. Of course, when the market exchange rate is used to compare GDP data, the US is still the largest economy in the world. Despite different views existing on the relevance of market-based or PPP-based data, and on the implication and significance of being the largest economy, the sheer speedy ascendant to the top of the league is a quite astonishing accomplishment for the Chinese authorities.[13]

---

[13] For discussions on China overtaking the US, see, for example, Frankel (2014), Pethokoukis (2014), Giles (2014), *The Economist* (2014), and Carter (2014). Ruoen and Kai (1995) presented an early comparison of the Chinese and US GDP using purchasing power parity adjusted data.

Echoing its growth momentum, China's real GDP per capita also has exhibited a strong performance since 1979. As evidenced in Figure 2.2, the improvement in China's real output per capita compares quite well relative to the four Asian economies and two developed economies. In local currency, China's real output per capita has an annual growth rate of 8.74% between 1979 and 2014. The growth in the 21st century is higher than that before (Figure 2.2 and Panel A of Table 2.2). The four newly developed Asian economies and the two developed economies, during the same period, have an average growth rate between 1 to 5.5%.

When the output is measured with PPP-based data, China's relative performance is even better — the real output per capita increased over 48-fold and has a growth rate over 11% (Panel B of Table 2.2). With the prolonged growth differential, China has caught up quite a lot with these economies in the last three-and-half decades. For instance, China's per capita GDP is only 2% of the US figure in 1979, and is about 24% in 2014. Nevertheless, because of its very low initial value, China is still poor in

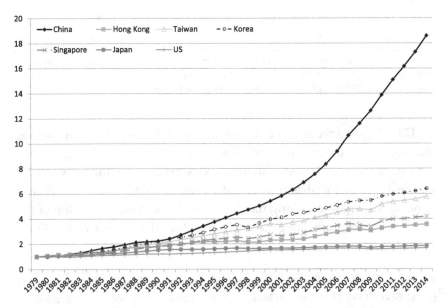

Figure 2.2   Real GDP per Capita in Local Currency (1979 = 1)

Table 2.2 Real Per Capita Gross Domestic Product

	China	Hong Kong	Taiwan	Korea	Singapore	Japan	Unites States
A. Real per capita GDP (local currency)							
1979	1,449	85,188	114,854	4,419,624	16,704	2,259,309	38,883
1991	3,489	162,884	252,057	10,692,858	31,357	3,534,139	46,655
2002	9,154	197,961	424,467	19,355,666	45,327	3,748,764	59,014
2014	26,949	302,712	661,304	28,290,924	69,580	4,148,686	64,594
Growth Rate (% p.a.)							
79–14	8.74	3.76	5.17	5.52	4.24	1.78	1.48
91–14	9.25	2.87	4.44	4.58	3.62	0.81	1.33
02–14	9.35	3.46	3.90	3.50	3.70	0.82	0.76
B. Per capita GDP (PPP $)							
1979	265	5,749	3,639	2,163	7,502	7,782	11,680
1991	1,063	18,679	11,139	8,489	23,764	20,328	24,366
2002	3,447	28,365	23,120	18,939	42,339	26,549	38,114
2014	12,880	54,722	45,854	35,277	82,762	37,390	54,597
Growth Rate (% p.a.)							
79–14	11.99	6.89	7.72	8.53	7.47	4.81	4.70
91–14	11.48	4.99	6.58	6.72	5.74	2.86	3.52
02–14	11.52	5.51	5.98	5.58	5.78	2.83	3.01

Note: Real per capita GDP in local currencies and per capita PPP-based GDP in selected years and their average annual growth rates over the 1979–2014, 1991–2014, and 2002–2014 periods are reported.
Source: CEIC, and IMF World Economic Outlook Database, World Bank.

terms of per capita income after a 35-year economic growth marathon. According to the World Bank data, China's per capita GDP in PPP ranked the 92th in 2014.[14]

In passing, we note that neither the size of the economy nor the per capita income offers a comprehensive welfare measure of an economy. The focus on the size and average income overshadows some economic and

---

[14] See http://data.worldbank.org/indicator/NY.GDP.PCAP.PP.CD/countries?display=default. China's rank is 88 according to the US$ based GDP data, http://data.worldbank.org/indicator/NY.GDP.PCAP.CD

societal issues that typically come along with rapid economic growth. China's experience is of no exception. Some side effects of China's rapid growth include the adverse impact on environment, inefficient uses of resources, unbalanced regional and provincial growth, and worsening income inequality.

The unbalanced growth and inequality, specifically, are lethal sources of social tensions that could be cumulated to political instability and unrest. Even though the economic reform has improved the general standard of living in China, the distribution of economic gains is uneven across regions and income classes.[15] Further, income inequality leads to inequalities in education opportunities and health care provisions that have adverse impacts on the economy.

According to the official Gini coefficient index, income inequality has been alleviated since the index reached a peak of 0.491 in 2008. The official figures are 0.469 for 2014, 0.473 for 2013, and 0.474 for 2012.[16] Despite the encouraging trend, China's official Gini coefficient — which is deemed to understate the degree of inequality — is quite large among developed countries, and higher than the informal warning mark of 0.4. To be fair, China, especially in the recent years, has implemented social and industrial policies to narrow the income gap, say, between the urban and rural areas, and between the coastal and inland provinces. The effort is reflected in the recent downward trend of the official Gini coefficient. Nevertheless, to create an equitable society, China has some serious work to do to improve income distribution across regions and citizens, which in turn, will lead China to a sustainable economic growth trajectory.[17]

---

[15] Some studies on uneven growth and inequality are Aziz and Duenwald (2001), Cevik and Correa-Caro (2015), Démurger *et al.* (2002), Fujita and Hu (2001), Jian *et al.* (1996), Jones *et al.* (2003), OECD (2010), Sicular (2013), Li, Sato and Sicular (2013), Xie and Zhou (2014).

[16] The Gini index implies "perfect" equality when it has a value of 0 and "perfect" inequality — one person takes all — when it assumes a value of 1.0. After an interruption of 12 years, China resumed in 2013 its release of the official Gini coefficient index. The 2012 official index, however, is quite noticeably lower than the 2010 figure of 0.61 estimated by the Chinese Household Finance Survey Center of Chengdu's Southwestern University of Finance and Economics. Before 2012, the latest officially published figure is 0.412 for 2000.

[17] See, for example, OECD (2015) and OCED (2013).

2.3 Trade Giant

In early 2013, the headline of China overtaking the US as the world's largest trading country affirmed its formidable strength in the world trade platform. China's total foreign trade (the sum of exports and imports) in 2012 surpassed the US total. Before that, the US was the world's biggest trading nation for over six decades.[18] Indeed, a main ingredient of the 1978 reform initiative is to end China's isolation policy and open it to the world. The open-door policy is proved to be a very potent dose of stimulus to the then sluggish Chinese economy.

Starting with preferential treatments for exports and foreign direct investment, China has set off a steady expansion in trade and foreign direct investment flows, albeit the initial amounts are meager and mostly with Hong Kong and other neighboring economies. The strong foundation of China's trade was gradually established around the manufacturing industry in the 1980s and 1990s; with capital, technical know-how, and management skills afforded by the continuous influx of foreign capital. China dramatically expanded both the scale and scope of its trading activities with the rest of the world and solidly established its prominent role in trade in the 2000s.

Figure 2.3 illustrates China's performance in trade between 1979 and 2014. The total foreign trade is given by the sum of exports and imports.[19] For comparison purposes, total foreign trade data of four Asian economies (Hong Kong, Taiwan, Korea, and Singapore) and two advanced economies (Japan and US) are included, and the data are normalized to 1 in 1979. Some specific trade data including total trade, exports, and imports are presented in Table 2.3. The figure clearly shows that, during these three-and-half decades, China's foreign trade growth dwarfed these economies by a wide margin. In the decade after the inception of reform initiative, China's expansion in the trade sector, though was higher than Japan and the US, was comparable with the four newly industrialized economies.

---

[18] China has been the largest exporters since 2009.
[19] The growing importance of global production chains makes it difficult to use the conventional trade data to examine, say, China's global trade share. Benkovskis and Wörz (2015), for instance, show that even allowing for the value-added and other issues of measuring trade performance, China's gain in global trade share is substantial.

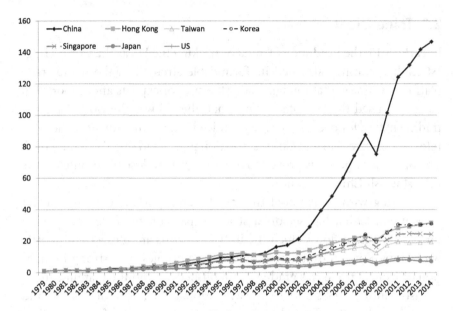

Figure 2.3   Total Trade (1979 = 1)

It started to take off in the 1990s, possibly benefiting from the concurring globalization trend and China's strategic position in the global production chain. The accession to the WTO in 2001 supercharged China's trade activity; the world witnessed China grew its trade sector in the 21st century by an astonishing average annual rate of 18%, which is far higher than the growth rates of the other economies in Table 2.3.

China's growth in trade can be illustrated from a few perspectives. For instance, between 1979 to 2014, China grew its total trade by over 145 times, exports by over 170 times, and imports by over 124 times; each category grew with an annual average rate of 16% or higher. The growth rate average is higher after joining the WTO in 2001.

Compared with the US and Japan, China's trade volume in 1979 was US$29,330 million, which is only about 7% of the US or 14% of the Japanese volumes. In a relatively short period of 33 years, China took over the crown of the world's largest trade nation — a position that the US held for over 60 years — in 2012. In 2014, China's total trade volume is 6.7% larger than that of the US and almost three times that of Japan. Similarly, China's trade grew much faster than the four vibrant Asian economies

Table 2.3   External Trade, Exports, and Imports (US$ million)

	China	Hong Kong	Taiwan	Korea	Singapore	Japan	United States
A. External Trade							
1979	29,330	32,267	30,337	35,396	31,877	212,131	408,588
1991	135,701	198,799	139,705	153,896	125,259	551,792	930,093
2002	620,766	407,736	248,562	314,555	241,625	753,920	1,893,333
2014	4,303,037	1,017,771	587,722	1,098,179	776,016	1,502,094	4,032,790
Growth Rate (% p.a.)							
79–14	16.67	11.42	8.97	11.57	11.20	6.74	7.57
91–14	16.92	8.28	7.61	10.07	9.22	5.22	6.74
02–14	18.73	7.93	8.27	11.57	10.46	6.41	6.51
B. Exports							
1979	13,660	15,140	15,829	15,057	14,233	102,300	186,363
1991	71,910	98,557	76,563	71,896	58,966	314,793	421,730
2002	325,596	200,092	135,317	162,484	125,177	416,726	693,103
2014	2,342,747	473,659	313,696	572,665	409,769	690,202	1,623,410
Growth Rate (% p.a.)							
79–14	17.12	11.45	8.91	11.73	11.77	6.20	7.35
91–14	17.05	7.93	7.28	10.09	9.79	4.42	6.42
02–14	19.12	7.58	7.96	11.47	10.73	5.16	6.83
C. Imports							
1979	15,670	17,127	14,508	20,339	17,643	109,831	222,225
1991	63,791	100,242	63,142	82,000	66,293	236,999	508,363
2002	295,170	207,644	113,245	152,071	116,448	337,194	1,200,230
2014	1,960,290	544,112	274,026	525,514	366,247	811,892	2,409,380
Growth Rate (% p.a.)							
79–14	16.58	11.41	9.20	11.67	10.72	7.55	7.81
91–14	16.96	8.63	8.04	10.35	8.71	6.19	7.10
02–14	18.33	8.26	8.68	11.73	10.21	7.79	6.34

Note: External trade (imports plus exports), exports, and imports in selected years and their average annual growth rates over the 1979–2014, 1991–2014, and 2002–2014 periods are reported.
Source: CEIC.

included in Table 2.3. That is, China's strong growth in trade is reflected in both absolute and relative terms.

Similarly, China's exports and imports demonstrated comparable growth performance with exports showed a stronger momentum. Indeed, China's exports overtook the US volume in 2007 and the Germany, the then largest exporter, in 2009. It has maintained its leading exporter position since 2009.

Table 2.4 offers an alternative view on China's progress in trade. It presents the degree of openness as measured by the ratio of trade to GDP of China and the selected economies. China has clearly made significant stride in integrating with the world economy through trade. Its degree of openness increased rapidly from 11% in 1979 to 41% in 2014, and became more open then the two advanced economies Japan and the US. However, China's openness is no match for the four relatively small open Asian economies. The two international finance centers, Hong Kong and Singapore, have a 2014 trade-to-GDP ratio of 3.5 and 2.5, respectively. The magnitudes of Taiwan's and Korea's volume of trade are comparable to their respective GDP in 2014. It is conceivable that, given the large size of China's economy, it is hard to lift its trade to output ratio beyond its current level.[20]

Figure 2.4 and Table 2.5 present yet another way to interpret China's increasing role in world trade. As evidenced in Figure 2.4, China's contribution to the world trade has started its steep climb since its accession to WTO in 2001. The evolution of China's share of the world trade is similar to its path of trade expansion: its share increased from less than 1% in 1979 to over 11% in 2014. China's gain apparently is at the expense of the US and Japan. The US and Japan ratios dropped; especially during the period of 2002 to 2014; the US from 14.6% to 10.7% and Japan from 5.8% to 4.0%. The other four Asian economies, in the meanwhile, contribute 1% to 3% to world trade in 2014. China's contribution to world trade essentially mirrors its accomplishment in its trade sector.

The evolution of China's bilateral trade with the selected economies is presented in Table 2.6. Over the period 1979–2014, China's bilateral trade with each selected economy maintains an average annual growth rate of

---

[20] Indeed, China's degree of openness has declined between 2012 and 2015.

Table 2.4   Ratios of External Trade, Exports, and Imports to Gross Domestic Product

	China	Hong Kong	Taiwan	Korea	Singapore	Japan	United States
A. External Trade							
1979	0.11	1.43	0.91	0.53	3.28	0.21	0.16
1991	0.34	2.23	0.75	0.49	2.75	0.16	0.15
2002	0.42	2.45	0.80	0.49	2.63	0.19	0.17
2014	0.41	3.50	1.11	0.81	2.52	0.33	0.23
Growth Rate (% p.a.)							
79–14	5.16	2.86	0.92	2.96	−0.08	2.19	1.66
91–14	1.68	2.29	2.10	4.63	−0.35	3.23	2.05
02–14	1.19	3.48	3.21	4.43	−0.02	5.35	2.39
B. Exports							
1979	0.05	0.67	0.48	0.23	1.46	0.10	0.07
1991	0.18	1.11	0.41	0.23	1.30	0.09	0.07
2002	0.22	1.20	0.44	0.25	1.36	0.10	0.06
2014	0.23	1.63	0.59	0.42	1.33	0.15	0.09
Growth Rate (% p.a.)							
79–14	5.70	2.90	0.93	3.12	0.46	1.56	1.47
91–14	1.89	1.98	1.86	4.61	0.20	2.43	1.72
02–14	1.52	3.14	2.98	4.19	0.21	4.13	2.73
C. Imports							
1979	0.06	0.76	0.44	0.31	1.82	0.11	0.08
1991	0.16	1.13	0.34	0.26	1.46	0.07	0.08
2002	0.20	1.25	0.37	0.24	1.27	0.08	0.11
2014	0.19	1.87	0.52	0.39	1.19	0.18	0.14
Growth Rate (% p.a.)							
79–14	4.96	2.85	1.01	3.07	−0.55	3.08	1.87
91–14	1.62	2.58	2.43	4.95	−0.83	4.21	2.32
02–14	0.86	3.78	3.52	4.73	−0.24	6.69	2.21

Note: Ratios of external trade (imports plus exports), exports, and imports to GDP in selected years and their average annual growth rates over the 1979–2014, 1991–2014, and 2012–2014 periods are reported.
Source: CEIC.

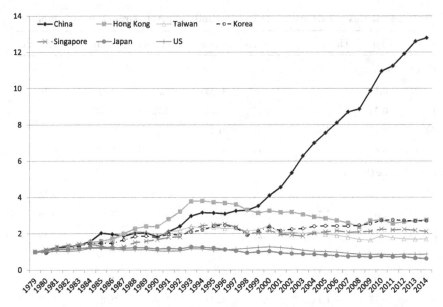

Figure 2.4   Total Trade as a Percentage of World Trade (1979 = 1)

over 10%, while the average growth rate of world trade is about 7%. That is, the average growth rate of China's trade with these selected economies is higher than that of world trade. The difference in growth rate underscores the increase of China's share in world trade in the past three-and-half decades. In 2014, China had the largest trade surpluses against Hong Kong (US$350,313 million) and the US (US$242,963 million), and it incurred the largest deficit against Taiwan (US$105,745 million) and Korea (US$89,884 million).

In passing, we note the change of Hong Kong's role in China trade. Before China opened itself to the rest of the world, Hong Kong was its main *entrepôt* and brokered most of its international transactions. In the early phase of China's open era, Hong Kong strengthened its middleman position, and its share of China trade reached 36.6% in 1991.[21] It is quite an accomplishment of an economy of Hong Kong's size. As China expanded its trading facility, and the scope and scale of trade activity, the relative role

---

[21] The ratio reached in 1993 its highest level of 49.51%.

Table 2.5   Contributions to World Trade

	China	Hong Kong	Taiwan	Korea	Singapore	Japan	United States
National Trade/World Trade							
1979	0.009	0.010	0.009	0.011	0.010	0.065	0.125
1991	0.019	0.028	0.019	0.021	0.017	0.076	0.129
2002	0.048	0.031	0.019	0.024	0.019	0.058	0.146
2014	0.114	0.027	0.016	0.029	0.021	0.040	0.107
Growth Rate (% p.a.)							
79–14	7.94	3.18	1.52	3.08	2.61	−1.39	−0.41
91–14	8.58	0.86	−0.22	1.99	1.26	−2.45	−0.71
02–14	8.38	−0.94	−1.24	1.77	0.70	−3.04	−2.63

Note: Ratios of individual country's trade volume to world trade selected years and their average annual growth rates over the 1979–2014, 1991–2014, and 2002–2014 periods are reported.
Source: CEIC, IMF International Financial Statistics Database.

of Hong Kong is diminishing. Indeed, after 2002, the shares of China's trade attributed to individual economies in Table 2.6 have declined.

China's triumph in international trade is a significant impetus to its phenomenal growth. It is underpinned by its policies and the concurrent trend of globalization. The successful foreign direct investment policy has brought in the needed capital and technical know-how to build up its manufacturing infrastructure, develop its trade network, and occupy a strategic position in the evolving global production chain. The manufacturing sector also benefits from the abundance of labor and low production costs.

Besides hardware, China is quite willing to leverage external forces to promote its reform schedule. The decision to join WTO and subject the country to international rules on trade arrangement is a good case in point. WTO accession in essence is China's statement of its commitment to international trade, willingness to follow the prevailing international practices, and policy direction of integrating into the global economy.

To consolidate its position in the global trade network, China has engaged in various bilateral trade agreements. The Framework Agreement on China–ASEAN Comprehensive Economic Co-operation signed in

Table 2.6   China's Trade with Selected Economies (in millions of US dollars)

	Hong Kong	Taiwan	Japan	US	Korea	Singapore
A. Exports from China to the Selected Economies						
1979	3,328	N.A.	2,764	595	N.A.	297
1991	32,138	595	10,252	6,198	2,179	2,014
2002	58,483	6,586	48,483	70,064	15,508	6,969
2014	363,223	46,285	149,452	397,099	100,402	48,707
Proportion of China's Total Exports						
1979	0.244	N.A.	0.202	0.044	N.A.	0.022
1991	0.447	0.008	0.143	0.086	0.030	0.028
2002	0.180	0.020	0.149	0.215	0.048	0.021
2014	0.155	0.020	0.064	0.170	0.043	0.021
Growth Rate (% p.a.)						
79–14	18.00	N.A.	13.70	22.47	N.A.	18.59
91–14	15.67	22.17	12.10	17.74	36.85	15.21
02–14	18.01	20.09	10.26	17.33	18.74	18.60
B. Imports of China from the Selected Economies						
1979	214	N.A.	3,944	1,857	N.A.	105
1991	17,543	3,639	10,032	8,010	1,066	1,063
2002	10,788	38,061	53,489	27,251	28,581	7,054
2014	12,920	152,030	162,686	154,136	190,286	30,535
Proportion of China's Total Imports						
1979	0.014	N.A.	0.252	0.118	N.A.	0.007
1991	0.275	0.057	0.157	0.126	0.017	0.017
2002	0.037	0.129	0.181	0.092	0.097	0.024
2014	0.007	0.078	0.083	0.079	0.097	0.016
Growth Rate (% p.a.)						
79–14	24.75	N.A.	13.20	19.34	N.A.	22.85
91–14	4.13	17.45	12.57	14.23	39.44	14.19
02–14	4.67	15.20	11.96	15.07	18.57	15.97

(*Continued*)

Table 2.6 (*Continued*)

	Hong Kong	Taiwan	Japan	US	Korea	Singapore
C. External Trade with China						
1979	3,543	N.A.	6,708	2,452	N.A.	401
1991	49,681	4,234	20,284	14,208	3,245	3,077
2002	69,271	44,647	101,972	97,315	44,089	14,023
2014	376,143	198,314	312,138	551,235	290,688	79,241
Proportion of China's Total External Trade						
1979	0.121	N.A.	0.229	0.084	N.A.	0.014
1991	0.366	0.031	0.149	0.105	0.024	0.023
2002	0.112	0.072	0.164	0.157	0.071	0.023
2014	0.087	0.046	0.073	0.128	0.068	0.018
Growth Rate (% p.a.)						
79–14	18.14	N.A.	12.61	20.84	N.A.	18.06
91–14	13.73	18.07	12.09	16.27	37.18	14.24
02–14	16.62	16.07	11.04	16.57	18.51	17.15

Note: The table presents the trade activities between China and selected economies in the years 1979–2014. "External Trade" refers to the sum of exports and imports.
Source: CEIC.

November 2002 is an example of China's early efforts in establishing a bilateral free trade arrangement. Table 2.7 lists China's existing free trade agreements that are skewed toward Asian economies.[22]

Despite all these efforts, there is not an uncommon view that the supercharged China trade is propelled by China's "predatory" foreign exchange policy that greatly depresses the value of China's currency. As a result, China has gained unfair competitive advantages in the global market; especially in manufacturing exports. We will discuss issues related to China's exchange rate policy in the next few chapters.

---

[22] Strictly speaking, the arrangements with Hong Kong, Macao, and Taiwan are not official trade agreements that are meant for economies of different sovereignties. China considers it has sovereignty over these three economies.

Table 2.7   China's Free Trade Agreements with Other Economies

Existing Agreements	Remarks
China–ASEAN[a]	1. In November 2004, signed the Agreement on Trade in Goods of the China–ASEAN FTA, which entered into force in July 2005. 2. In January 2007, signed the Agreement on Trade in Services, which entered into effect in July of the same year. 3. In August 2009, signed the Agreement on Investment and became effective from January 2010.
China–Pakistan	1. Reached the FTA in November 2006 and took effect in July 2007. 2. On February 21, 2009, signed the Agreement on Trade in Service of the China–Pakistan FTA, which has entered into effect since October 10, 2009.
China–Chile	1. In November 2005, after five rounds of negotiations, signed the FTA, which entered into effect in October 2006. 2. On April 13, 2008, signed The Supplementary Agreement on Trade in Services of the Free Trade Agreement, which was implemented on August 1, 2010.
China–New Zealand	On April 7, 2008, after 15 rounds of negotiations, signed the China–New Zealand FTA, which became effective on October 1, 2008.
China–Singapore	1. Signed FTA on October 23, 2008 after eight rounds of negotiations. 2. Signed four documents on new cooperative projects in Singapore in November 2009.
China–Peru	Signed on April 28, 2009 after 8 rounds negotiations and came into effect on March 1, 2010.
Mainland and Hong Kong Closer Economic and Partnership Arrangement[b]	1. In 2003, the Central Government of China signed the Closer Economic Partnership Arrangement (CEPA) with the Government of the Special Administrative Region of Hong Kong. 2. Supplement I, II, III, IV, V, and VI were signed in 2004, 2005, 2006, 2007, 2008, and 2009, respectively.

(Continued)

[a] ASEAN countries include Indonesia, Malaysia, Philippines, Singapore, Thailand, Brunei, Myanmar, Cambodia, Laos and Vietnam.
[b] Strictly speaking the arrangements with Hong Kong and Macau are not free trade agreements, which are typically signed between sovereign nations.

Table 2.7 (*Continued*)

Existing Agreements	Remarks
Mainland and Macao Closer Economic and Partnership Arrangement	1. In 2003, the Central Government of China signed the Closer Economic Partnership Arrangement (CEPA) with the Government of the Special Administrative Region of Macao. 2. Supplement I, II, III, IV, V, and VI were signed in 2004, 2005, 2006, 2007, 2008, and 2009, respectively.
China–Costa Rica	Signed the agreement in April 2010, and became effective on August 1, 2011
China–Iceland	Signed the FTA on April 15, 2013 after six rounds of negotiations, and officially went into effect on July 1, 2014.
China–Switzerland	Signed the FTA in July 2013, which became effective on July 1, 2014
China–Taiwan	Cross-Straits Economic Cooperation Framework Agreement, signed on June 29, 2010
China–Australia	Trade and Investment Minister Andrew Robb and Chinese Commerce Minister Gao Hucheng signed the China–Australia Free Trade Agreement (ChAFTA) in Canberra on June 17, 2015
China–Korea	The FTA was officially signed on June 1, 2015
Under Negotiation	
China–GCC[c]	In July 2004, China and the Gulf Cooperation Council (GCC) announced the launch of China–GCC Free Trade Agreement negotiations. Till now, the two parties have held five rounds of negotiations and have reached agreements on the majority of issues concerning trade in goods. Negotiations on trade in services have been launched.
China–Norway	The first round of negotiations was held on September 18, 2008 and the latest eighth round was held on September 14–16, 2010.
China–Japan–Korea	1. On November 20, 2012 announced the China–Japan–Korea FTA negotiations. 2. The first round of negotiations was held on March 26–28, 2013 and the fourth round was held on March 4, 2014. 3. The fifth round of negotiations was held in Beijing on September 1, 2014.

(*Continued*)

[c] GCC (Gulf Cooperation Council) includes Saudi Arabia, UAE, Kuwait, Oman, Qatar, and Bahrain.

Table 2.7   (*Continued*)

Existing Agreements	Remarks
	4. The sixth round of negotiations was held in Tokyo, Japan, on January 16, 2015.
	5. The seventh round of negotiations was held in Seoul, Korea, on May 12, 2015.
Regional Comprehensive Economic Partnership (RCEP)[d]	1. A regional trade agreement plan put forward and driven by ASEAN in 2011.
	2. Negotiations were formally launched in November 2012.
	3. Until the end of August 2015, there were nine rounds of negotiations.
China–ASEAN FTA Upgrade Negotiations	1. Proposed by China during the China–ASEAN Leadership Summit in October 2013.
	2. First Round of Upgrading Negotiations of the China–ASEAN FTA was held in Hanoi, Vietnam, on September 23–24, 2014.
China–Sri Lanka	1. A joint feasibility study between China and Sri Lanka began in Beijing in August 2013, and ended in March 2014.
	2. In September 2014, signed a memorandum to formally launch FTA negotiations.
	3. First round of negotiations was held in Colombo, on September 17–19, 2014.
	4. The second round of negotiations was held in Beijing on November 26–28, 2014.
China–Maldives	Joint feasibility studies on the China–Maldives Free Trade Area were held in Male, capital of Maldives, on February 4–5, 2015.
China–India	1. In 2003, established the Joint Study Group.
	2. In October 2007, the Joint Task Force finalized the feasibility of a China–India Regional Trading Arrangement (RTA).
China–Georgia	1. In March 2015, signed a joint declaration of launching the feasible studies on China–Georgia free trade agreement negotiations.

Sources: News and the official Chinese FTA website.

---

[d]The partnership involves Brunei, Burma (Myanmar), Cambodia, Indonesia, Laos, Malaysia, Philippines, Singapore, Thailand, Vietnam, China, Japan, Korea, Australia, New Zealand and India.

One key issue here, in addition to whether the Chinese currency is significantly undervalued or not, is the link between exchange rate and trade in the case of China. Studies abound about the difficulty of characterizing China's empirical trade behavior. Part of the difficulty is attributed to the fast growth of the Chinese economy and its dynamic interactions with the rest of the world. In general, it is hard to nail down the exact exchange rate effects on Chinese exports and imports. The empirical exchange rate effect varies across the choice of real exchange rate, the type of exports/imports, and the ownership of trading companies.[23] The phenomenon has a favor of the so-called elasticity pessimism that questions the effectiveness of depressing exchange rate value to spur exports and, hence, growth. Alternatively, one can say that the exchange rate can be one but not the only factor that affects China's trade. It may be over-simplified to credit China's success in trade solely to its exchange rate policy.

As noted earlier in the chapter, China's manufacturing sector that is a key driver of its amazing trading performance and economic rise has to fend off competition from new emerging markets in Asia and Africa in the midst of increasing domestic wages. In addition to competition at the low end, China struggles to move up the quality ladder and competes with advanced manufacturing countries including Germany, Japan, and the US. Compared with these manufacturing giants, China suffers anemic core technologies, limited high-end innovation, and inefficient production.

To address these drawbacks, and prepare for the coming decades, China's State Council in May 2015 published an ambitious 10-year plan "Made in China, 2025" to upgrade its industrial sector. The objective is, with similar plans after this one, to transform China to a global manufacturing powerhouse that excels not just in quantity but also in production

---

[23] See, for example, Ahmed (2009), Aziz and Li (2008), Cheung, Chinn and Fujii (2010a), Cheung, Chinn and Qian (2012, 2016), Eichengreen *et al.* (2007), Frankel (2010), Garcia-Herrero and Koivu (2007), Gaulier *et al.* (2006), Kwack *et al.* (2007), Mann and Plück (2007), Marquez and Schindler (2007), Thorbecke (2006, 2013, 2014), and Thorbecke and Smith (2010), and Thorbecke and Zhang (2009). However, a recent IMF study — Leigh *et al.* (2015) — asserts that a real effective exchange rate depreciation is associated with an increase in real net exports.

efficiency and quality. The plan lists nine tasks and five key projects to promote breakthroughs in 10 identified sectors.[24]

Similar to China's previous initiatives to develop its manufacture capacity, the "Made in China, 2025" presents both challenges and benefits to the global economy. While the incumbent leaders in global manufacturing have to face increased competition, consumers around the world will benefit. Indeed, China's presence in selected advanced manufacturing sectors such as computer networking and high-speed rail is felt in recent years. The advanced countries have to prepare themselves for China's move to up its technology play.

2.4 Foreign Direct Investment

2.4.1 Inward flows

Foreign direct investment (FDI) into China widely conceived a main driver of China's blistering growth in the last few decades. Since 1978, China has encouraged foreign capital to invest in China. Attracted by favorable policies and the huge domestic market, foreign corporations have migrated to China and set up their footholds in the world's most populous country. The FDI does not only upgrade the production technology and capacity and introduce modern management practices, it helps China to explore markets in different continents and industries.

---

[24] The "Made in China, 2025" document in Chinese is available at http://www.gov.cn/zhengce/content/2015-05/19/content_9784.htm (accessed July 10, 2015). The nine tasks are: improving manufacturing innovation, advancing the integration of information technology and industry, strengthening the industrial base, fostering quality and building up brands, expanding green manufacturing capacity, making breakthroughs in key industries, promoting the restructuring of the manufacturing sector, enhancing service-oriented manufacturing and manufacturing-related service industries, and internationalizing the manufacturing industry. The five key projects are: the construction of innovation centers, intelligent transformation, industrial foundation improvement, green manufacturing, and high-end equipment innovation. The 10 identified sectors are: next generation information technology, computerized tools and robotics, aerospace equipment, marine engineering equipment and high-tech ships, advanced railway equipment, energy-efficient and alternative energy vehicles, electrical equipment, and agricultural equipment, new materials, and biomedicines and high-performance medical devices.

While domestic and external economic hard times have interrupted the appetite of investing in China from time to time, they do not alter the basic strong trend. Table 2.8 shows the global FDI inflows to China, and some performance ratios. Similar data for selected economies are included for comparison purposes.

The minuscule amount of FDI received by China in 1980 reflects its near-autarky environment at the time. Benefited from the extremely low base, China has grown its FDI over 2200 times since 1980, with an amazing expansion of almost 76 times in the 1980s.[25]

A large proportion of China's FDI is from Hong Kong. Hong Kong's role in brokering FDI into China follows quite naturally from the fact that it is the main *entrepôt* for China trade. Besides its extensive contacts in China and the rest of the world, Hong Kong's well-regarded legal and financial systems further strengthen its ability to channel FDI into China.

Foreign investors, especially in the early reform period, have used Hong Kong as the beachhead. Taiwan investors, for example, use Hong Kong as the springboard to invest in China because of legal issues in the early days. Further, Hong Kong is a popular place that receives capital from China that is invested back in China — the so-called round-trip investment — to enjoy the preferential treatments not available to China's own local capital.

Against this backdrop, Hong Kong has greatly enjoyed the economic spillovers from China's open door policy and its rise. Its FDI inflow recorded an impressive growth rate of over 38% for the period 1991–2014, and grew over 158 times during the similar 35-years period.[26]

The other economies in the Table 2.8 registered 35-year growth rates of around 20–30%, which are far less than China's and Hong Kong's growth multiples.

According to the United Nations Conference on Trade and Development (UNCTAD) FDI database, China for the first time surpassed US in attracting FDI in 2003 (US$53,505 million vs US$53,146 million). Despite variations in its ranking, China has consistently been

---

[25] Some studies on FDI into China and its distribution are Chantasasawat *et al.* (2003), Cheng and Kwan (2000), Fung *et al.* (2002, 2003, 2004), Hale and Long (2011), Hu and Owen (2005), Tseng and Zebregs (2002), Prasad and Wei (2007), Sauvant (2011), Xu and Sheng (2012), Sethi *et al.* (2011).

[26] See, for example, Sung (1997) and Chantasasawat *et al.* (2003, 2004).

Table 2.8   Foreign Direct Investment Inflows

	China	Hong Kong	Taiwan	Korea	Singapore	Japan	United States
A. FDI (US$ million)							
1979	57 *	648	126	172	836	239	8,700
1991	4,366	1,021	1,271	1,455	4,887	1,284	22,799
2002	52,743	6,748	1,445	5,475	6,157	9,239	74,457
2014	128,500	103,254	2,839	9,899	67,523	2,090	92,397
Growth Rate (% p.a.)							
79–14	35.17 +	55.74	25.81	22.64	34.44	41.52	22.05
91–14	20.75	37.82	24.07	16.41	32.76	44.56	18.08
02–14	8.61	24.71	39.96	7.11	33.81	8.94	12.37
B. FDI/GDP							
1979	0.0002 *	0.0288	0.0037	0.0026	0.0860	0.0002	0.0033
1991	0.0103	0.0115	0.0068	0.0045	0.1075	0.0004	0.0037
2002	0.0362	0.0406	0.0047	0.0090	0.0670	0.0023	0.0068
2014	0.0124	0.3565	0.0054	0.0070	0.2192	0.0005	0.0053
C. FDI/ World FDI							
1979	0.0011 *	0.0153	0.0030	0.0041	0.0198	0.0057	0.2057
1991	0.0281	0.0066	0.0082	0.0094	0.0315	0.0083	0.1467
2002	0.0839	0.0107	0.0023	0.0087	0.0098	0.0147	0.1184
2014	0.1046	0.0841	0.0023	0.0081	0.0550	0.0017	0.0752
D. FDI/ FDI in DdC(DpC)							
1979	0.0076 *	0.0762	0.0148	0.0202	0.0983	0.0071	0.2575
1991	0.1096	0.0256	0.0319	0.0365	0.1227	0.0111	0.1977
2002	0.3061	0.0392	0.0084	0.0318	0.0357	0.0207	0.1669
2014	0.1886	0.1515	0.0042	0.0145	0.0991	0.0042	0.1853

Note: FDI flows to individual economies in selected years and their average annual growth rates over the 1979–2014, 1991–2014, and 2002–2014 periods are reported in Panel A. The ratios of FDI to GDP, FDI to the World FDI, and FDI to the FDI in the developed (or developing) countries are given in Panels B to D, respectively. "*" indicates 1980 figures and "+" indicates 1981–14 growth rates. Japan and the United States are classified as a developed country (DdC) while the others are classified as a developing country (DpC).

Source: United Nations Conference on Trade and Development (UNCTAD) Database, World Investment Report 2015, World Economic Outlook (WEO) Database April 2015.

one of the main attractors of global capital since then. Indeed, in 2014, China became the world's largest FDI recipient, receiving an estimate of US$128 billion inflow, followed by Hong Kong (US$103 billion) and the US (US$92 billion).[27]

Sections B, C, and D of Table 2.8 presents some ratios that describes China's FDI performance. Section B of Table 2.8 shows that China's FDI to GDP ratio increased from less than 0.1% in 1980 to the high of 3.6% in 2002, and then dwindled to 1.2% in 2014. The downward trend is a reflection of China's eminent growth in the 21st century rather than the weakening of FDI inflow. Among the six economies selected for comparison purposes, both Hong Kong and Singapore registered, respectively, a strong eightfold and three-and-half-fold increase in their FDI/GDP ratios during the 2002–2014 period. As shown later, the increase is likely a reflection of their middleman function of brokering capital flows into China.

China's share of global FDI flow that reached a high level of 10.4% in 2014 affirms its status as an attractive destination of global capital (Section C, Table 2.8). Surveys conducted by the United Nations usually put China on the list of top foreign investment destinations.[28] Also, the global survey conducted by Pricewaterhouse Coopers (PwC) and the China Development Research Foundation (2013) notes that China is a top destination for foreign investment in 2013, and the attractiveness survey of Ernst & Young (2015) finds that China ranks the third after the Western Europe and the North America on the list of the most attractive FDI destination in 2015.

Again, during the 2002–2014 period, Hong Kong and Singapore experienced a substantial increase in their global FDI shares from, respectively, 1.1–8.4% and 1.0–5.5%. Indeed, China, Hong Kong and Singapore are the three developing economies among the top five host economies of the 2014 FDI inflows (UNCTAD, 2015). Later in the chapter, we see that both Hong Kong and Singapore, especially Hong Kong, are notable sources of FDI into China. The other four selected economies display either a small increase or a drop in their shares of global FDI flows.

China's share of FDI to developing countries following a time pattern that is similar to its FDI/GDP ratio (Panels B and D). Both ratios show a

---

[27] See UNCTAD (2015).

[28] See, for example, UNCTAD (2010a, 2012a. 2013a).

hump-shape and have a value in 2014 lower than those in the beginning of the 21st century. The decline of the FDI/GDP ratio can be attributed to China's strong growth and the rise of other attractive host economies, especially developing economies that compete for global capital. Even China is investing in developing economies with a lower cost structure. The developing and transition economies accounted for half of the top 20 host economies from 2010 and 2014.[29] Nevertheless, China still commands a large share of global FDI flows to developing countries.

Table 2.9 presents guesstimates of the rate of return of FDI to China from 1991 to 2014. Specifically, the ratio of repatriated profit to the stock of FDI is used as a proxy for the return on FDI investment. The reported profit repatriation (with a few exceptions — 1997, 2002, and 2004) has increased steadily. The indicated annual returns are quite respectable. The return is hovering around 10% or above from 1991 to 2003. After 2004, the ratio rapidly increased from around 10% to nearly 20% in 2005 and then gradually went up to over 27% in 2013. The average annual return from 1991 to 2014 reached 17%, which is relatively high compared with other economies.[30] If we take these return estimates literally, they then rationalize the huge inflow into China in term of profitability, and are in accordance with the continuous strong FDI inflow to China.

We have to point out that the ratio of repatriated profit to the FDI stock is affected by, say, China's regulations governing profit repatriation, the choice of repatriation and reinvestment by foreign corporations, and the reliability of FDI data. The restrictions on repatriating profit are relaxed over time. The data on reinvestment (and depreciation allowances) are not readily available. Also, similar to reservations about the reliability of official economic data, there are concerns about the accuracy of official FDI data. For instance, OECD (2003) shows that the Chinese official data on FDI from OECD countries are larger than those reported by OECD countries. The ratio has its limitations in measuring returns on China's FDI; we consider the ratio mainly because of the lack of a better

---

[29] See, for example, UNCTAD (2011, 2012b, 2013b, 2014, 2015).

[30] The average return for Hong Kong from 1998 to 2014 is around 8%, for Taiwan from 1991 to 2014 is also around 8%, for Korea from 1991–2014 is around 7.7%, for Japan from 1996 to 2014 is around 7.6%, and for the US from 1991 to 2014 is around 3%.

Table 2.9   Estimated Returns on Foreign Direct Investment in China

	Repatriated Profit	FDI, stock	Return, %
1991	2,879	25,057	11.49
1992	5,347	36,064	14.83
1993	5,674	63,579	8.92
1994	6,774	74,151	9.14
1995	16,965	101,098	16.78
1996	19,755	128,069	15.43
1997	16,715	153,995	10.85
1998	22,024	175,156	12.57
1999	22,278	186,189	11.97
2000	26,537	193,348	13.73
2001	27,711	203,142	13.64
2002	22,339	216,503	10.32
2003	25,193	228,371	11.03
2004	24,307	245,467	9.90
2005	53,569	272,094	19.69
2006	57,377	292,559	19.61
2007	72,939	327,087	22.30
2008	80,471	378,083	21.28
2009	114,732	473,083	24.25
2010	166,868	587,817	28.39
2011	212,967	711,802	29.92
2012	185,136	832,882	22.23
2013	260,701	956,793	27.25
2014	242,916	1,085,293	22.38

Note: Annual estimated returns on FDI in China based the stock of FDI and repatriated profits for the period 1991–2014 are reported.
Source: United Nations Conference on Trade and Development (UNCTAD) Database, World Investment Report 2015, CEIC.

alternative. Thus, we have to interpret the increasing trend of these return estimates with caution.

Table 2.10 shows the breakdown of FDI flows to China from the selected source economies. The case of Hong Kong deserves some

Table 2.10   Selected Foreign Direct Investment Flows to China (in millions of US dollars)

	Hong Kong	Taiwan	Korea	Singapore	Japan	US
Inflow into China						
1991	2,405	466	119 *	58	533	323
2002	17,861	3,971	2,721	2,337	4,190	5,424
2014	81,268	2,018	3,966	5,827	4,325	2,371
Proportion						
1991	0.55	0.11	0.01 *	0.01	0.12	0.07
2002	0.34	0.08	0.05	0.04	0.08	0.10
2014	0.68	0.02	0.03	0.05	0.04	0.02
Growth Rate (% p.a.)						
91–14	22.96	17.67	25.14 +	32.51	13.19	15.46
02–14	13.95	−0.90	7.57	10.00	2.70	−3.51

Note: FDI flows into China from the selected source economies during the years 1991, 2002, and 2014 are presented. "Value" gives the US dollar amount of investment and "Proportion" gives the ratio of the investment amount to China's total foreign direct investment.
"*" is the 1992 figure and "+" is the 1993–2014 figure.
Source: CEIC.

comments. First, even China has sovereignty over Hong Kong, investment from Hong Kong is recorded as FDI to China. Second, Hong Kong is the most important source of FDI to China. Indeed, it always accounts for a lion share of China's FDI — the lowest indicated in the table is 34% in 2002. Third, the decline of Hong Kong's share in the 1990s is likely due to the diminishing role of *entrepôt* trade when China aggressively penetrated into the global market. Fourth, when China has speeded up its financial market reform efforts in the 21st century, Hong Kong is the designated testing ground for new Chinese policies. While these Chinese policy experiments take advantage of Hong Kong's developed financial sector, they has strengthened Hong Kong's status as the international finance center and revitalized its role in brokering Chinese businesses. As a result, Hong Kong's share of China's FDI has increased, as it has attracted global capital that would like to make use of its comparative advantages and participate in China's financial liberalization process. These FDI figures highlight the relative importance of Hong Kong to China's economic activity.

Singapore is an economy in the sample that records a gain in its share of China's FDI from 1991 to 2002, and then to 2014. The other four selected economies all experienced a decline in their shares of China's FDI between 2002 and 2014.

In sum, a lion share of FDI to China is coming from Hong Kong, Taiwan, and Singapore, which that are not typical FDI-source economies.[31] It lessens the concern that China's rise is displacing other developing countries in the global foreign direct investment market. Several studies in the 2000s, for example, find no evidence that China gains FDI flows at the expense of other neighboring economies; see, for example, Eichengreen and Tong (2007), Fung *et al.* (2003), Fung *et al.* (2004), Hsu and Liu (2004), Liu *et al.* (2001), OECD (2003), Mercereau (2005), and Zhang (2005).

2.4.2 Outward flows

The 1978 open door policy has changed China's FDI policy. In the first two decades of the modern economic reform era, we witnessed the stunning rate at which China absorbed foreign capital. The success of attracting FDI inflows has overshadowed the other prong of the FDI policy — the deployment of capital overseas. The *de facto* evidence is that, about a decade after the reform initiative, the ratio of FDI inflow to outward direct investment (ODI) is about 4.7 (Tables 2.8 and 2.11). By 2002, the ratio was increased to almost 21. The jump in the ratio reflects the relative success in bringing in foreign capital than deployment capital overseas. Two studies in the 1990s (Sung, 1996; Wall, 1997) suggested that China's FDI outflows appear to be concentrated in certain economies including Hong Kong.[32]

China's ODI policy has evolved in tandem with other economic reform policies. A notable milestone is the "going global" or "stepping out" initiative

---

[31] Macao, a former Portuguese colony that China regained sovereignty in 1999, is another provider not active in the global capital market but has a share of China's FDI large relative to its size.

[32] Early studies on China's ODI are mostly descriptive in nature and policy oriented; they include Buckley *et al.* (2007), Morck *et al.* (2008), UNCTAD (2003), Wong and Chan (2003), and Wu and Chen (2001). Asia Pacific Foundation of Canada (2005, 2006) offered some insights on China's ODI behavior from the perspectives of the Chinese enterprises.

announced in 2002.[33] The going global strategy is meant to complement and sustain the economic momentum of the reform process, and to promote global industry champions. Since then, policies have been introduced to simplify the rules governing Chinese enterprises making investment aboard. The policy effort has paid off; the FDI/ODI ratio dropped from 21 in 2002 to 1.1 in 2014. That is, in 12 years, China accelerated its pace of investing in markets overseas to catch up with its strong FDI inflow.

Besides China, Hong Kong, Taiwan, and Korea expanded their overseas investments quite impressively in the last three decades. Taiwan, for example, benefited from a very low base in 1979 and exhibits an overall growth in ODI higher than that of China. The two developed economies, Japan and the US, also logged some good increases in their ODI activities. To some extent, the rapid expansion of global ODI has ridden on the globalization trend.

The performance ratios presented in Section B, C, and D of Table 2.11 offer alternative perspectives on the swift expansion of China's ODI activity, especially after 2002. The conscientious policy has not only increased the volume of the Chinese investment overseas, it has established China as a key supplier of global capital; especial in the post-crisis contraction period. In 2014, China's ranked number three on the list of top ODI providers, after the US and Hong Kong but before Japan. It also accounted for over 24% of global capital from the developing world. Looking forward, China is positioned to be a key global capital provider and play a significant role in the world capital market.

The potential role of China's ODI in the global capital market was recognized soon after its adoption of the going global policy. The surveys presented in UNCTAD (2004, 2005), for example, indicate that China is expected to be among the top five leading FDI source economies. The concentration of China's investment in other developing countries, especially those in Africa has drawn some attention from the international community.[34] Since 2009, the share of China's ODI received by developed

---

[33] The 2002 "*Almanac of China's Foreign Economic Relations and Trade*" discusses the effort to implement vigorously the "going global" policy.

[34] The United Nations reports (UNCTAD, 2007, 2010b), for example, notes that China is one of the major capital providers for developing countries in Africa.

Table 2.11 Outward Direct Investment Flows

	China	Hong Kong	Taiwan	Korea	Singapore	Japan	United States
A. ODI (US$ million)							
1979	44**	82*	4	16	167	2,898	26,493
1991	913	2,825	2,055	1,591	526	31,638	32,696
2002	2,518	16,249	4,886	3,437	3,113#	32,281	134,946
2014	116,000	142,700	12,697	30,558	40,660	113,629	336,943
Growth Rate (% p.a.)							
79–14	60.22++	59.46+	80.68	40.74	58.95	17.82	33.93
91–14	56.55	34.57	8.95	18.80	53.26	8.61	13.27
02–14	34.86	25.06	11.23	23.46	51.09	14.79	9.18
B. ODI/GDP							
1979	0.0002**	0.0028*	0.0001	0.0002	0.0172	0.0029	0.0101
1991	0.0022	0.0318	0.0110	0.0049	0.0116	0.0089	0.0053
2002	0.0017	0.0977	0.0158	0.0056	0.0321#	0.0081	0.0123
2014	0.0112	0.4927	0.0240	0.0216	0.1320	0.0246	0.0193
C. ODI/ World ODI							
1979	0.0016**	0.0016*	0.0001	0.0003	0.0027	0.0462	0.4222
1991	0.0046	0.0141	0.0103	0.0080	0.0026	0.1584	0.1637
2002	0.0048	0.0308	0.0093	0.0065	0.0054#	0.0611	0.2555
2014	0.0857	0.1054	0.0094	0.0226	0.0300	0.0839	0.2488
D. ODI/ ODI in DdC(DpC)							
1979	0.0217**	0.0287*	0.0133	0.0547	0.5585	0.0464	0.4242
1991	0.0708	0.2189	0.1592	0.1233	0.0407	0.1693	0.1750
2002	0.0564	0.3637	0.1094	0.0769	0.0601#	0.0673	0.2815
2014	0.2478	0.3048	0.0271	0.0653	0.0869	0.1381	0.4095

Note: ODI flows from individual economies in selected years and their average annual growth rates over the 1979–2014, 1991–2014, and 2002–2014 periods are reported in Panel A. The ratios of ODI flow to GDP, ODI flow to the World ODI, and ODI flows to the ODI in the developed (or developing) countries are given in Panels B to D, respectively. "*" indicates 1980 figures, "**" indicates 1982 figures, "+" indicates 1981–2014 growth rates, and "++" indicates 1983–2014 growth rates. "#" indicates 2003 figures. Japan and the US are classified as a developed country (DdC) while the others are classified as a developing country (DpC).
Source: United Nations Conference on Trade and Development (UNCTAD) Database, World Investment Report 2015, World Economic Outlook (WEO) Database April 2015.

countries has been on an upward trend. Attention has shifted to China's investment in, say, the European Union and the US, and its potential impacts on the global economy, especial in light of the deleveraging trend formed after the global financial crisis.[35]

The quick expansion of Chinese outward investment, especially in strategic areas including natural resources and energies has drawn attentions from academics and policymakers. The discussion typically focuses on the motivations behind China's investment overseas, and its implications for the host economy.[36] While the outcomes depend on the adopted analytical framework, it is commonly agreed that the motivation tends to move away from political to economic considerations over time, and the global economy has to prepare to work with, if not to embrace, the Chinese capital.

In passing, we note that ODI is only one of the ways China deploys its capital aboard. Contracted engineering projects are an important channel through which China put its money to work overseas, especially in Africa.[37] For instance, in 2010 China's contracted engineering projects and ODI in various African countries are in the amounts of, respectively, $38.3 billion and $2.1 billion.

2.5 Participation in the Global Economy

China is undertaking an extraordinary journey of transferring its autarkic economy to an active member of the global market. Accompanying the growing trade prowess is the question of China's role in the world economy. China's reemergence on the global stage has shifted not only the economic focus but also the geopolitics the region, and the world.

During its early days, the modern China's close relationship with the former Soviet Union and engagement in the Korean War led to a severe

---

[35] See, for example, *The Economist* (2015), Hanemann *et al.* (2015), and National Committee on US–China Relations and Rhodium Group (2015).

[36] Some studies on China's ODI are Cheung and Qian (2009a), Cheung, de Haan, Qian and Yu (2012, 2013), Qian (2013), Kolstad and Wiig (2012), Ramasamy *et al.* (2012), Huang and Wang (2011), Wang *et al.* (2014), Wong and Chan (2003), and Yang and Su (2012).

[37] See, for example, Bhaumik and Co (2011), Bräutigam (2009), Broadman (2007), Cheung, de Haan, Qian and Yu (2014), Corkin *et al.* (2008), and Foster *et al.* (2008).

cutback in its interactions with the Western world. Gaining the United Nations membership at the expense of Taiwan in 1971 was a key step for China to rejoin the world. Since then, China has been conscientiously, if not aggressively, joining various international organizations.

In developing its economic ties with the rest of the world, China always emphasizes its peaceful development policy and five principles of peaceful coexistence.[38] Following the 1997–98 Asian financial crisis and the 2001 accession to WTO, China has noticeably fostered its global economic relationship; especially with the Asian economies, and stirred up the concern of its regional hegemony.

One early China's footprint in regional economic businesses is the signing of the Bangkok Agreement in 2000, which aimed at promoting the intraregional trade through exchange of mutually agreed concessions by member countries (Economic and Social Commission for Asia and the Pacific, 2003).

In 2002, a year after its accession to WTO, China signed the Framework Agreement with ASEAN to lower the tariff and promote regional trade and cooperation.[39] The framework agreement prepared for the formation of the world's largest free trade area by population. The planned China–ASEAN free trade area came into effect in January 2010. The free trade area initiative affirmed China's desire to play an active role in the regional trade activity. Indeed, as noted earlier, China's existing free trade agreements are heavily loaded with economies in the Asia-Pacific area (Table 2.7).

In addition to trade-promoting cooperation, China has participated in regional monetary cooperation efforts. For instance, after the 1997–98 Asian financial crisis, China signed the Chiang Mai Initiative (CMI) in 2000 and the subsequent expanded version; the Chiang Mai Initiative Multilateralization (CMIM) Agreement in 2009. While the CMI has set up a series of bilateral swap arrangements to manage regional short-term liquidity, the

---

[38] See, for example, China's Ministry of Foreign Affairs on the Five Principles of Peaceful Co-Existence (http://www.fmprc.gov.cn/mfa_eng/ziliao_665539/3602_665543/3604_665547/t18053.shtml).

[39] The Framework Agreement — "Framework Agreement on Comprehensive Economic Co-Operation Between ASEAN and the People's Republic of China" — is downloadable from http://asean.org/?static_post=framework-agreement-on-comprehensive-economic-co-operation-between-asean-and-the-people-s-republic-of-china-phnom-penh-4-november-2002-4.

CMIM framework aims to strengthen the region's capacity to safeguard against increased risks and challenges in the global economy. The core objectives of the CMIM are (i) to address balance-of-payments and short-term liquidity difficulties in the region and (ii) to supplement the existing international financial arrangements. The CMIM provides financial support through currency swap transactions to the CMIM participants facing balance-of-payments and short-term liquidity difficulties.

More recently, in promoting the cross-border use of its currency, China has signed bilateral local currency swap agreements with economies around the world. We will discuss these local currency swap arrangements that involve the Chinese currency in Chapter 5.

China's global engagement goes beyond regional affairs. Over time, China has increased its level of involvements in the key international organizations including the United Nations, IMF, and the World Bank, and joined various international organizations of different natures. According to the *CIA World Factbook*, China has taken part, albeit in different manners, in hundreds of international organizations.[40]

Joining the global economy offers China the synergy that helps to advance its economic agenda. For instance, China has gained access to aid programs, technology, and management know-how via its memberships in, for example, the United Nation, World Bank, IMF, and the WTO. Through these international institutions, China can promote its agenda and influence others. Nevertheless, with its relentless economic expansion, China has outgrown the existing global economic order that is shaped by the dominating international organizations including the World Bank and IMF. The existing international economic system is largely designed by the incumbent economic powers, and, thus, is commonly perceived to serve the interest of incumbents. A large developing nation like China that has experienced rapid economic growth will feel the constraints, if not the restrictions, imposed by the existing establishment.

Soon moving into the 21st century, China's role in the global economy has gradually evolved from being a passive adopter of the existing system

---

[40] See https://www.cia.gov/library/publications/the-world-factbook/fields/2107.html, the *CIA World Factbook* for a list of international organizations that China is a member or participates in some other way.

to an active stakeholder who is willing to take initiatives to make changes to facilitate its own economic development, and geopolitics. Despite its autarkic past, China has to find ways to move beyond the existing international setting and influence the world that it is integrating into. A rising China with the accompanying increase in its global strengths presents challenges to incumbent powers and stirs up the fear of hegemony, say, in the Asian region. The US and Japan, for example, are quite explicit about their concerns about implications of China's policies on the global economic order and geopolitics.

China's initiative to set up the Asian Infrastructure Investment Bank illustrates its efforts to develop an international organization beyond the existing international order. Despite the explicit opposition of the US, the Asian Infrastructure Bank solicited over 50 founding member countries. The establishment of the China-centered development institution — that is considered a rival to the Asian Development Bank — is China's triumph over the incumbent. The Asian Infrastructure Investment Bank is also complementary to China's other efforts to establish international institutions, which include the BRICS New Development Bank and the Shanghai Golden Exchange, which promotes gold trading in the RMB, to expand its reach in different areas of the global market. In a nutshell, China is not necessarily satisfied with being a participant of an existing organization, and is ready to launch one to compete with or supplement it.

Despite its incredible pace of linking up with the world economy, China's neighbors are quite antagonistic toward its apparent hegemonic behaviors. A case in point is the territorial disputes between China and its neighboring countries including India, Japan, Philippines, Malaysia, and Vietnam. The disputes, especially those that took place in the South China Sea in the 2010s, have revived historical animosities between these countries, and do not help China to promote its cooperative development agenda in the Southeast Asian region. Given its size and communist background, China has a lot to do to convince its neighbors that it is neither an economic nor a security threat. A 2015 survey conducted by the US-based Pew Research Center indeed indicates that the territorial disputes undermined China's popularity in the region.[41]

---

[41] See Stokes (2015).

2.6 Conclusion

Three decades after the reform and opening up policy, the Chinese economy has been successfully transformed in different areas: from a closed economy to the world's largest trading nation, from a centrally planned economy to one that market forces play a role, and from a relatively inefficient agricultural economy to the world's manufacturing powerhouse. Although the rise of China may not be the most important event in the last century, its emergence has no doubt changed the global economic landscape.

Similar to other historical episodes of the coming of age of a new economic power, China's spectacular economic growth has created both opportunities and challenges to the existing global economic order. Both the scope and scale of economic expansion have generated serious pressure for competitors, and opened up new business possibilities to other. The Chinese phenomenon and the rising of other dynamic economies in the region have shifted the economic gravity to Asia, and made the 21st century the Asian century.

Following its success in upgrading its production capacity and liberalizing trade, China has broadened and deepened its financial liberalization policy. Its level of integration with the world has been slowly expanded from trade interactions to include financial activity. China is gradually integrated into the international financial system. The trend is quite reasonable — it is hard to perceive a full global economic integration in the absence of financial market integration.

The foreign exchange policy is a key component of China's overall financial liberalization agenda. Since the 2007–08 global financial crisis, China has been quite aggressive in revamping its exchange rate policy and promoting the use of its currency in cross-border transactions. Note that the role of a national currency in the modern world goes beyond its textbook economic functions — it measures not only the nation's sovereignty and global prestige; it has implications for its economic well-being. After all, "Great powers have great currencies."[42] In the next few

---

[42] Mundell's (1993) quote as cited by Cohen (2009). See, for example, Hockenhull (2015) for a historical account of evolution of 10 currencies, though the RMB is not included.

chapters, we discuss China's foreign exchange policy, with a focus on some recent developments.

In the process of climbing up (or back) to the league of elite global economies, China has intensified its interaction with countries around the world, and flexing its muscles in handling international economic and political issues. There is no doubt that China could contribute substantially to the global economy. A not uncommon concern is, however, whether China would be a responsible participant and stakeholder.

Anecdotal evidence shows that China does not confine itself to the current international architecture; it is both willing and able to put together new international institutions to promote its visions. To further enhance its economic and political relationships with the rest of the world, China has to overcome hurdles hidden behind historical antagonisms and animosities, and its communist background. Conceivably, China is going to hit some roadblocks in further building up its roles in the international community. It is not an overstatement to say that, moving forward, China's strength is certain. Its future position in the global economy, even though expected to be contrastive, is not necessarily be 100% certain given the evolving economic and geopolitical tectonics.

Chapter 3
Exchange Rate Policy

Initiated in 1978, China's reform policy agenda has propelled its economy to an astonishing growth trajectory and promoted its integration with the rest of the world. Over the last few decades, China has been gaining economic ascendancy and become an increasingly important player in the global economy. The growing influence has put China's policies under close scrutiny. An archetypal example is China's exchange rate policy that has drawn increasingly intense attention from the international community since the 1990s.

Before the 1990s, there was not much discussion about China's exchange rate or the Chinese currency the renminbi (RMB) in the global market. In midst of China's ballooning trade surplus and surging volume of foreign exchange reserves, the RMB valuation became one of the intensely debated economic issues around the turn of the 21st century. When China stepped up efforts to reform its exchange rate policy in the late 2010s, the global economy has anxiously embraced its initiative of promoting the use of the RMB overseas.

There are a few defining moments in the modern history of China' exchange rate policy. The first one is the decision of not linking the value of the currency to gold when the RMB was introduced with the advent of the People's Republic of China. The decision went against the convention in the 1940s. Second, in January 1994, China unified its official rate and swap (market) rate into a single one, and managed its value against the

US dollar. The unified rate, relative to the official rate, was depreciated to RMB8.70 per US dollar. Third, in December 2003, China appointed the Bank of China (Hong Kong) as the RMB clearing bank in Hong Kong. It is the first local RMB clearing arrangement outside mainland China. Looking back, the arrangement prepared for the pilot scheme in Hong Kong and the subsequent efforts to establish offshore RMB markets and facilitate the use of RMB in cross-border transactions.

Fourth, China announced in July 2005 that it will manage the RMB value against an unspecified basket of currencies taking market demand and supply into consideration. The announcement signaled the intention to weaken the tie between the RMB and the US dollar.[1] Upon the change, the RMB was appreciated 2.1% against the dollar. The stated currency basket approach was temporarily abandoned in the midst of the global financial crisis — between July 2008 and June 2010. Fifth, in April 2009, China launched the pilot scheme that encourages the use of RMB to denominate and settle cross-border trade transactions. Since then, the Chinese currency has become increasingly accessible to non-residents, and swiftly ascended to the league of the most used world payments currency.[2]

Sixth, in August 2015, China revamped the central parity formation mechanism and replaced the officially determined daily fixing with a fixing determined by the closing rate in the previous day, market demand and supply factors, and the rates of other major currencies. Following the change in fixing mechanism, the RMB's central parity rate was depreciated in three days from 6.1162 (August 10) to 6.4010 (August 13). The relative sharp depreciation confused the market about China's actual policy intention. On December 11, 2015, China reiterated the July 2005 message of managing the RMB value against a basket of currencies and posted the composition of a currency basket on the web.[3] Seventh, the RMB was

---

[1] Despite the stated policy intention, studies including Frankel (2006, 2009) found that the RMB value is still largely linked to the US dollar.

[2] In August 2015, the RMB became the fourth most used world payments currency before it fell back to the fifth position in September 2015 (SWIFT, 2015a, b). China ranked number 13 in January 2013.

[3] See the commentary posted on http://www.pbc.gov.cn/english/130721/2988680/index.html.

granted the status of being one of the IMF's basket of special drawing rights currencies. China's elite currency basket membership will officially begin in October 2016.

In view of the general reform agenda, it is not surprising to observe that most of changes in exchange rate policy took place in the 21st century. Since the establishment of the People's Republic of China, China has managed its exchange rate to serve national economic objectives with some ideological twists. The importance of ideological factors has varied over time, and has been declining slowly relative to economic considerations during the reform period. Under the closed and isolated pre-reform regime, the exchange rate was deployed to adjust the external and internal accounting balances, and did not respond much to demand and supply forces.

In the early reform period, market incentives were gradually introduced to the RMB exchange rate determination mechanism to guide and promote trade competitiveness and external balances. When the reform is deepened and spread to financial markets, China is conscientious in modifying the institutional framework and bringing in market forces to liberalize the exchange rate. The initiative to promote the international use of the RMB makes the exchange rate policy an integration part of the overall liberalization strategy that generates feedback to reform policies in other sectors.

Since the RMB was introduced in 1948, China's exchange rate policy has undergone some significant changes, especially in the last decade. The evolution of exchange rate policy, however, has its root in the history. The policy, in historical context, always has a trait of proactiveness, independence, gradualism, and controllability.[4] Indeed, China's reform initiatives are typically imbued with these characteristics. Policy changes are strategically introduced to broaden, deepen, and coordinate reforms in different areas. Independence echoes the principle of self-reliance, which was popular in the 1960s and 1970s, and emphasizes policy autonomy.

---

[4] In 2005, the then Premier WEN Jiabao pointed out the principles of proactiveness, gradualism, and controllability underlying China's exchange rate policy; 中国人民银行货币司: "2005 年中国货币政策大事记"。http://www.pbc.gov.cn/zhengcehuobisi/125207/125227/125963/ 2892706/index.html.

Gradualism and controllability focus on the operational effectiveness and the ability to manage the policy effects.

In the following sections, we briefly discuss the evolution of the policy of the Chinese currency.[5]

3.1 The Pre-reform Era

After the People's Republic of China was established on October 1, 1949, China engaged in the 1950–53 Korean War. At the same time, it underwent a large-scale domestic economic and political reform in a rather hostile external environment. During its first three decades, the communist China had cold relationships with the capitalist US, the communist USSR, and allies of these two countries. These are only a few other countries outside the US and USSR blocs. That is, China was quite isolated from the global economy, and only befriended some selected third world countries. Against this backdrop, China's established the stringent view on national security and the cherished policy of self-reliance. The exchange rate policy was guided by economic and political considerations and received limited attention from the rest of the world.

3.1.1 1948–1952

The Chinese currency RMB was introduced before the official founding of the People's Republic of China. The central bank — the People's Bank of China — was established on December 1, 1948, and issued the RMB to consolidate money issuance under the communist rule.[6] The Bank of China was the designated foreign exchange bank. Note that "renminbi" is the name of the currency, and "yuan" is the unit of the currency.

---

[5] The history of the RMB and related policies are discussed in, for example, Huang and Wang (2004), Liew and Wu (2007), Lin and Schramm (2003), Miyashita (1966), Shi (1998), Wu and Chen (2002), and Xu (2000).

[6] Before the RMB, bianbi (border regional money) was used in regions controlled by the Communist Party. Fabi (legal money) and gold yuan certificate were circulated in regions controlled by the Kuomintang government.

One unique policy decision about the new currency is that the value of the RMB is not linked to gold. The decision is not in accordance with the general and IMF practice prevailing at that time. The adoption of a fiat money instead of a commodity-backed one was the outcome of serious internal policy debates (Shi, 1998; Wu and Chen, 2002). While the decision was unconventional at that time, it was a practical and operational one because, after the imperialist adventures of foreign powers, the 1937–45 war of resistance against Japanese aggression, and the civil war, China had limited gold (or silver) reserves. Delinking the value of the RMB from gold allowed China the flexibility to fix its exchange rate by decree. In a sense, the delink decision predated the collapse of the gold exchange Bretton Woods system in 1973.

In the aftermath of prolonged political and economic turmoil amplified by wars and conflicts, the new China was busy in rebuilding its economy, and to institute its own economic, political, and social orders. The RMB exchange rate, against this backdrop, was adjusted quite frequently in its first few years of its existence. For instance, the currency depreciated from one US dollar to 600 RMB in January 1949, to 42,000 RMB in March 1950, and then to 22,380 in May 1951 — it changed its value 52 times over the period. The exchange rate variations mostly reflected the heavy demand for imports during the recovery phase, and changes in the domestic and foreign price levels.

Since the RMB is not officially pegged to gold, its exchange rate against, say, the US dollar could not be determined by referring to the official gold price of the US dollar.[7] Instead, the RMB exchange rate was determined by comparing the relative purchasing power. Specifically, the three main relative prices that affect the RMB exchange value are the relative price of exports, the relative price of imports, and the relative domestic and foreign costs of living. In addition to trade (exports and imports), the relative foreign cost of living was included in the exchange rate calculation process because, at that time, overseas remittances were a main source of foreign exchanges. The weights of these three relative prices in

---

[7] When two currencies have their official prices of gold, say, under the gold standard, their exchange rate is determined by the mint parity defined by the ratio of their official prices of gold.

the exchange rate formulae were administratively determined based on policy considerations.

In sum, the exchange rate policy at that time was driven by the paucity of foreign exchange reserves and the need to rebuild the devastated economy. It was designed to favor the generation of foreign income from exports and from overseas remittances.

3.1.2 1953–1972

By 1953, China managed to restore viable levels of commercial, industrial, and agricultural activities. The socialist transformation process including land reform was largely completed. China entered the centralized economic planning era; all economic activities and prices were centrally determined.

During this period, there are a few dramatic economic and political events taking place in China. China's first five-year plan that exemplified the Soviet Union's style of economic development with state-owned enterprises, collective farms, and industrial-biased growth was implemented from 1953 to 1957. Apparently, the Soviet Union economic model did not work well. The switch to the Great Leap Forward program right after the first five-year plan, however, brought about severe economic hardship. Even though the infamous Cultural Revolution in the mid-1960s was mainly a political movement, its adverse impact on the economic front was harshly felt. After the high wave of the Cultural Revolution campaign, the economy activity stabilized in the late 1960s and growth resumed in the 1970s.

There are three episodes about the RMB worth mentioning. First, in March 1955, China issued the new (second) series of RMB notes — the conversion rate is one new RMB to 10,000 old RMB. Since then, the "new" RMB has become the RMB.[8]

Second, in 1968, China used RMB to invoice and settle trade with Hong Kong and Macau. The practice was later extended to other economies in other regions. Before that, China typically used the British

---

[8] Other "new" series of RMB were issued in 1962, 1987, and 1999. Beginning with the 1999 series, the RMB notes feature the Mao Zedong image.

sterling, which was China's main foreign exchange reserve currency at that time to invoice its trade. The policy change was triggered by an unexpected 1967 pound devaluation that took place during the Cantor Fair (Wu and Chen, 2002).[9] In the following years, however, the practice was reverted back to the use of foreign currencies for trade invoicing and settlement. Almost 40 years later, in 2009, China, for different reasons, launched its aggressive promotion of using RMB to settle cross-border transactions (see Chapter 5).

Third, China signed bilateral agreements with other socialist and communist economies to determine the terms and the exchange rates for nontrade transactions. These nontrade transaction exchange rates were derived from weighted averages of relative domestic retail prices of designated goods and services in the respective countries. The exchange rates were adjusted quite infrequently. A sample of the exchange rates for nontrade transactions are given in Wu and Chen (2002).

In the midst of these turbulent domestic economic conditions and the split up with the former Soviet Union in the 1960s, China maintained a low level of economic interactions with the rest of the world. Further, by adopting the social planning system, government agencies set the prices of most goods and services, and seldom change them in responses to demand and supply conditions. Goods were exported and imported according to the centrally designed economic plan; and government agencies, and not individual trading firms, managed the resulting profits and losses. The role of the RMB exchange rate in regulating trade was greatly marginalized, and the role of relative prices in setting the RMB exchange rate was weakened. The exchange rate was set mainly for internal accounting purposes, facilitating nontrade transactions, and preparing national economic plans.

The exchange rate was quite stable throughout this period. It was, for instance, managed at around a level of RMB2.4618 per US dollar between 1955 and 1972. The stable rate gives the impression that China's exchange rate policy during this period was mainly a US dollar peg. The observed stability, nevertheless, is in line with the general exchange rate stability

---

[9] The Canton Fair — currently known as China Import and Export Fair — is a main trade fair held twice a year.

observed under the Bretton Woods exchange rate system. In December 1971, when the US revised up the US dollar price of gold, China revaluated the RMB against the US dollar to 2.2673.[10]

3.1.3 1973–1978

The fixed exchange rate regime under the Bretton Woods system collapsed in 1973. Even before the landmark change of the international financial system, China's interactions with the world underwent a momentous change in October 1971 when the United Nations officially recognized the People's Republic of China (referred to as China here) as the only legitimate representative to the United Nations.[11] Since then, China has gradually expanded its global network and established diplomatic relationships with other countries. The event prepared China's expansion into the global stage.

The period represents the six years before China embarked upon its new economic reform program. In 1976, the death of Zhou Enlai (January) and Chairman Mao (September), and the subsequent purge of the gang of four (October) marked the beginning of the post-Mao era. The reinstatement of the legendary reformist Deng Xiaoping in July 1977 prepared the launch pad of the "long march" of economic reforms program in December 1978.

In response of the volatile global foreign exchange market after the collapse of the Bretton Woods system, China switched its foreign exchange policy and adopted the currency basket approach to determine the RMB exchange rate. The composition of currencies and their weights in the currency basket depended on China's trade intensities with these countries, exchange rate volatility, and other policy considerations. Pegged to currencies of its main trading partners, China reduced the volatility of the RMB exchange rate and mitigated the adverse volatility effect on trade.[12]

---

[10] Against increased exchange rate uncertainty, Bank of China offered currency forward contracts to foreign merchants in 1971 (Wu and Chen, 2002).

[11] On October 25, 1971, the United Nations General Assembly passed the Albania's Resolution 2758, and replaced the then representative of China — Republic of China — with People's Republic of China.

[12] According to Wu and Chen (2002, p. 26), the composition and the currency weights were adjusted seven times between 1973 and 1984.

While the exchange rate policy was adjusted according to developments in the world market, China maintained its tight grip on prices and international trade during the pre-reform period. The exchange rate still mainly served the accounting and planning needs of the centrally planned economic program, and supported the national development policy.

3.2 The Post-Open-Door Policy Era

3.2.1 1979–1993

Deng Xiaoping, the mastermind behind China's modern reform movement, articulated the objective of the reform is not to dismantle communism but to morph it to an enhanced version of socialism with Chinese characteristics. It is done by reducing the level of government controls and, at the same time, increasing the role of market forces. The emphasis is on improving the economic system and economic well-being. It is of interest to note that right from the beginning the basic policy directive is "改革開放," which literally means "reform and opening up." In addition to enhancing the economic system and its efficiency, the authorities encouraged the opening up of China via trade and scholar–student exchanges with the rest of the world.

Introducing market forces to the most populous centrally planned economy is not an obvious task. On top of the scale and scope of the Chinese economy, it is difficult to reconcile communist ideology with capitalist undertakings. Further, the lack of historical precedent, and the historic antagonism between China and Western countries do not help. The authorities chose the gradual, instead of the shock therapy, approach to rewire China's lethargic state-controlled and closed economy. Sometimes, the old Chinese adage "feel the rock, wade across the river" is used as a metaphor of the experimental nature of China's reform program.

The reform policies are typically carried out in a controlled manner, and in small and incremental steps. To guard against major unpleasant surprises, they are tested in designated local geographical regions. Successful experiences are then introduced and implemented at the national scale. A well-noted example is the establishment of the Shenzhen

Special Economic Zone in the Guangdong Province in May 1980. Based on its success, the authorities have subsequently established special economic zones in other regions in China.

As China is moving away from central planning protocol toward market economy, its exchange policy evolves along the way. Roughly speaking, the period of 1979–1993 is characterized by dual exchange rate arrangements. The official exchange rate and the rate for internal settlements constituted the official dual rates prevailing between 1981 and 1984; the former was a managed rate based on a currency basket formulation and the latter was conceptualized in August 1979 and instituted in January 1981 for settling trade-related transactions and assessing the performances of all units dealing with foreign trade. Between 1985 and 1993, the official rate and the partially market-determined "swap" exchange rate coexisted.[13] The swap exchange rate was from the experimental foreign currency swap (adjustment) centers, which will be discussed later in the subsection.

The era of dual exchange rate arrangement was succeeded by a managed exchange rate arrangement when the official and swap rates were merged in 1994.

Before offering some remarks on exchange rate policies, let us look at a few main events took place in the first 15 years of the reform period. The first is establishment of the State Administration of Foreign Exchange (SAFE) in March 1979 to manage foreign exchange reserves, foreign exchanges, and related policies. With a few intervening changes, SAFE was officially put under the jurisdiction of the central bank, the People's Bank of China, in March 1998. The formation of SAFE highlights the important role of foreign exchange reserves management and foreign exchange policies in reforming the Chinese economy. Since its inception, SAFE has managed an increasingly large amount of China's foreign exchange reserves and participated in designing policy measures for advancing the flexibility and convertibility of the RMB.

Second, the Foreign Exchange Retention Scheme was introduced in 1979 and was in operation until the beginning of 1994. Under the centrally

---

[13] Before the presence of the internal settlement rate, and between the time the internal settlement rate was abandoned (January 1, 1985) and the introduction of swap centers, transactions were settled using the official rate.

planned regime, all earnings of foreign exchanges were surrendered to the government at the official rate. The scheme introduced certain flexibility and allowed an individual trading enterprise to keep a pre-assigned percentage of its foreign exchange earnings. The retained foreign exchange earnings can then be used to settle allowable transactions or be sold to others.[14] Given the general shortage of foreign exchanges at that time, the scheme is meant to enhance the incentive of earning foreign exchanges – which enterprise earns more foreign exchanges will have more for its own uses. The scheme cracked the state's monopoly on foreign exchanges. In addition, by allowing individual enterprises to trade their retention quotas, the scheme brought the market forces, albeit via an indirect mode, back to exchange rate trading.

Third, on April 1, 1980, the Bank of China was authorized to issues foreign exchange certificates, which were withdrawn from circulation in the beginning of 1994. Strictly speaking, the foreign exchange certificate is not a legal tender even though it was denominated in the RMB value. Despite the stated purpose of strengthening exchange controls,[15] the foreign exchange certificate is effectively a market discriminative device intended to be sold to nonresidents at official exchange rates for foreign currencies. Foreigners are not supposed to hold the RMB but use these certificates to pay for goods and services at designated venues in China.

A holder of these certificates is privileged to purchase goods and services that are of good quality, in short supply, and out of reach of individuals using the RMB. Even though they are meant for uses by visitors from overseas and no private dealings are allowed, these certificates in practice could be used by any individuals including local Chinese residents. As a result, these privileged foreign exchange certificates commanded a value higher than its par value, that is, its printed RMB value, in the unofficial foreign exchange parallel market in China.

Indeed, the foreign exchange certificate premium exemplifies a problem commonly observed under a system with foreign exchange controls

---

[14] The retention ratio varied across regional and industries.
[15] Bank of China (1980).

and an overvalued official exchange rate.[16] In addition to the foreign exchange certificate, there were individual "money-changers" buying and selling the RMB at off-the-official exchange rates. These furtive transactions were mostly carried out in areas where foreigner and tourists congregated. The official US dollar exchange rate of the RMB was always overvalued relative to its parallel (black market) rate (Reinhart and Rogoff, 2004). Different valuations of foreign currencies created problems. It was reported, for instance, in some places, that the same product commodity was priced in three "currencies" — the RMB, the foreign exchange certificate, and a foreign currency; typically Hong Kong dollar in the southern part of China. As expected, the RMB pricing is the least favorable one.

China stopped the issuance of foreign exchange certificates when it moved to a different stage of exchange rate reform in 1994. Those in circulation were gradually removed from the market.[17]

Fourth, the foreign currency swap (adjustment) centers were created to experiment with bringing in market forces to the foreign exchange market. China's first swap center was established in the Shenzhen Special Economic Zone in November 1985. Since then, swap centers popped up across the country. They were phased out and their roles were largely subsumed under the China Foreign Exchange Trading Center and National Interbank Funding Center established in April 1994.

The foreign currency swap centers had their roots in the Foreign Exchange Retention Scheme introduced in 1979. The retention scheme offered individual enterprises to trade retention quotas and to adjust the allocation of foreign exchanges. Initially, Bank of China was the designated financial institution to handle adjustment trades on retention quotas with references to the official exchange rate. After the People's Bank of China relaxed it's rules on foreign exchange trading in March 1988, the swap rate

---

[16] The authorities recognized problems related to the circulation of foreign exchange certificates quite early. The State Council (1981), for instance, introduced measures to strengthen the "administration of foreign exchange certificates."

[17] The People's Bank of China issued on November 22, 1994 a circular (in Chinese, 中国人民银行关于外汇兑换券停止流通和限期兑换的公告, http://fgk.chinalaw.gov.cn/article/bmgz/199411/19941100271618.shtml) on withdrawing all foreign exchange certificates from circulation by the deadline December 31, 1995. These certificates can be exchanged into the RMB or the US dollar from the Bank of China before June 30, 1995.

was determined by demand and supply forces subject to interventions. That is, the swap rate can be materially different from the official rate. Indeed, the RMB official rate was always overvalued relative to its swap rate during the period of 1988 and 1993.[18]

Things changed quite fast in the first 15 years of the post-Mao reform period. In moving away from the rigid central planning regime, the role of the RMB exchange rate has to go beyond the function of an accounting price serving the economic planning process. Despite the apparent heavy-handed approach, there is an obvious trail of evidence that the economy is gradually pushed toward the market-determined spectrum. Market elements were introduced to the foreign exchange policy of a tightly controlled communist and planned economy, and their impacts were evaluated and assessed before the next policy change. The developments clearly illustrate the process of trial and error and the "feel the rock, wade across the river" spirit. Throughout the process, the authorities maintained a high degree of policy autonomy and closely monitored the operation and its effectiveness. While the country is politically controlled, the role of central planning is gradually replaced with demand and supply forces.

The dual rate system comprised the official rate based on price comparison and the internal settlement rate based on trade cost considerations was introduced to improve the foreign exchange reserve position and balance the internal and external demands. The system was supplemented by the Foreign Exchange Retention Scheme, which incorporated some incentive elements to enhance efficiency. Nevertheless, it was largely tilted in favor of planned economy. The internal settlement price that was meant to facilitate imports and exports did not perform its economic roles well because most prices used to construct it were administratively determined and did not appropriately reflect market demand and supply factors. The internal settlement rate was abandoned when the growing importance of external trade aggravated the rate's limitations (Wu and Chen, 2002).[19]

---

[18] The two officially endorsed rates are different from the black market exchange rate. That is, the number of available exchange rates was beyond the official dual rate arrangement.
[19] The total trade (imports plus exports) to GDP ratio increased from 12.6% in 1980 to 23.1% in 1985.

Then, the swap rate derived from the retention scheme foreign exchange quota trading was used side-by-side with the official rate. Market forces were allowed to price a designated type of foreign exchanges in a confined circumstance. The swap center experiment offered a glimpse of the difference between the (partially) market-determined exchange rate and the officially declared rate. In practicing the dual rate system in different forms with restricted market forces, the authorities faced the difficulties of managing the economy in an efficient manner, especially in the presence of black markets. The big question is whether China is ready for a freely floated exchange rate arrangement. With the benefit of hindsight, we know China's answer to the question was "no." Instead of fully liberalizing its exchange rate policy, China consolidated the multiple rate system and adopted an alternative exchange rate management mechanism.

3.2.2 1994–2005

Arguably, 1994 is an eventful year of China's exchange rate history. After experimenting with the dual rate arrangement and realizing its limitations and adverse side effects, the authorities replaced it with a managed floating exchange rate arrangement. On January 1, 1994, China merged the official rate and the swap center rate into one, and set the unified rate at the then prevailing swap rate of RMB8.72 per US dollar. Effectively, the official RMB rate was devalued by over 33%.[20] Since then, China's exchange rate reform has been conducted under various forms of managed floating exchange rate arrangement.

The RMB was allowed to be traded within a defined band around its daily official fixing announced by the People's Bank of China. Initially, the daily trading band against the US dollar was set to 0.3% around the fixing. The policy, on the one hand, permits the presence of market forces and, on the other hand, retains the authorities' ability to manage and stabilize the RMB. Over time, the trading band was widened to ±0.5% on May 21, 2007, to ±1 % on April 16, 2012, and ±2 % on March 17, 2014.

---

[20] The deeply devalued exchange rate became the source of the contentious debate on RMB valuation 10 years later; see the next chapter for discussion on the debate.

The abandoning of the dual rate system was accompanied by the termination of a few other related foreign exchange policy measures including the abolishment of the Foreign Exchange Retention Scheme, and the phasing out of foreign currency swap centers. At the same time, measures were introduced to make the currency current account convertible. In December 1996, China achieved the RMB current account convertibility.

The China Foreign Exchange Trading System (CFETS), which is an interbank platform for trading RMB, was established on April 18, 1994. The phased-out foreign currency swap centers were "absorbed" into the system, and turned into its regional subcenters. The CFETS is under the direct jurisdiction of the People's Bank of China. The membership-based foreign exchange trading vehicle affords People's Bank of China to efficiently regulate market participants and operations, manage exchange rate stability, and implement related policy measures.

Since its inception, the CFETS has been developed to be the main institutional framework for organizing and supporting interbank RMB trading. For instance, authorized by the central bank, the CFETS calculates and publishes the central parities — the so-called daily fixings — of the RMB against the US dollar and other major foreign currencies on each business day. In addition, it also calculates the benchmark RMB interest rate — the Shanghai Interbank Offered Rate (Shibor) — and publishes it on the National Interbank Funding Center platform.[21]

Between 1994 and 2005, the stability of RMB exchange rate against the US dollar attested China's inclination to maintain a stable environment to experiment with its reform measures and expand its external sector. However, the RMB stability understated the volatile nature of exchange rates. A few years after unifying its exchange rate, China had to deal with adverse market shocks triggered by the 1997 Asian financial crisis. The crisis inflicted huge pressures on exchange rates of developing and emerging economies. Economies depreciated their currencies and triggered the fear of competitive devaluations. China, at that time, as a transitional economy relying quite heavily on exports, boldly decided to hold steady its

---

[21] While it is usual known as CFETS, its complete name is China Foreign Exchange Trade System and National Interbank Funding Center. See, for example, http://www.chinamoney. com.cn/en/index.html for information on functions and services provided by CFETS.

exchange rate against the US dollar. The move affirmed China's commit-ment of not engaging in the bout of competitive devaluations and helped to stabilize the nervous global foreign exchange market.

After 15 years of negotiation, China became a member of the World Trade Organization (WTO) on December 11, 2001. China's accession to the WTO was lauded as its strong commitment to continue reforming its economy and to accept the rules governing global trade. Leveraging on commitments to WTO to open up and liberalize, China has continued its efforts to reform various sectors of its economy, and expand into the global economy. The combination of open and reform, and the concurrent trend of globalization has worked out quite well for China. From 2001 to 2004, its economy grew by 40% and its degree of openness measured by the ratio of trade to GDP increased from the level of 0.43 to 0.70. At the same time, China experienced strong growth in foreign direct investment inflow, trade volume, and holding of foreign exchange reserves.

China's continued strong economic performance after its accession to WTO led other economies to contemplate its roles in the global economy. By then, China is far too large to be kept out of the global economy. Exports from China have flooded the world and become formidable chal-lenges to local industries overseas. At the same time, the Chinese market has become important markets for others, especially the resources export-ing economies. Together with the expanding trade sector, China's trade surplus and holding of foreign exchange reserves are increasing at a brisk rate, which led to accusations that China was manipulating its currency value to gain an unfair competitive advantage in the global market. The US is arguably the most vocal advocate of the view that China manipulates its currency. In the midst of the contentious debate, China modified its exchange rate policy in July 2005. We will discuss the debate on RMB valu-ation in the next chapter.

In the roughly 12-year period, China acted quite independently to manage its foreign exchange policy. It is apparent that China prefers a stable exchange rate to develop foreign trade and attract foreign invest-ment. Against this backdrop, China fine-tuned its policy and managed the RMB rate within a narrowly defined band, especially after the crisis experi-ence. It, at the same time, moved along its reform path and gradually widened the trading band of the RMB. Throughout the process, China gave the impression that it was in control and the economy was quite well managed even when the global economy was severely tempered by the 1997 Asian financial crisis.

3.2.3 2005–2015

On July 21, 2005, China re-tuned its exchange rate formation mechanism and instituted a "managed floating exchange rate regime based on market demand and supply with reference to a basket of currencies." Since China has trade and investment interactions with the global economy beyond the US, the RMB value against a basket of currencies, instead of against only the US dollar, offers an appropriate measure of the currency's global value and competitiveness. Indeed, in theoretical studies, an exchange rate index with appropriate weights of its constituents is a preferred comprehensive measure of the relative value of a currency. Further, by referencing to a basket of currencies, China can move the RMB out of the US dollar's shadow, and step in the right direction of RMB exchange rate flexibility. Under a currency basket setting, depending on the performance of component currencies, the RMB can appreciate or depreciate against the US, and, thus, it is flexible against the US dollar in both directions.

Despite the official stance, the RMB movement between 2005 and 2015 mostly gives the impression that it was managed against the US dollar — or the US dollar has a very large relative weight in the currency basket.[22] After the initial 2% revaluation against the US dollar from 8.28 to 8.11 on July 21, the RMB experienced a gradually appreciation until July 2008. Some studies characterize the arrangement as effectively similar to a crawling peg arrangement. The daily trading band was initially kept at the level of 0.3% and widened to 0.5% on May 21, 2007.

In the midst of the 2008–09 global financial crisis, China emphasized the stability of RMB exchange rate, a policy stance that was similar to the one taken during the 1997 Asian financial crisis. The rate was tightly managed around the level of RMB6.83 against one US dollar from July 2008 to

---

[22] See, for example, Frankel (2006, 2009) and Sun (2010). Funke and Gronwald (2008) use a nonlinear framework to illustrate the slow varying nature of China's exchange rate regime during the period.

June 2010. Essentially, China halted the appreciation of RMB against the US dollar and, at the same time, did not join the bout of currency depreciations of developing economies. The stability of RMB helped to stabilize the global financial market then.

On June 19, 2010, China announced to further reform its exchange rate formation mechanism based on measures taken in 2005. In essence, it reiterated the 2005 declared policy of managing the RMB against a basket of currencies. The announcement was taken as an affirmation of the established policy of managed floating rate arrangement. Again, the authorities did not give specific information of the currency basket composition — neither the component currencies nor their weights — under consideration.[23] It is perceived that, without disclosing the currency basket, the authorities have an extra degree of freedom to manage the exchange rate.

Further, the basket of currencies is used as a reference but not as a pegging anchor in determining the RMB value. That is the exchange rate formation mechanism makes reference to but does not have to peg to the currency basket. Upon the further reform initiative, the RMB embarked upon its new gradual appreciation path. The daily trading band, after being adjusted to 0.5% in 2007, was further widened to 1.0% on both sides of the daily fixing on April 16, 2012, and to ±2 % on March 17, 2014.

The gradual widening of the trading band signifies China's confidence in its exchange rate reform strategy. A widened band adds flexibility to the RMB exchange rate, allows for a role of demand and supply forces in determining the rate, and increases the probability of two-way fluctuations of the RMB. Since the RMB resumed its exchange rate reform, the market has made substantial bets on one-way RMB appreciation under the tightly guarded exchange trading. A wider trading band means the RMB can deviate further away from the daily fixing set by the authorities and, thus, heightens the risk of making one-way bets. Indeed, in both 2012 and 2014, the RMB showed two-way volatility with some downward movements, albeit for a short time period, around the time the trading

---

[23] The PBoC Governor Zhou Xiaochuan in 2005 indicated that the US dollar, the euro, the Japanese yen, and the Korean won are included, though specific currency weights are not revealed. Further there is no official information on whether there are changes in component currencies and their weights over time.

band was widened. That is, China engineered two-way volatility via managing the trading band.

In 2015, China cumulated its financial market reform efforts and lobbied heavily to have the RMB included in the International Monetary Fund's special drawing rights basket.[24] Before the widely expected announcement by the International Monetary Fund on November 30 to formally admit the Chinese currency to its currency basket,[25] China carried out a number of policy changes to enhance its odd.[26] For instance, on August 11, 2015, China fine-tuned the RMB exchange rate formation mechanism. Specifically, the People's Bank of China announced that the daily fixing will be set by referencing to the previous day's closing rate, market demand and supply, and valuations of other currencies.[27]

The change in procedure was meant to assign market forces a big role in setting the daily official rate. The RMB depreciated 1.9% against the US dollar the first day the new fixing procedure was adopted and experienced a cumulated depreciation of 4.4% in the first three trading days after the change. The degree of depreciation, which is relatively large and unexpected, stirred up unrest in the global financial market. Some countries, including the US, worried that it was the beginning of a currency war, while the IMF viewed it is "a welcome step as it should allow market forces to have a greater role in determining the exchange rate."[28] While the change in the daily fixing procedure is meant to move the RMB exchange rate formation mechanism toward the market-oriented objective, the resulted depreciation made the global market quite nervous.

---

[24] The special drawing rights is a supplementary reserve asset created by the IMF under the Bretton Woods regime in 1969. See Chapter 6 for discussions on the RMB and the special drawing rights currency basket.

[25] The new SDR basket came into use 10 months later on October 1, 2016.

[26] Examples of these policy changes include developing offshore RMB trading centers, relaxing interest rate controls, and permitting full participation by foreign central banks and sovereign wealth funds in the domestic bond market.

[27] CFETS is authorized by the People's Bank of China to calculate and publish the central parity (à la the fixing) of the RMB. Before August 11, 2015, the fixing is based on a trimmed weighted average of prices from designated liquidity providers, and the weights are set discretionally; see http://www.chinamoney.com.cn/fe/Channel/2781516.

[28] See https://www.imf.org/external/country/CHN/rr/2015/0811.pdf (IMF Press Line on PBC's Announcement on the change to the RMB fixing mechanism, August 11, 2015).

For foreign central banks, the RMB became technically convertible when the People's Bank of China announced in September 2015 that they will be allowed to participate in the onshore interbank RMB market.[29] The change followed a similar relaxation of restrictions on foreign central banks' participation in the domestic bond market. The full participation in the onshore foreign exchange and bond markets greatly facilitates these institutions to manage their investment denominated in RMB. Five days before the announcement of the special drawing rights membership, the first batch of seven institutions completed the procedure to participate in China's interbank foreign exchange market.[30]

On December 11, 2015, in less than two weeks after the RMB was accepted to the special drawing rights currency basket, CFETS published a commentary on its website together with a RMB exchange rate index.[31] And, the People's Bank of China reproduced the commentary on its own website.[32] In essence, the commentary points out the deficient of focusing on the bilateral RMB and US dollar exchange rate, and advocates the appropriateness of looking at the RMB value relative to a currency basket. The point of referencing the RMB to a currency basket was openly announced back in 2005 and, at least, again in 2010. What is new is that the CFETS RMB index is published together with its component currencies and their weights.[33] Among the 13 component currencies, the US dollar has a weight of 26.4%, euro 21.39%, the Japanese yen 14.68%, and the remaining currencies less than 10% each.[34]

---

[29] Sovereign wealth funds and international financial organizations were offered similar treatments.

[30] Three of the seven institutions are central banks: Hong Kong Monetary Authority, Reserve Bank of Australia, and National Bank of Hungary. The other four institutions are The International Bank for Reconstruction and Development, International Development Association, World Bank Group Trust Funds, and Government of Singapore Investment Corporation.

[31] See http://www.chinamoney.com.cn/fe/Info/15850969.

[32] See http://www.pbc.gov.cn/goutongjiaoliu/113456/113469/2988677/index.html.

[33] The RMB indexes based on BIS and SDR weights are included for comparison.

[34] The remaining ten currencies are HKD (6.55%), GBP (3.86%), AUD (6.27%), NZD (0.65%), SGD (3.82%), CHF (1.51), CAD (2.53%), MYR (4.67%), RUB (4.36%), and THB (3.33%).

Nevertheless, there is no information on how these currencies are selected into the index, and how their weights are determined. The Korean won and Taiwanese dollar that have the fourth and fifth largest weights in the BIS RMB index, for instance, are not included in the CFETS RMB index. Further, it is not clear if the CFETS currency basket is the one that the People's Bank of China (or Chinese authorities) uses to guide the RMB exchange rate movement. Despite all these, the revelation of the CFETS RMB index stirred up concerns that China uses the reference to the index to mitigate criticisms against further RMB depreciation against the US dollar.[35]

China's exchange rate policy is not a stand-alone policy but is part of its overall reform architecture. For instance, to prepare for the exchange rate formation mechanism reform, China restructured its financial sector via the joint-stock reform of state-owned banks in the 1990s. When restructured large financial intuitions were essentially in place in 2005, China revamped its exchange rate policy and followed the currency basket approach.

Around the same time, China prepared for the use of the RMB overseas, and stealthily began its initiative to develop offshore RMB centers in 2003 by setting the RMB clearing bank in Hong Kong — the first facility of this kind outside mainland China. After the 2008–09 global financial crisis, China has stepped up its efforts to promote the cross-border use of the RMB while continued to reform its domestic sectors.[36] All these policy initiatives are introduced addressing the specific economic scenarios faced by China. On the one hand, exchange rate reform is an established policy — over time, market factors are playing an increasingly important role in determining the RMB exchange rate. On the other hand, the pace and details of policy changes are dictated by China's needs and conditions, and not by pressure from outside.

3.3 Some Reflections

In the previous sections, we outlined China's foreign exchange policy between 1949 and 2015. Before 1979, the exchange rate policy was designed

---

[35] Cheung, Hui and Tsang (2016) empirically assesses the relative roles of the US dollar and the CFETS RMB index in determining the RMB daily fixings.

[36] See Chapters 5 and 6 on China's policies of globalizing its currency.

in accordance to, in addition to economic considerations, ideology issues under a rather hostile external environment. Under a centrally planned system in which prices and quantities are set from a top-down approach, the RMB exchange rate played a limited economic role in regulating imports and exports.

To operationalize the communist ideology, China launched several political, social, and economic movements in the 1950s and 1960s to build up a prosperous socialist Chinese economy. The exchange rate was used as an administrative tool to tackle the economic reality as perceived by the authorities, and was usually effectively used as an accounting variable for completing central planning exercises. Despite the exchange rate is an important price linking China to the rest of the world, it was set administratively and was inelastic to market forces. The exchange rate determination process then was mainly driven by ideological and political reasoning rather than economic considerations, and did not yield desirable economic effects.

After the 1979 reform initiative, the basic philosophy underlying the economic policy making has been shifted toward economic factors, and the role of political considerations weakened. Market forces have been gaining their weights in discussions of economic matters. Demand and supply factors are slowly introduced to the centrally planned economy to achieve economic efficiency. The exchange rate formation mechanism is gradually guided to the goal of flexibility. And the RMB exchange rate is playing an increasingly important role in supporting the economy, and regulating the external and internal sectors.

Reforming the world's most populous country is not an easy undertaking. The mission is complicated by the charge to build an affluent socialist society with Chinese characteristics under the communist rule. Almost by definition, there is no precedent for China's ambitious reform. As said earlier, China has taken the gradual approach and adopted the experimental "feel the rock, wade across the river" strategy to carry out its various reform initiatives. The evolution of China's exchange rate policy exemplifies its general reform philosophy. In general, China does not rush to achieve full flexibility of its currency.

Even before the inception of the reform era, China designed its exchange rate arrangement according to China's economic and political circumstances. Since 1979, China has revamped its exchange rate formation mechanism to support and complement its efforts in reforming the economy. It dictates the timing and the specifics of policy changes to address China's own economic conditions. The controllability of policy is also an important factor to consider. When the existing exchange rate policy is out-grown by developments in the economy, new policy initiatives are introduced to further reform the exchange rate policy.

Even under the so-called gradual approach, the role of RMB in both the local and global economy has grown quite noticeably since the Chinese style managed floating rate arrangement was stipulated in 2005. For instance, under China's carefully orchestrated campaign to promote the cross-border uses of the RMB, the Chinese currency has ascended quickly in the global financial market and become one of the world's most commonly used trade settlement currencies. The reforming and liberalizing efforts were recognized by the IMF in late 2015 when it announced the RMB to be the new fifth component currency of the SDR basket.[37] That is, with self-initiated and gradually changed policies, China has managed the RMB exchange rate formation mechanism quite well in serving its economy and pushing its currency to the global financial system.

---

[37] The four incumbent SDR currencies are the US dollar, euro, British pound and Japanese yen.

Chapter 4

RMB Valuation

Managing the exchange rate value has been part of China's reform agenda. Before the 21st century, however, the world did not pay much attention to the global value of the RMB. The sharp increase in China's trade surplus, after a dip in 2004, has changed the scene (Figure 4.1). The size of China's trade surplus has alarmed its trading partners of the adverse implications for their domestic economies. Since then, the appropriate level of the RMB exchange rate has become a controversial topic among policymakers and academia.

On the one hand, the US and other countries have accused China of manipulating the RMB exchange rate and setting it at an artificially low level, which gives Chinese exporters an "unfair" advantage when competing in the US market, as well as exporting "deflation" to global market.[1] The US government, for instance, has exerted political pressure on the Chinese government to revalue the RMB and increase its flexibility so that an appropriate level could be achieved by market forces. Even after 2005, the year China loosened its tight grip on the RMB and allowed the currency to

---

[1]Commentators also refer to China's holding of foreign exchange reserves, which has exhibited a blast of increase since 2005 as another indicator of undervaluation of the RMB. Some recent studies on hoarding of international reserves are Aizenman and Lee (2007), Aizenman and Marion (2003, 2004), Aizenman et al. (2007, 2015), de Beaufort Wijnholds and Kapteyn (2001), Cheung and Wong (2008), Cheung and Ito (2008, 2009a), Cheung and Sengupta (2011), Cheung and Qian (2009b), Flood and Marion (2002), and Genberg et al. (2005).

USD bn

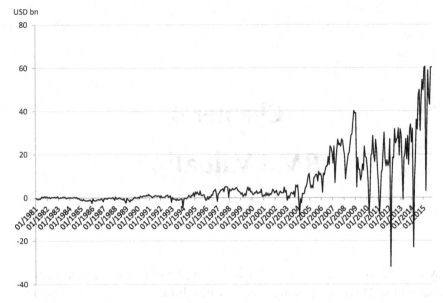

Figure 4.1   Trade Balance of China (1981M1 to 2015M9)

slowly appreciate, the US has repeatedly asserted that the RMB is still closely managed and demanded China to further liberalize the RMB.

On the other hand, China claims that the country is opening up its capital account in measured steps to avoid unnecessary mishaps and market chaos. The exchange rate mechanism reform is conducted accordingly, and policies that allow market forces to play an increasing role are introduced over time. It is not practicing a predatory policy to promote its export trade. Indeed, since 2005, the RMB has been appreciated steadily even when currencies in the 2010s including the euro, the Japanese yen, and other emerging market currencies engineered some noticeable degree of depreciation.

In the first decade of the 21st century, studies by academicians and think tanks usually favored the view that the RMB is undervalued, if not seriously undervalued. A sample of these studies includes Bergsten (2007, 2010a, 2010b), Bergsten and Gagnon (2012), Cline and Williamson (2008a, 2008b, 2010), Funke and Rahn (2005), Hufbauer and Brunel (2008), Gagnon and Hufbauer (2011), Goldstein and Lardy (2009), Korhonen and Ritola (2011), Stupnytska et al. (2009), Subramanian (2010), Tenengauzer (2010), and Wang and Hu (2010). Indeed, the 2005 Schumer–Graham bipartisan bill that proposes to impose an across the board tariff on all imports from China to force China to stop currency manipulation is claimed to use estimates of the level of the RMB undervaluation provided by economists to come up with the proposed tariff rate of 27.5%.[2]

In May 2015, the International Monetary Fund (IMF), in its end of Article IV consultation mission press release, stated that the RMB is at a level that is no longer undervalued while urging China to make "rapid progress toward greater exchange rate flexibility."[3] The IMF "no longer undervalued" assessment is also shared by a long-time critic of China's foreign exchange policy (Cline, 2015).[4] The IMF's point of view, however, was not in line with its largest shareholder. The US Treasury Department, in a few hours after the IMF press release, reiterated its view that the RMB is still substantially undervalued.

In this chapter, we discuss the valuation of RMB from an alternative perspective. Instead of arguing whether the RMB is under- or over-valued, we focus on the basic issues of assessing whether a currency in general, and the RMB in particular, is misaligned. First, we discuss some typical theoretical and empirical issues encountered in modeling equilibrium exchange rates. Second, we consider a few methods that are commonly used to investigate the degree of RMB misalignment. The uncertain and imprecise nature of these exercises is highlighted. Third, we recap some of the recent studies on the valuation of RMB. The discussions, we hope, could offer a useful backdrop for an informed debate on and assessment of the valuation of the RMB.

4.1 Modeling Equilibrium Exchange Rate[5]

The inability of structural economic and time-series models to explain exchange rate movements is documented by the well-cited study of Meese

[2] See http://schumer.senate.gov/SchumerWebsite/pressroom/press_releases/2005/PR4111.China020305.html.

[3] International Monetary Fund Communications Department (2015).

[4] Since Cline and Williamson (2008a), William R. Cline has engaged in preparing a semi-annual exchange rate misalignment assessment exercise using a fundamental equilibrium exchange rate framework, which will be discussed later in the chapter.

[5] Some of the materials are drawn from Cheung (2012), Cheung, Chinn and Fujii (2007b, 2011), and Cheung and Fujii (2014).

and Rogoff (1983a). The so-called Meese and Rogoff puzzle becomes a challenge for academics to provide evidence to beat the performance of a naïve random walk model specification. The effort to resolve the puzzle is arguably in vain so far. Attempts to resolve the puzzle include the works of Bacchetta *et al.* (2010), Cheung *et al.* (2005), Meese and Rogoff (1983b), and Rogoff (1996).[6] Recently, Rossi (2013) affirmed that, under the floating exchange rate regime, it is difficult to find a model that consistently outperforms the random walk specification for all exchange rates, for all periods, and for alternative evaluation criteria. One implication of the robustness of Meese and Rogoff puzzle is that it is difficult to find a commonly agreed framework to assess equilibrium exchange rates.

Even though journalistic writings typically refer to nominal exchange rates, academic studies on currency misalignment focus on real exchange rates. While the Meese and Rogoff results pertain to nominal exchange rates, the same conclusions typically apply to real exchange rates — an unsurprising outcome given the close correspondence of nominal and real exchange rates, except in countries experiencing rapid inflation.

In the following, we discuss the difficulties of assessing the degree of RMB misalignment. However, as the difficulty of modeling exchange rates is generic, these difficulties are relevant to the general discussion of estimating currency misalignment.

4.1.1 Theoretical considerations

Given the growing economic power of China, the extent of RMB misalignment and its implications are of great relevance to policymakers and financial institutions. For economists, the RMB is undervalued (overvalued) when it can be exchanged for a smaller (larger) amount of US dollar than what economic fundamentals suggest. In the technical jargon, the amount suggested by economic fundamentals is the equilibrium exchange rate. With the equilibrium value, we can then predict whether the market

---

[6] Also see Alquist and Chinn (2008), Berkowitz and Giorgianni (2001), Cerra and Saxena (2010), Chen *et al.* (2010), Cheung and Erlandsson (2005), Chinn and Meese (1995), Engel *et al.* (2008), Molodtsova and Papell (2009), and Rogoff and Stavrakeva (2008).

rate is overvalued or undervalued, and by how much. Thus, the overarching issue is the determination of the equilibrium value of RMB.

Which exchange rate model is appropriate for evaluating RMB's fair value? In exchange rate economics, however, there is very limited consensus on which is the right exchange rate model. Different models might be relevant for economies with different economic structures and over different time horizons. A related issue is that standard or conventional equilibrium exchange rate models may not work for an emerging economy or an economy in transition. China has undergone rapid structural changes, and has been transitioning from a central planning economy toward a market-oriented one over the last couple of decades. Despite the reform effort, China is still a hybrid economy characterized by attributes of both "planned" and "market" systems, and non-negligible capital control measures. These characteristics lead to concerns about the choice of an appropriate RMB exchange rate model. In the absence of a consensual exchange rate model, we should interpret any currency misalignment estimates with caution.

When the observed exchange rate is different from its equilibrium value, does it mean that the currency has been manipulated to stay at, say, an artificially low level? The well-known Dornbusch (1976) overshooting model is a useful setting to expound the role of time horizon in interpreting deviations from the equilibrium exchange rate. Under the overshooting framework, the exchange rate in the short run can deviate from its long-run equilibrium value and, at the same time, is consistent with market fundamentals. That is, the equilibrium path of the exchange rate can deviate from its long-run value in the short run, and the observed misalignment does not necessarily imply a disequilibrium scenario that requires a corresponding policy remedy.

Even when the observed exchange rate is different from its long-run equilibrium rate, one should not jump to the conclusion that the market rate is inappropriate, and intervention is required to restore the correct exchange rate value. The time horizon consideration definitely increases the complexity of the misalignment assessment exercise.

Whether there is misalignment or not depends on which economic model or what time horizon is being used as the benchmark. Undervaluation, overvaluation, or currency misalignment, in general, can be in the eye of the beholder.

As summarized in Cheung, Chinn and Fujii (2010b, 2010c), most of the extant studies on RMB misalignment adopt some theoretical framework that can be placed in the categories of relative purchasing power parity, the Penn effect, the fundamental equilibrium exchange rate approach, and the macroeconomic balance effect approach. We will briefly comment on results from these approaches in Section 4.2.

In addition to theoretical considerations, the challenge of valuing the RMB is compounded by the usual difficulties encountered in empirical exercises.

4.1.2 Empirical considerations

Even if a theoretical exchange rate specification is chosen, the ability to infer the actual level of misalignment is hindered by some practical statistical considerations. Let us consider a few here. For a given theoretical framework, researchers have to derive an empirical specification and choose an estimation technique, preferably based on theory. It is not uncommon that empirical studies based on the same theoretical framework employ different estimation specifications and econometric techniques. It is quite common to observe that estimates of currency misalignment vary substantially with estimation specification and econometric techniques. Dunaway, Leigh, and Li (2009), for instance, show that a small change in model specification could give rise to very different equilibrium estimates.

The preciseness of a misalignment estimate is also affected by the usual statistical caveats, including sampling uncertainty and data uncertainty.

Given an estimate of the degree of misalignment, what do we know about the probability that the currency under consideration is misaligned? This is a standard statistical question of sampling uncertainty, which arises from the fact that the data included in the estimation process do not contain all the information of interest. The confidence interval is a typical measure of the level of sampling uncertainty. The more (less) informative the data, the narrower (wider) will be the interval. As noted by Cheung, Chinn and Fujii (2007b), the data used to assess RMB misalignment typically are not very informative in the sense that the misalignment estimate usually comes with a very wide confidence interval, which makes a clear-cut statistical statement on overvaluation or undervaluation impossible.

Data uncertainty is another factor that may affect the estimation of the degree of currency misalignment. Indeed, the quality and accuracy of Chinese economic data is a subject of concern for most empirical studies.[7] These concerns are exacerbated by the occasionally large changes in the accounting methodologies used in generating some of major macroeconomic indicators. For instance, China has routinely revised the economic data based on its National Economic Census, which was first conducted in 2004. The first such revision took place in December 2005 based on the new nationwide economic survey, and China revised its 2004 GDP figure upward by 17%. These data revisions are sufficiently massive that results based upon pre-revision data could be overturned.

In addition to uncertainty associated with economic data provided by the Chinese statistical agencies, international organizations revise data in a manner that could affect the calculations of the equilibrium RMB exchange rate. A case in point is the sensitivity of empirical RMB misalignment estimates obtained from price and output data derived from various International Comparison Program surveys. In 2007, World Bank, together with Asian Development Bank, released the 2005 International Comparison Program benchmark and revised the corresponding data.[8] The new release came with a substantial revision of some national data. For example, China's PPP-per capita gross domestic product data were revised down by 40% as the price level was revised upward. In the subsequent sections, we will discuss the implications of the change in the International Comparison Program benchmark for the debate on RMB valuation.

4.2 Estimating the Degree of RMB Misalignment

As pointed out in the previous section, the assessment of exchange rate misalignment is impaired by both theoretical and empirical impreciseness.

---

[7] On the reliability of Chinese, see footnote 10 of Chapter 2. Also, see the discussion in Section 4.2.3.2.
[8] See Asian Development Bank (2007), International Comparison Program (2007), and World Bank (2008a).

Table 4.1   Some Recent RMB Misalignment Estimates

Estimate	As of	Source
+45.6%	January 2016	*The Economist* (2016), Big Mac Index
+33%	March 2009	Cline and Williamson (2010), FEER
+31%*	2005	Subramanian (2010), Penn effect
+21%**	End of 2008	Goldstein and Lardy (2009), external balance
+17.5**	2009	Wang and Hu (2010), FEER, external balance
+10%	2010Q1	Tenengauzer (2010), external balance
+2.56%	2009Q4	Stupnytska *et al.* (2009), BEER
−5%	2008	Cheung *et al.* (2010c)
−13.4%	2008Q4	Hu and Chen (2010), FEER
−16.8%	September 2009	Cheung *et al.* (2010c), relative PPP, real US exchange rate
−36%	December 2009	Cheung *et al.* (2010c), real PPP, trade-weighted exchange rate
−(>)100%	—	Schnatz (2011), FEER

Notes: The "Estimate" column lists the RMB misalignment estimates, with a positive sign indicates undervaluation and a negative sign overvaluation.
* The average of estimates from adjusted data.
** The average of estimates.

Some consequences of the impreciseness are illustrated by Table 4.1, which presents some recent RMB misalignment estimates reported in the literature.[9] The dispersion of these misalignment estimates is strikingly large. The estimates range from a 46% undervaluation (*The Economist*, 2016, Big Mac Index)[10] to an over 100% overvaluation (Schnatz, 2011, FEER). The differences in the estimates come not only from different model specifications and different sample periods, but also from models with similar

---

[9] See also Table 27.1 of Cheung (2012), and Table 1 of Cheung, Chinn and Fujii (2010b).
[10] The large degree of undervaluation is obtained by comparing the prices of big mac in China and the US. The undervaluation is shrunk to 9.4% when the income differential of these two countries is accounted for, see http://www.economist.com/content/big-mac-index/ for additional information.

theoretical underpinning. Even if we drop the extreme overvaluation cases, the remaining estimates still cover a rather wide range.

Most studies and debates on the issue did not explicitly address the notorious difficulty of determining the extent of RMB undervaluation, and the impreciseness of empirical RMB misalignment estimates. Finding a solution to the problem is not easy. Nevertheless, we think it is important to acknowledge the problem, and understand its relevance in practical situations.

In the next subsection, we use a simple setup to illustrate the sensitivity of empirical estimates of the degree of RMB misalignment. Then, we discuss the difficulties encountered by some commonly used exchange rate models.

4.2.1 Deviations from average and trend estimates

There is no shortage of estimates of the degree of RMB misalignment, which vary considerably from one study to other. Some basic issues related to multiple misalignment estimates can be highlighted using the relative purchasing power parity (relative PPP) and the deviation from the trend framework.

Relative PPP asserts that, in the long run, the nominal exchange rate moves with the relative price level of the two countries under consideration, up to a constant.[11] The concept could be expressed as follows:

$$S = \left(\frac{P}{P^*} \right) \times \Psi \tag{4.1}$$

where S is the exchange rate expressed in the amount of RMB per unit of foreign currency. P is the general price index (say, the consumption price index, CPI) of China, P^* is the foreign price index, and Ψ is a proportional constant. Although relative PPP may not be valid in short run, it holds approximately in the long run. Therefore, equation (4.1), as a long-run

---

[11] See, for example, Rogoff (1996) for a review. Some studies on relative PPP are Apte *et al.* (1994), Cheung and Lai (2000), Holmes (2000), Aizenman (2004), Cheung, Lai and Bergman (2004), Taylor and Taylor (2004), and Coakley *et al.* (2005).

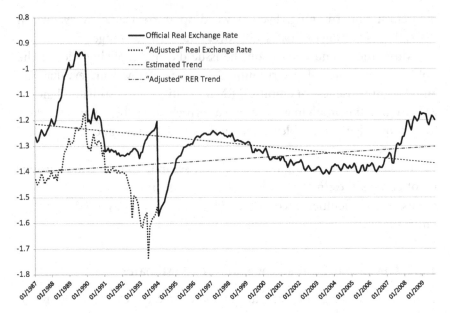

Figure 4.2   RMB Real Exchange Rates and Trends (1987M1 to 2009M9), in logs

relationship, implies that the real exchange rate (RER) would converge to the average of Ψ:

$$S = \left(\frac{P}{P^*}\right) \times \Psi \qquad (4.2)$$

Figure 4.2 shows the official real exchange rate series from January 1987 to September 2009, deflated by the US and Chinese CPIs.[12] The official rate is defined in such a way that higher values of the rate indicate a stronger Chinese currency. The solid black line shows the official real exchange rate and the dotted line represents the "adjusted" real exchange rate.[13] As shown

---

[12] See also Cheung, Chinn and Fujii (2010b, 2010c).

[13] As with the case with many economies experiencing transition from controlled to partially decontrolled capital accounts and from dual to unified exchange rate regimes, there is some dispute over what exchange rate measure to use. It turns out that in the years leading up to 1994, increasingly large amounts of RMB transactions were taking place at "swap rates" — rather than the official rate — so that the 1994 "mega-devaluation" is actually better described as a unification of different rates of exchange (Fernald *et al.* 1999). The "adjusted" rate in Figure 4.2 is a weighted average of the official and swap rates.

in the figure, the value of RMB has declined for a number of years after the Asian financial crisis in 1997 as expected. After a policy change in 2005, we observe a steady appreciation of the RMB.

However, the major problem with real exchange rates based on price indexes is that it provides no information on the level of the equilibrium rate. It is difficult to determine the extent of currency misalignment from the real exchange rates. Therefore, we need to compare its movement with its own trend. In the early warning system literature that developed in the wake of the financial crises of the 1990s, a typical measure of currency misalignment was the deviation from a deterministic trend.

The linear trends fitted to the official and "adjusted" exchange rates are indicated by the two broken lines in Figure 4.2. As we can observe from the figure, the main difference between the official and adjusted rates is their trending behavior. The RMB based on the official rate shows a downward trend while the adjusted rate displays an upward trend. Despite the official and adjusted rates have trends of different signs, the trend deviation measure of misalignment indicates that both rates represent an overvaluation of RMB: the "adjusted" rate shows an overvaluation of 10.4% and the official rate shows an overvaluation of 16.8% in September 2009. Note that, around the turn of the 21st century, most people believed that the RMB was undervalued, not overvalued.

When the sample period is updated to the end of 2014, the corresponding estimated trend lines of the official rate and adjusted rate show an upward momentum, though with different slopes (Figure 4.3). That is, a change in the sample period alters the inference about the trending behavior of the exchange rate. Based on these new trend estimates, both the official and adjusted rates represent an RMB overvaluation — the "adjusted" rate displays an overvaluation of 15% and the official rate an overvaluation of 22% — in November of 2014.

Up to this point, some readers may believe that, despite the usual undervaluation claim, the inference of the RMB overvaluation is robust. Figure 4.4, however, portrays a different scenario. When we look at, say, the period of January 2006 to November 2014 in which only the official rate is the relevant rate, the evidence of misalignment changes. Although the estimated trend of the official rate is still upward sloping, the implied degree of misalignment is that the RMB is undervalued by 3.3%! That is,

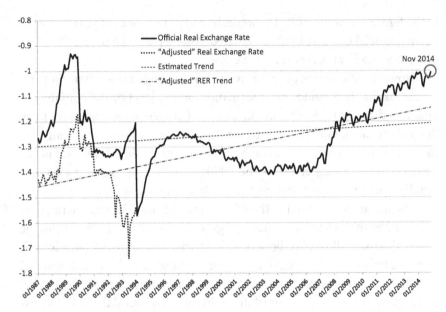

Figure 4.3   RMB Real Exchange Rates and Trends (1987M1 to 2014M11), in logs

one could change the evidence on, say, overvaluation to undervaluation by simply selecting the appropriate sample period.

Another noticeable observation from Figure 4.4 is that the evidence of misalignment depends on the reference point. In this case, the benchmarks based on the estimated mean and trend yield, respectively, an overvaluation and an undervaluation estimate. In anticipation of the discussions in the following subsections, the choice of an estimated mean or an estimated trend in a sense is analogous to the choice of alternative empirical exchange rate models in determining the equilibrium exchange rate.

Instead of examining the bilateral exchange rate, some people may argue that trade-weighted effective exchange rate indexes are more preferable since focusing on the bilateral exchange rate may overlook the overall competitiveness.[14] However, appealing to trade-weighted exchange rates would not necessarily resolve matters. Figure 4.5 depicts the RMB real

---

[14] See, for example, Chinn (2006) for a primer on real effective exchange rates. Since the early 2000s, China has mentioned a few times its preference for assessing the RMB value against a currency basket rather than against a single currency, say, the US dollar.

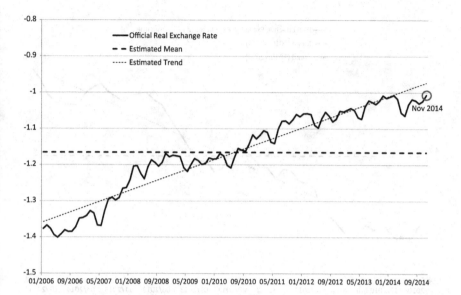

Figure 4.4 RMB Real Exchange Rate, Its Mean, and Trend (2006M1 to 2014M11), in logs

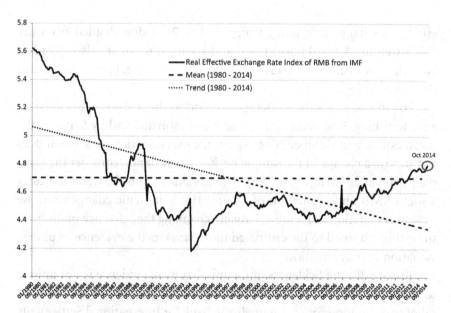

Figure 4.5 RMB Real Effective Exchange Rate Index from IMF, Its Mean, and Trend (1980M1 to 2014M10), in logs

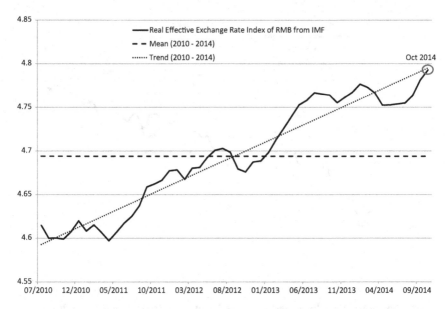

Figure 4.6   RMB Real Effective Exchange Rate Index from IMF, Its Mean, and Trend (2010M07 to 2014M10), in logs

effective exchange rate index from 1980 to 2014 downloaded from the IMF's website. A fitted linear trend and a sample mean are also included. Note that the estimated trend line is downward sloping, instead of upward sloping as in Figure 4.3.

For this real effective exchange rate index, the RMB is overvalued by an astonishing 57% according to the trend estimate, and by 9.4% by the mean estimate in October 2014. Again, the overvaluation conclusion does not survive a change in the sample period. For instance, consider the sample period after 2010 (Figure 4.6). The deviation from the trend indicates a slight RMB undervaluation of around 1%; a dramatic change from the 52% overvaluation in Figure 4.5. Again, changing the reference point from the estimated trend to the estimated mean reverses the evidence of undervaluation to overvaluation.

Apparently, the fickleness of the misalignment evidence is not unique to the IMF data. The RMB real effective exchange rate indexes from the other two common sources, namely the Bank for International Settlements (BIS) and the World Bank display similar patterns. The BIS case depicted

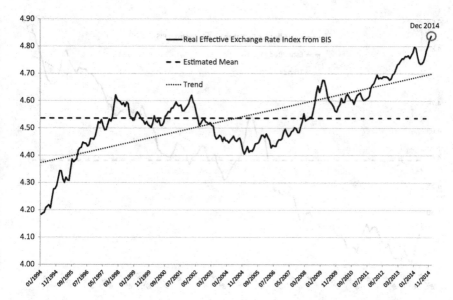

Figure 4.7 **RMB Real Effective Exchange Rate Index from BIS, Its Mean, and Trend (1994M1 to 2014M12), in logs**

in Figures 4.7 and 4.8, and the World Bank case depicted in Figures 4.9 and 4.10 again illustrate the conclusion on whether the RMB is overvalued or undervalued depends on the choices of the sample period and the benchmark.[15]

What is the moral of these trend- and mean-based misalignment estimates? The obvious message is the fragility and sensitivity of a misalignment estimate — both in term of its magnitude and direction. Despite some believing that the setup is oversimplistic, the framework highlights how easy

---

[15] Regarding the case of RMB real effective exchange rate index from BIS for the period 1994 to 2014 (Figure 4.7), the RMB is overvalued by 14.9% according to the trend estimate, and by 35.2% by the mean estimate in December 2014. For the period after September 2004 (Figure 4.8), the RMB is overvalued by 5% according to the trend estimate, and overvalued by 27.4% by the mean estimate in December 2014.

Regarding the RMB real effective exchange rate data from the World Bank for the period 1980 to 2013 (Figure 4.9), the RMB is overvalued by 52.1% according to the trend estimate, and by 4.6% by the mean estimate in 2013. For the period after 1994 (Figure 4.10), the RMB is overvalued by 9.6% according to the trend estimate, and by 25.5% by the mean estimate in 2013.

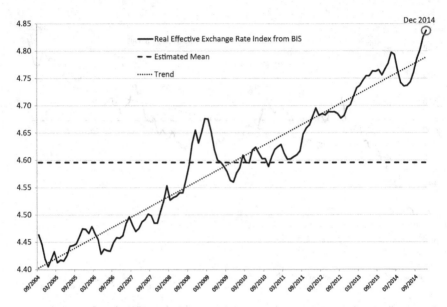

Figure 4.8   Log of RMB Real Effective Exchange Rate Index from BIS, Its Mean and Trend (2004M9 to 2014M12), in logs

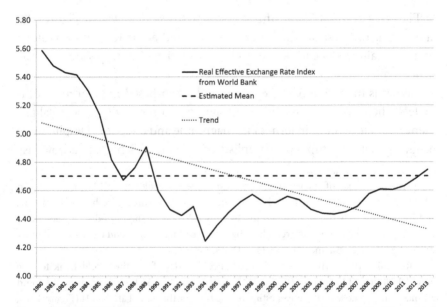

Figure 4.9   RMB Real Effective Exchange Rate Index from World Bank, Its Mean, and Trend (1980 to 2013), in logs

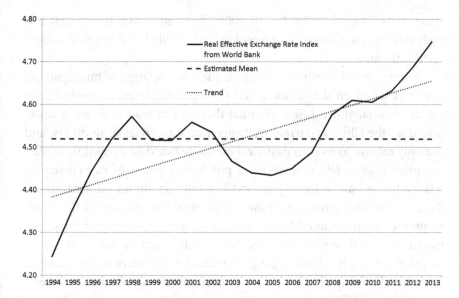

Figure 4.10   RMB Real Effective Exchange Rate Index from World Bank, Its Mean, and Trend (1994 to 2013), in logs

the conclusion on misalignment could be changed. There is no complicated estimation technology and complex data interaction. With "appropriate judicious" choices of sample period and reference point (a la empirical models), one can completely turn the misalignment result around.

Even within the simple framework adopted above, there are a few other factors in addition to the choices of sample period and benchmark that complicate the effort of determining the level of misalignment. For instance, the use of, say, non-linear trend lines or moving averages, which are more sophisticated than the simple trend and average methods, can generate different estimates of the level of misalignment.[16] The choice of a price deflator to derive the real exchange rate is another factor. While the CPI is a common choice, there are real exchange rates based on alternative deflators including producer price index, GDP price deflator, and unit

---

[16] Cheung, Chinn and Nong (2016) and Hassan (2014), for example, show that the presence of a nonlinear term in Penn effect regression affects inferences about exchange rate misalignment.

labor costs (Rogoff, 1996; Chinn 2006). It is quite safe to say that real exchange rate data based on different deflators will give different misalignment estimates.

Another point worth mentioning is the interpretation of misalignment estimates based on data constructed from price indexes. In assessing the extent of misalignment, it is essential that we can read from an estimate how does the Chinese current exchange rate stand relative to others, and not only relative to its own past. Real exchange rate data derived from relative price indexes tell us the relative purchasing power of two currencies relative to the base years of price indexes, but contain no information on the actual relative purchasing power. The trend lines plotted in the aforementioned figures should be appropriately interpreted as trend lines relative to the actual equilibrium value. Thus, with a real exchange rate based on price indexes, it is hard to gauge the actual deviation of the market rate from the desirable or the actual equilibrium rate. Consequently, assessments of the RMB misalignment based on models incorporating the relative PPP and the empirical exchange rate models using price indexes have to be interpreted carefully.

Do we get a more robust misalignment estimate with more elaborated theoretical models and statistical procedures? The answer is unfortunately not positive. As illustrated in the following subsections, sophisticated models may involve additional choice variables that further complicate the analysis.

4.2.2 Fundamental equilibrium exchange rate

Standard textbook models for exchange rates including the flexible price monetary model and the overshooting model are typically designed for countries in which economic outcomes are mainly determined by market forces. These models are deemed not to be appropriate for emerging and transitional economies that are subject to non-negligible government interventions.

For emerging and transitional economies, including China, the fundamental equilibrium exchange rate (FEER) approach is commonly used to estimate the degree of exchange rate misalignment. Here, we outline the main features of the FEER approach before discussing what we can learn about the FEER estimate of RMB misalignment.

The FEER approach is closely related to the macroeconomic balance approach,[17] which takes the perspective of saving and investment rates. Beginning with the national saving identity,

$$CA \equiv (S - I) + (T - G)$$

where CA is the current account balance, S is the private saving, I is the private investment, T is the government revenue, and G is the government expenditure. The accounting identity shows that the current account balance given by the difference between exports and imports is equal to the sum of (a) the public net saving given by the budget balance $(T - G)$, and (b) the private net saving given by the saving-investment gap $(S - I)$.

To draw policy implications and inferences, one has to impose some structure and causality on the identity. One approach is to assume the budget balance is exogenous (or use the cyclically adjusted budget balance), and then include the determinants of investment and saving.

One feature of the FEER approach is that it does not impose the restriction of a balanced current account in, say, the medium term. That is, for a policy relevant horizon, the "norm" of the current account could be non-zero. The norm that is usually expressed as a percentage of national output could either be determined by a research's prior belief or estimated empirically. When the observed balance is higher (lower) than the predetermined norm, the exchange rate is typically considered to be undervalued (overvalued). In such a case, information about trade elasticities is used to back out the "equilibrium real exchange rate" that can eliminate the gap. Assuming that the Marshall–Lerner condition is met, an appreciation (depreciation) of the currency is recommended to deal with the observed surplus (deficit). The degree of misalignment is then given by the difference between this "equilibrium real exchange rate" and the market rate.

Under the FEER approach, whether a currency is undervalued or overvalued depends on the relative position of the actual current account and the perceived norm. For a given level of exchange rate, the larger the norm of China's current account, the less likely the RMB is undervalued. The degree of misalignment, on the other hands, depends on trade

---

[17] Some early references on the FEER approach are Clark *et al.* (1994), Clark and MacDonald (1998), and Williamson (1994).

Figure 4.11   China's Real Effective Exchange Rate and Its Trade Balance (2003M1 to 2014M12)

elasticities. The larger the trade elasticities, the smaller will be the level of misalignment.

Do we have a consensus on China's current account norm? Apparently we do not. From the writings in this area, the value of norm covers quite a wide range; from a low of a 2.8% of GDP deficit (Williamson and Mahar, 1998) to a high of a 8.4% surplus (Medina, *et al.*, 2010). The norm of 8.4% is a projected value for 2014 (Medina *et al.*, 2010, Table 4). China's current account surplus was 4.0% in 2010 and 1.9% in 2013 (International Monetary Fund, 2014). If the norm is assumed to be near or at the high end of 8.4%, then the RMB is not undervalued but overvalued. Even if we consider the norm is 4%, a value that some people considered as a level that shall trigger intervention,[18] the evidence points that the RMB is over-valued rather than undervalued.

---

[18] For instance, it was reported that the then US Secretary of the Treasury Tim Geithner proposed to keep the magnitude of current account imbalance below 4% in the October 2010 G20 meeting. However, the suggested 4% target was not included in the G20 Communiqué (http://www.g20.utoronto.ca/2010/g20finance101023.html.)

Let us assume that we agreed on the current account norm. Still using trade elasticities to infer the degree of RMB misalignment is not that easy. It is a quite formidable empirical task to estimate China's trade behavior; that is, the exchange rate effect on China's trade. Figure 4.11 plots China's real effective exchange rate (an increase implies appreciation) and its trade balance. It is quite apparent that the RMB exchange rate moves with China's trade surplus in a "procyclical" manner — specifically, the RMB appreciation after the 2005 policy change was met with an increase in the trade surplus. The circumstantial evidence indicates the Chinese data may not follow the Marshall–Lerner condition. Indeed, a problematic phenomenon is that some of the Chinese trade elasticity estimates reported in the existing studies do not satisfy the Marshall–Lerner condition. When the Marshall–Lerner condition is violated, we have to entertain the "awkward" scenario of RMB depreciation, instead of appreciation is required to shrink China's trade surplus.

In general, the price elasticities of Chinese exports and imports are not very precisely and robustly estimated. Some difficulties encountered in studying China's behavior are the paucity of relevant price data on China's imports and exports, and the estimates tend to be quite sensitive to the inclusion of time trends and control variables in the regressions.[19] Further, Cheung, Chinn and Qian (2012, 2016) note that, in studying the price effect on China's exports and imports, it pays to consider alternative measures of real exchange rate and to use an appropriate estimation method to account for the (non)stationarity property of data.

Recall that the derivation of the equilibrium exchange rate under the FEER approach relies on trade elasticities. Given the high level of uncertainty surrounding the price elasticity estimates of China's exports and imports, there are concerns about the reliability of RMB misalignment estimates provided by FEER models.

Figure 4.12, which is adopted from Schnatz (2011), provides a striking picture of the sensitivity of a misalignment estimate to trade elasticity estimates. With a few China's trade elasticities found from the existing

---

[19] See, for example, Ahmed (2009), Aziz and Li (2008), Cerra and Anuradha (1999), Cerra and Saxena (2002), Fung *et al.* (2009), Kwack *et al.* (2007), Thorbecke and Zhang (2009), Mann and Plück (2007), Marquez and Schindler (2007), and Wang and Ji (2006). Some earlier studies are reviewed in Cheung, Chinn and Fujii (2010a).

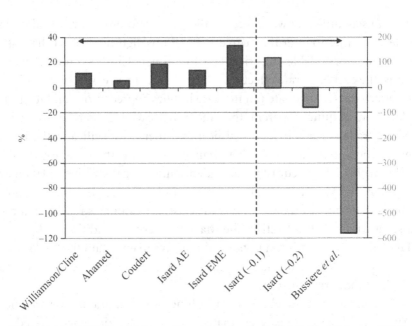

Figure 4.12   FEER Sensitivity to Changes in the Trade Elasticities (Schnatz, 2011)

Source: Schnatz (2011).

Note: Positive indicates undervaluation; Negative indicates overvaluation.

studies, the misalignment estimates range from an undervaluation of 40% to an overvaluation of near 600%. Although several extreme results may be implausible, the figure clearly shows that both the sign and the magnitude of an exchange rate misalignment estimate are sensitive to the values of trade elasticities used to make the inference.

In addition to the predetermined values of the current account norm and trade elasticities, the sign and the magnitude of RMB misalignment estimates could be affected by the ways these estimates are obtained (Dunaway *et al.*, 2009; Hu and Chen, 2010; Wang and Hu, 2010). Dunaway *et al.* (2009), for example, demonstrates that equilibrium RMB real exchange rate estimates obtained by approaches and models that are commonly used in the literature exhibit substantial variations in response to small perturbations in model specifications, explanatory variable definitions, and sample periods. In other words, inferences regarding currency misalignment can be very sensitive to small changes in the way the equilibrium exchange rate is estimated.

4.2.3 Penn effect estimates

The Penn effect regression is another approach commonly employed to study RMB misalignment. The basic Penn effect regression equation is given by

$$r_i = \beta_0 + \beta_1 y_i + u_i \qquad (4.3)$$

where r_i and y_i are, respectively, country i's national price level and real per capita income in logs and relative to the corresponding US variables. In the setup, the price levels refer to price indexes that allow direct cross-country comparison of purchasing powers. In most studies, the empirical analysis is conducted using the internationally comparable price indexes derived from surveys conducted by the International Comparison Program (ICP). The ICP conducted surveys on national prices in 1970, 1973, 1975, 1980, 1985, 1993, 2005, and 2011; which covered, respectively, 10, 16, 34, 60, 64, 117, 146, and 199 countries and economies. See World Bank (2008c, 2015) and International Comparison Program (2004, 2007) for a detailed discussion of the ICP surveys.

The survey results are used to produce internationally comparable price indexes, which are labeled purchasing power parities (PPPs). Using, say, the US as the numeraire country, a country's national price level is given by its PPP normalized by its US dollar exchange rate. The terms PPP and national price level are potentially confusing for those who are not familiar with the ICP data. In this context, the PPP is a local currency price measure and the national price level is a relative price, which is equivalent to the inverse of the real exchange rate. We will use these terms interchangeably in the following text.[20]

The Penn effect, a term coined by Samuelson (1994), refers to the robust empirical positive association between national price levels; that is, the real exchange rates, and real per capita income levels across countries documented by a series of Penn studies.[21] Anecdotal evidence lends support to the Penn effect phenomenon. For instance, haircut and dinning

---

[20] The PPP-based gross domestic product (GDP), which enables international comparison of real incomes and economic sizes, is the GDP in local currency units normalized by its national price level.

[21] See, for example, Kravis and Lipsey (1983, 1987), Kravis *et al.* (1978), Summers and Heston (1991), and Samuelson (1994).

tend to be more expensive in developed than developing countries, and in big metropolitan cities than rural areas. Alternatively speaking, a high income country/locality tends to have a high real exchange rate. Theoretical explanations of the Penn effect based on cross-country differences in relative productivities between the tradable and nontradable sectors are offered by, for example, Balassa (1964) and Samuelson (1964), or on the factor-endowment approach argument developed by Bhagwati (1984) and Kravis and Lipsey (1983).

The inference of currency misalignment based on equation (4.3) hinges upon the robust positive Penn effect and the implicit assumption that some real exchange rates relative to the US may be overvalued or undervalued, but they are at the equilibrium level on average. Specifically, for a given currency, the empirical level of misalignment is given by the estimated residual from equation (4.3). A positive (negative) estimated residual implies an overvaluation (undervaluation) since a high national price level means a high real exchange rate.

Figure 4.13 shows a scatter plot presented in Cheung, Chinn and Fujii (2007b) — the dots in the background are observations on the

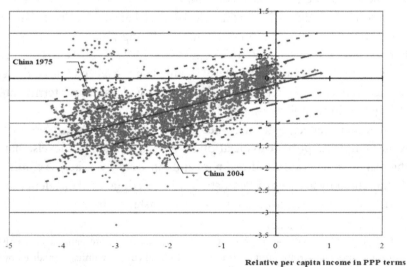

Figure 4.13   The Rate of RMB Misalignment Based on the 2006 Vintage Data on the PPP-based Per Capita Income

national price level against the per capita income of over 160 countries during the period 1975–2004. These data were from World Development Indicators. If absolute PPP holds, then the national price level should be 1 and uncorrelated with the per capita income of individual countries. Therefore, one would expect that the scatter plot of the observations to align horizontally. In fact, we can clearly observe that the observations tend to display a positive slope — in other words, higher income countries have stronger real exchange rates.

The real values of the RMB as measured by the PPP-adjusted national price level in the period 1975–2004 are traced in the figure. It is clear that the value of the RMB is declining over time. Additional information on the figure will be discussed later.

Instead of viewing the Penn effect as a problem of violating the absolute PPP, we can exploit this relationship and adopt it to assess the degree of RMB misalignment.[22] However, it is important to acknowledge the limitations of the relative-price–income relationship.

Theoretically, the equilibrium exchange rate in the Balassa–Samuelson model is the one that is consistent with both internal and external balances. In the short to medium term, however, internal or external balance is not guaranteed. Thus, the estimated exchange rate measure is properly interpreted as a long-run measure and is ill-suited (on its own) to analyzing short-run phenomena. One potential remedy is to include control variables that are relevant for (short-run) variations in internal and external balances. This remedy is explicitly discussed later.[23] Further, it is worthwhile mentioning that the Penn effect framework tends to yield the largest estimated degree of RMB undervaluation (Cairns, 2005a, 2005b). That is, the use of the Penn effect framework does not bias the results against RMB undervaluation.

In the next few subsections, we will use the Penn effect framework to illustrate a few issues encountered in estimating the level of exchange rate misalignment.

---

[22] Also see the discussion of Frankel (2006), Cheung, Chinn and Fujii (2007b), and Coudert and Couharde (2007) on this issue.

[23] Frankel (2006) discusses whether one can speak of an "equilibrium exchange rate" when there is more than one sector to consider. Engel (2009) argues that "external balance" needs to be defined in terms of efficiency in global resource allocation, rather than trade balances in the usual sense.

4.2.3.1 Sampling uncertainty

Cheung, Chinn and Fujii (2007b) use the Penn effect setup to study RMB misalignment. Using the PPP-based data on real exchange rates and GDPs plotted in Figure 4.13, they estimated equation (4.3) and reported the following Penn effect regression result:

$$r_i = -0.134 + 0.299y_i + \hat{u}_i \qquad (4.4)$$

The coefficients are statistically significant. The positively significant coefficient estimate of y_i affirms the Penn effect.

In addition to the data and China's real exchange rate series, Figure 4.13 includes the regression line given by (4.4) and the one-standard and two-standard error confidence intervals of the estimated real exchange rate. Thus, by comparing actual RMB and predicted RMB real exchange rate of the corresponding GDP level, we infer that the RMB was initially overvalued in 1975. Then the rate drifted down and its magnitude of overvaluation was shrinking in the following three decades. Then, the RMB became undervalued and amounted to 53% undervaluation in 2004.

Was the RMB undervalued? To answer the question, we have to consider both the magnitude of the misalignment estimate and the level of estimation precision (or, sampling uncertainty). The standard error confidence interval is the usual statistical device to capture sampling uncertainty associated with an estimator and is indicative of the possible range in which the true value of the variable of interest could be found. The wider the confidence interval, the less informative the data, and the less precise the estimation exercise. If the actual observation is outside the confidence interval around the predicted value, then the actual observation is deemed statistically different from the predicted value; otherwise, these two are statistically indistinguishable. Alternatively speaking, if the confidence interval contains the actual observation, the information embedded in the data is not conclusive enough to differentiate the actual and the predicted values. This is the criterion that applied economists commonly use to assess the statistical significance of empirical evidence.

One important feature of Figure 4.13 is the width of the confidence bands. Even though the RMB was lower than the estimated equilibrium value, and suggested it was undervalued in the 2000s, the RMB value stayed within the two-standard error confidence interval. That is, statistically speaking, the evidence is not significant or is not strong enough to make a definite conclusion. Obviously, the wide dispersion of the scatter plot and the wide confidence interval band displayed in the figure that signify weak information offered by data are the reasons for the inability to draw a statistically significance.

In sum, if we take sampling uncertainty into consideration, then we could not conclude that the empirical evidence on RMB undervaluation is statistically significant. That is, using the usual statistical criterion, we cannot rule out the possibility that the RMB exchange rate is consistent with its estimated equilibrium rate.

4.2.3.2 Data uncertainty

The accuracy of estimating equation (4.4) crucially depends on the quality of the price and output data used in the regression. While data quality affects all the empirical exercises, the concern regarding the reliability of the Chinese official data has been quite acute since 1980s.[24] A case in point is the accuracy of China's GDP and economic growth rate data. The general perception is that the data quality is better after the 1978 open door policy. However, China was accused of inflating its growth rate especially during the 1990s.[25] Cheung, Chinn and Fujii (2007a, p. 98), for example, shows that compared with other data sources, the Chinese official data usually give the highest growth rate.

The discussion on Chinese data reliability has reached a different level in late 2005. On December 20, 2005, the state agency the Chinese National Bureau of Statistics announced a 16.8% upward revision of the China's GDP in 2004 and put it at the level of 15.988 trillion yuan. The revision is based on the first National Economic Census conducted in 2004. The upward revision is mainly due to the previously under-reported services sector. The first economic census found that the services sector accounts for about 40%, instead of the previously reported 32%, of China's GDP in

---

[24] Some recent discussions of the reliability of the Chinese official data are Holz (2014) and Koch-Weser (2013). See also the related discussion in Chapter 2.

[25] Nevertheless, China at times in the 2000s was said to under-state its growth rate to hide the evidence of an over-heating economy; see, for example, Bradsher (2004).

2004. The refined assessment of China's services sector gives an improved measurement of the size of the Chinese economy but does not clear all the doubts about the reliability of official data.[26]

Subsequently, the second and third National Economic Census were conducted in 2008 and 2013. On December 19, 2014, the National Bureau of Statistics based on the 2013 Census revised up China's 2013 GDP by 3.4% from RMB56.9 trillion to RMB58.8 trillion.

Even the regression results in the previous subsections are based on data derived from ICP surveys, instead of the official Chinese data, the issue of data uncertainty remains. Specifically, the presented Penn effect results are based on data derived from the 1993 ICP benchmark, which is based on the 1993 ICP survey. Some emerging economies, including China and India, however, did not fully participate in the 1993 survey. For these economies, their PPP-based data are estimated and projected using partial or incomplete information.

The release of the 2005 ICP survey results in 2008 offers an opportunity to evaluate the possible drawbacks of using data derived from the 1993 ICP benchmark.[27] In the case of China, it participated in the 2005, but not the 1993, survey. Comparing data based on the 2005 survey with those derived from the previous survey, the revised China's PPP-based per capita GDP in 2005 was about 40% below the previously reported figure.[28] Indeed, large revisions resulting from the release of the new survey results are not unique to China; some countries have their 2005 per capita GDPs revised up or down by 50% or more (World Bank, 2008b).

Before the release of the latest (2011) survey results, there are modifications of the PPP-based data. While these changes are not as dramatic as those from the release of the 2005 survey data, they have some material implications for estimations using these PPP-based data. The implications

---

[26] It is noted that large revisions in output data also take place in developed countries (Faust *et al.*, 2000).

[27] The 2005 survey was conducted by the World Bank in cooperation with the Asian Development Bank. See Asian Development Bank (2007), Elekdag and Lall (2008) and International Comparison Program (2007) for discussions about the survey and data update program.

[28] That is, the 2005 ICP survey shows that China's PPP-based real exchange rate is higher than previously estimated.

Real exchange rate

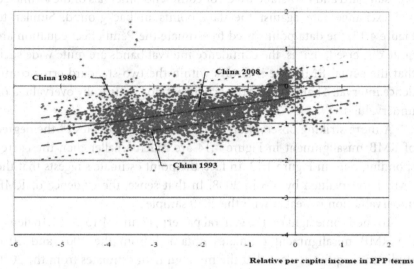

Relative per capita income in PPP terms

Figure 4.14 The Rate of RMB Misalignment Based on the 2010 Vintage Data on the PPP-based Per Capita Income

of these data revisions for assessing RMB misalignment are discussed in, for example, Cheung, Chinn and Fujii (2009, 2010b, 2010c).[29] In essence, these studies show that the estimation of RMB misalignment is quite sensitive to these data revisions.

Let us consider Cheung, Chinn and Fujii (2010c), which used data available in 2010 that are derived from the 2005 ICP survey to illustrate the degree of sensitivity. The Penn effect regression result is given by

$$r_i = -0.295 + 0.174y_i + \hat{u}_i. \qquad (4.5)$$

The estimated Penn effect is significant though its magnitude is smaller than the one reported in equation (4.4), which is derived from data available in 2006. Figure 4.14 plots the regression line of (4.5) and the

---

[29] In addition to misalignment estimation, different vintages of ICP survey data have implications for GDP (growth) estimates, the negative growth volatility effect, growth determinants, poverty measures, and inequality assessment; see, for example, Chen and Ravallion (2010a, 2010b), Ciccone and Jarocinski (2010), Johnson *et al.* (2009), Milanovic (2009), and Ponomareva and Katayama (2010).

one-standard and two-standard error confidence intervals of the estimated real exchange rate against the data points in background. Similar to Figure 4.13, the data points used to estimate the Penn effect equation are quite dispersed; that is, the confidence interval bands are quite wide such that the actual RMB rate is always within the two-standard error confidence interval. That is, the RMB exchange is not statistically overvalued or undervalued.

A more striking observation is that the point estimates of the degree of RMB misalignment in Figure 4.14 are much smaller than the corresponding ones in Figure 4.13. In fact, the point estimate suggests that the RMB is overvalued by 5% in 2008. In that sense, the evidence of RMB undervaluation is weaker with the 2010 sample.

To shed some light on the general pattern, Figures 4.15 and 4.16 depict the RMB misalignment estimates obtained from the 2007 and 2010 studies. It is quite evident that the misalignment estimates from the 2010 studies are, in general, smaller in magnitude than those from the 2007 studies. For the period of the late 1990s and early 2000s, the estimates from the newer dataset are half of those from the older dataset. The main difference between these estimates is that they are generated from different data vintages.

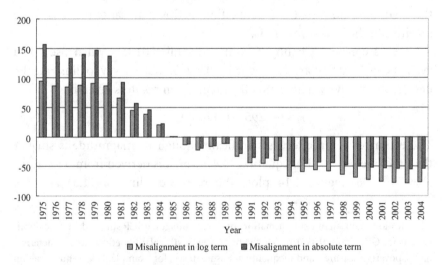

Figure 4.15 The 2007 Panel Point Estimates of RMB Misalignment in % Terms (PPP-based Per Capita Income)

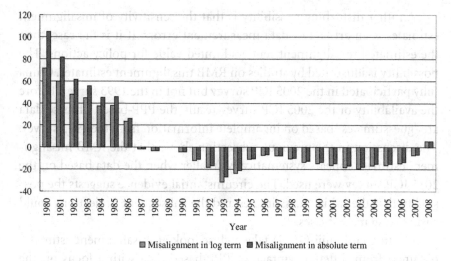

Figure 4.16 **The 2010 Panel Point Estimates of the RMB Misalignment in % Terms (PPP-based Per Capita Income)**

To be sure, both the sampling uncertainty discussed in the previous subsection and the data uncertainty noted here make it hard to obtain strong statistical evidence for exchange rate misalignment. The weak evidence, however, does not exclude the possibility of RMB undervaluation. The takeaway, however, is that we have to recognize the difficulty of assessing misalignment, and it is prudent to follow the established statistical standard to assess claims based on empirical evidence.

4.2.3.3 Economic or non-economic reasons

The sensitivity of the RMB misalignment estimate to data revision casts doubts on its relevance for policy discussions. Since the policy measure to rectify misalignment depends on the degree of deviation, the policy for a large deviation from the equilibrium is different from a small one. When the magnitude of the misalignment estimate varies with data revision, it is hard to devise an appropriate policy to correct the misalignment. The situation is even more complicated if data revision can alter the sign of a misalignment estimate and, thus, give different undervaluation or overvaluation inferences. Drastic revisions undoubtedly raise concerns about the relevance of exchange rate misalignment estimates for policy debates.

Another disturbing possibility is that the sensitivity of misalignment estimates is an artifact of data measurement errors. If it is the case, then the estimated misalignment renders limited value for policy actions. The possibility is illustrated by studies on RMB misalignment estimates. China fully participated in the 2005 ICP survey but not in the 1993 survey. Before the availability of the 2005 ICP survey result, the PPP-based Chinese data are "guesstimates" based on incomplete information from the 1993 survey. The discussion in the previous subsection shows that the RMB misalignment estimate appears systematically smaller when the data based on the 2015 ICP survey were used. The circumstantial evidence suggests the possibility that the initial guesstimates and the subsequent projections could sustain systematic biases.[30]

Cheung and Fujii (2014) take a close look at misalignment estimates obtained from different vintage of PPP-based data with a focus on the release of the 2005 ICP survey results. Specifically, they compared the currency misalignment estimates of 2005 obtained from two PPP-based cross-country datasets: one incorporates the 2005 ICP survey results and the other one does not. The two datasets are labeled WDI 2008 and WDI 2007; the former dataset incorporates information of the 2005 survey.

The misalignment estimates of 154 countries are graphed in Figure 4.17. The ordering of countries is set according to the size of misalignment according to the WDI 2007 dataset. It is apparent that the ICP data revision has pronounced implications for the estimated degree of misalignment — misalignment estimates of individual countries differ widely across these two datasets. The differences appear more pronounced at both ends (most undervalued and most overvalued currencies) than in the middle of the graph. For a given country, both the magnitude and the sign of its misalignment estimate from the WDI 2008 dataset could be different from the WDI 2007 dataset; that is, even an overvaluation result could turn into an undervaluation result, or vice versa. Indeed, the correlation between these two sets of misalignment estimates is 0.49. The dramatic change in empirical misalignment estimates

---

[30] The Chinese data from the 2015 ICP survey are not free from quality concerns. Deaton and Heston (2010) and Chen and Ravallion (2010b), for example, suggest the Chinese price data could be inflated.

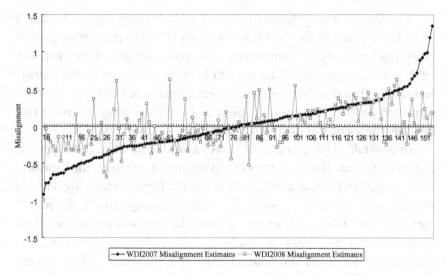

Figure 4.17   Misalignment Estimates

Notes: Plots of misalignment estimates obtained by Penn effect regression (1) in main text using WDI 2007 and WDI 2008 datasets from (Cheung and Fujii, 2014).

noted in the previous subsection is not unique to the Chinese RMB; instead, the effect of data revision on misalignment estimates is a pervasive phenomenon for most, if not all, currencies.

Are these changes attributable to economic or non-economic factors? Cheung and Fujii (2014) use two measurement-related factors and four economic factors to explain the changes in the misalignment estimates. A comparison of the explanatory powers of these two group allow us to infer the relevance of economic interpretations of misalignment estimates derived from these PPP-based data.

The two measurement-related factors are the participation status and data quality. If a country participates in the survey, it belongs to the group of benchmark countries. Otherwise, it is a non-benchmark country. China belongs to the non-benchmark group in the 1993 ICP survey and the benchmark group in the 2005 survey. Data quality refers to the quality of economic data reported in Summers and Heston (1991).[31]

---

[31] Data quality was shown to affect empirical analyses. See, for example, Cheung and Chinn (1996) and Dawson *et al.* (2001).

The four economic factors included in their study are (a) the initial output level given by the 1993 real per capita GDP, (b) the average growth rate given by the average annual real per capita GDP growth rate between 1993 and 2005, (c) the average growth in openness, given by the average annual growth rate of degree of openness, as measured by the ratio of the sum of exports and imports to GDP, and (d) the average inflation rate given by the average annual inflation rate between 1993 and 2005.

In general, Cheung and Fujii (2014) found that, while both types of factors contribute to the changes in misalignment estimates, the measurement-related factors compared with economic factors offer a higher level of (marginal) explanatory power. The finding is suggestive of the role of measurement errors in determining both the sign and size of misalignment estimates and, thus casts doubt on the usefulness of these empirical estimates for economic and policy debates. If economic factors are not the main reason for revisions in misalignment estimates, does it mean that the estimates themselves are heavily influenced by measurement-related factors? If it does, then these estimates do not provide a good guideline to devise economic policies for correcting (the actual level of) misalignment, and the implied global imbalances.

4.3 A Few Recent Studies

To further illustrate the complexity of assessing the RMB misalignment, we provide synopses of a few recent studies.

4.3.1 Schnatz (2011)

As discussed in Section 4.2, there are various reasons for obtaining different estimates of the level of RMB misalignment from different models and different sample periods. One of these reasons is related to the assessment of the fair (or equilibrium) value, which is the reference point for determining the direction and the magnitude of misalignment. Despite its importance, the sensitivity to the underlying equilibrium value assumption is not well articulated in most studies on RMB misalignment.

Using the FEER approach that relates misalignment to trade imbalances as an example, Schnatz (2011) highlights the complexity of estimating the equilibrium exchange rate. The paper also points out the difficulty of assessing the nature of imbalances and devising the related policy remedies when trade elasticity is imprecisely estimated.

In the case of the RMB, it acutely noted that the estimates of China's current account norm cover a wide range; from a deficit value of 2.8% to a surplus value of 8.4% surplus, and these norm estimates typically vary with the observed current account figures. Specifically, the norm estimates reported in the early 2000s — a period during which China experienced large surpluses — typically are surplus numbers, while those in the 1990s are smaller and could be a deficit value. Note that, under FEER, the equilibrium exchange rate is the one that is consistent with the current account norm. That is, the extent of RMB undervaluation (*à la* deviation from the equilibrium rate) is determined by the current account norm estimate, *ceteris paribus*. The uncertainty around the norm value leads to uncertainty about the level of misalignment.

Suppose the norm value is determined. How to close the gap between the observed current account balance and the norm? Under normal circumstances, exchange rate appreciation is prescribed to narrow a surplus gap. The extent of required appreciation, however, depends on the exchange rate (price) elasticity of trade. If trade elasticity of China is only imprecisely estimated, then it is hard to determine the exchange rate value that will align the actual current account balance with the norm.

Indeed, Schnatz (2011) demonstrates that small changes in the assumptions of the norm of current account and trade elasticities can lead to very different assessments of RMB misalignment. Therefore, it is prudent to recognize the sensitivity and imprecision of misalignment estimates and the implications for academic and policy discussions.

4.3.2 Bergsten and Gagnon (2012)

It is not difficult to find a study that presents a strong argument for the RMB is extremely undervalued. Bergsten and Gagnon (2012) is one of these studies. These authors assert that China has been intervening in the foreign exchange market to depress the value of the RMB to boost its competitiveness in the global market and, hence, has sustained a huge trade surplus. For instance, the study shows that China's daily intervention volume is about $1.5 billion in 2007 and $250 million in 2012. Although China slowed the pace of intervention over the past few years, its heavy intervention in the past has kept the level of the RMB exchange rate lower than it should be. The study cites the IMF forecasts that if China's real exchange rate remains constant, which requires a large scale of currency intervention, its current account surplus will increase to more than 4% of GDP by 2017.

Bergsten and Gagnon (2012) note that there are more than 20 other countries engaged in similar currency manipulation activities, with China being the most influential one in terms of its economic importance and the amount of intervention. According to their estimation, the total amount of intervention conducted by these countries in 2011 amounted to $1 trillion. The level of currency undervaluation sustained by the intervention, in turn, has increased the total trade surpluses of these countries by $400 billion to $800 billion per year. The US is perceived to be the largest victim of the manipulation — suffering 1 million to 5 million job losses, and incurring increases of trade and current account deficits of $200 billion to $500 billion per year. Therefore, they suggest that the US and other non-manipulating countries should seek a voluntary agreement from the manipulators to desist from intervening and to develop new sources of sustainable domestic-demand-led growth in their economies.

4.3.3 Dekle and Ungor (2013)

Dekle and Ungor (2013) consider a modified Balassa–Samuelson framework to assess the implication of productivity for the RMB misalignment. Under the usual Balassa–Samuelson approach, the (real) exchange rate is driven by the relative productivity of tradeables and non-tradeables. When the productivity in the tradeables sector is higher than the one in the non-tradeables sector, the productivity differential tends to drive up the general price level and, thus, lead to a real appreciation of its currency. It is known as the Balassa–Samuelson effect. In the case of the RMB and US dollar exchange rate, if the productivity growth of the relative tradeables and non-tradeables is higher in China than the US, then the Chinese general price will grow faster than that in the US, and the RMB will experience real appreciation.

In recognizing the importance of the agricultural sector in China, Dekle and Ungor (2013) extend the usual two-sector setup to a three-sector model that comprises agriculture, manufacturing, and services. The agricultural products and manufacturing goods are labeled tradeables, and services non-tradeables. The model is used to study the relative productivity growth and the real exchange rate of the Chinese RMB against the US dollar.

If we only consider the relative productivity of manufacturing goods (tradeables) and services (non-tradeables) sector, then the US relative productivity was 1.1% while the Chinese one was 3% during the period of 1985 to 2010. According to the Balassa–Samuelson approach, the RMB real exchange rate should have appreciated. The actual rate, instead, depreciated between 1985 and 2010.

The picture is quite different when the relative size of China's agricultural sector and its low level of productivity are incorporated in the analysis. Once the agricultural sector is included in the productivity comparison exercise, it is found that the Chinese relative productivity of tradeables and non-tradeables sectors is not larger than that of the US one. That is, we should not expect the RMB to appreciate over time. Taking all factors into consideration, Dekle and Ungor (2013) assert that, relative to the equilibrium exchange rate that takes the agricultural sector into consideration, the RMB-dollar exchange rate could be over-appreciated and over-valued.

4.3.4 Fischer and Hossfeld (2014)

Similar to Dekle and Ungor (2013), Fischer and Hossfeld (2014) follow the Balassa–Samuelson reasoning and adopt the productivity approach to compare real exchange rates. Fischer and Hossfeld, however, focus on the construction of measures of price competitiveness and its implications for misalignment evaluation. Specifically, they propose internationally comparable price measures that have multilateral consistency, and are derived from data on the levels rather than indexes of prices and productivities. Up to 32 years of data of 57 developed and emerging economies including China are considered.

In the case of China, Fischer and Hossfeld find that its price level and relative productivity increased gradually in the past 10 years. Starting from

2008, however, China's price competitiveness changed from being favorable to unfavorable. The price competitiveness deteriorated because China's price level increased faster than its productivity. As a result, the RMB is not undervalued given the unfavorable level of Chinese price competitiveness. The finding of Hossfeld and Fischer mirrors that of, say, Dekle and Ungor (2013) that infers China's currency was not undervalued in the 2000s, but is in stark contrast to, say, Bergsten and Gagnon (2012) who assert that China is gaining price competitiveness via currency manipulating.

Again, it is not our intention to draw a definite inference from these few studies on whether the RMB is under- or overvalued. These few studies reveal that alternative perspectives and approaches can be used to assess exchange rate misalignment. Given the desire to rebalance the global economy, the appropriate policy remedy should be based on fair evaluations of currency misalignment. These few selected papers, coupled with the evidence presented in the previous subsections, illustrate the difficulty of pinning down the precise level of the RMB misalignment. The message to take home is, at the risk of repeating, that we have to exercise caution in formulating policies based on an empirical estimate of currency misalignment, which typically comes with a fog of uncertainty.

4.4 Discussions

In the last few decades, China's economic activity has advanced at a blistering pace. Its importance to the global economy is growing with its trade linkages with the world. The foreign exchange value of the RMB that connects China's economic activity to the world has drawn serious attention from the global community. China's large trade surplus and economic hardship experienced by other countries before and after the 2007 global finance crisis have aggravated the contentious debate on whether the RMB is excessively undervalued or not. The debate is further fueled by China's political rise and its increasing involvement in international geopolitics.

In this chapter, we attempt to abstain from political rhetoric and focus on basic economic issues of assessing exchange rate misalignment. The current status of exchange rate economics is essentially characterized by the well-known, if not the consensual, empirical finding that there is no convincing structural or time series model that can offer a consistent explanation for exchange rate dynamics across currencies and historical time series. Again this backdrop, it is not surprising to find that, based on strict statistical reasoning, the evidence on misalignment could be fickle in the absence of a commonly agreed exchange rate specification that can be precisely estimated.

The previous sections have noted both the theoretical and empirical issues that make it difficult, if not impossible, to determine the precise degree of the RMB misalignment. Indeed, the large variability of RMB misalignment estimates affords researchers and politicians to draw on empirical evidence that suit their own prior beliefs.

We, at the risk of repeating ourselves, have to re-emphasize that our elaborations should not be interpreted as supporting evidence for no RMB undervaluation. Our theme is not to argue whether the RMB is undervalued or not. Rather, we bring to the foreground the limitations of the models and the data that can prevent us from making a sharp inference. Without a strong theoretical model and statistically significant evidence, assertions about currency misalignment should be interpreted with great caution.

For academic researchers, the uncertainty of misalignment estimates is an important topic to explore. For policymakers and financial professionals, who have to conduct their operations in the real world, what could they do in the absence of a clear verdict on RMB misalignment? Should they do nothing? The inability to nail down the precise level of misalignment can be interpreted positively. While it is typical to devise a remedy policy based on misalignment assessment exercise, it is important to realize our limits and know what we do not know. Given these considerations, it is not advisable to demand a drastic and swift exchange rate move without taking the uncertainty surrounding a misalignment estimate into consideration.

The fickleness of market view on RMB valuation is quite well illustrated by the change in the sentiment towards the Chinese currency in 2015. As mentioned in the introduction, when IMF said in May 2015 that the RMB is no longer undervalued, there is no shortage of dissenting voices. The market sentiment, however, experienced a swift change when the RMB was depreciated after the new fixing mechanism was introduced in August. Since then, there are claims that the currency is significantly overvalued and has lost its competitiveness. Devaluations up to 10% to 20% are required to restore China's strength in the international market.

It is debatable that whether the sentiment shift is due to changes in (subjective) expectations or is underpinned by changes in China's real economic activity. Nevertheless, the swift u-turn in the assessment of RMB valuation is a warning sign that reminds us to be cautious about interpreting claims about currency misalignment.

Chapter 5
RMB Internationalization: I

China's economic performance in the last three decades is quite astonishing. When China launched economic reform in 1978, it was essentially a closed economy inflicted by severe misallocation of resources and inefficiencies. In the 1980s, there was no shortage of skeptics on the effectiveness of economic reform. However, when the Chinese economy picked up steam in the 1990s, the world felt the economic dynamism of its reform policies. The momentum was strong and carried into the 21st century.

The accession to the WTO in 2001 serves as China's affidavit on its commitment to liberalize trade and set the path toward a market-based economy. China has continued its expansion in the global trade arena. And the efforts paid off. China became the largest exporter in 2009 and overtook the US and became the largest trading nation in 2012.

In 2014, the world is stunned by the IMF estimates that put the Chinese economy slightly ahead of the US one, and ranked it the largest economy in the world. Despite the IMF estimates using purchasing power parity adjusted figures as the basis — the US still has the largest economy in the absence of the purchasing power parity adjustment — the news has stirred a wave of heated discussions on China and its role in the global economy.[1]

---

[1] See, for example, Frankel (2014). Ruoen and Kai (1995) presented an early comparison of the Chinese and US GDP using purchasing power parity adjusted data.

With its increasing economic prowess and trade activity, China is becoming a key player on the world stage. Despite its extensive trade network, China has a rather rudimentary level of integration with the global financial market. Partially, it is because in the early phase of the reform process, the focus is on promoting economic well-being via revamping the real economy and international trade. Compared with its relatively advanced trade sector, China's financial markets are underdeveloped and subject to severe capital control measures. For instance, there is current account convertibility, but capital account is not convertible.

Rapid economic growth calls for advances in the financial markets. A complete global integration process involves integration at the levels of trade and financial sectors. It is either a natural development process or part of its grand reform agenda. China has been proactive in liberalizing its financial markets since its accession to the WTO. In addition to liberalizing its financial sector, China is conscientious in joining the international financial community. Evidently, China is following its usual gradual approach in reforming its financial markets and venturing into the global financial world.

5.1 Joining the Global Financial Community

The promotion of the use of the Chinese currency renminbi (RMB) overseas is arguably an intensively discussed initiative taken by China to advance its dealing with the global financial community. In hindsight, the initiative was planted back in 2003 when China assigned in Hong Kong the first clearing bank for RMB transactions outside mainland China, and started the offshore RMB business there. Despite Hong Kong being politically under China's sovereignty, its economy is segregated from China, and it is a *de facto* offshore market for RMB transactions.

Since the advent of the 2007–08 global financial crisis, China has been active in setting up the infrastructure for using the RMB overseas. The crisis critically illustrated the danger of assigning a pivotal role to the US dollar and operating a US-centric global financial system. The dollar shortage experienced in 2008 is more severe than that of the 1950s (McCauley and McGuire, 2009; McGuire and von Peter, 2009). The sharp drop in international dollar liquidity seriously curtailed global trade and pressured banks when they had to roll over their dollar liabilities. The global financial system was under acute stress.

In response, the US authorities mitigated the shortage by arranging dollar swaps with central banks on an unprecedentedly broad scale and, with some major central banks in unlimited amounts (Aizenman and Pasricha, 2010; Aizenman, Jinjarak and Park, 2011; Committee on the Global Financial System, 2010). Before long, the global economy, especially the emerging economies, bleated on the excessive international dollar liquidity triggered by the US quantitative easing, which is aimed at reviving the anemic US economy. To contain the adverse effect, economies outside the United States tried to build dams to divert away excessive dollar inflows (Strategy, Policy and Review Department, International Monetary Fund, 2010a; McCauley, 2010). The temporary but acute dollar shortage and the subsequent abundant supply of dollar liquidity highlight the fragility of an international monetary architecture that is built upon a national currency, and provide another anecdotal evidence of the Triffin dilemma.[2]

The crisis experience apparently has prompted China to actively implement measures of promoting the cross-border use of RMB to reduce its reliance on the US dollar. Since its inception in 2009, China's scheme of cross-border trade settlement in RMB has encouraged denominating and settling its international trade in RMB. As the largest trading nation in the world, China's program has benefited from its extensive trade network. To enhance the RMB cross-border trade settlement program, China has actively pursued various complementary policy measures that include establishing offshore RMB centers, signing RMB-based bilateral currency swap agreements, designating RMB clearing banks in offshore centers, and developing direct cross-currency trading platforms.

Five years after launching the cross-border trade settlement program, China settled about a quarter of its cross-border trade in the RMB in 2014.

---

[2] While the dilemma was pointed out by Triffin (1960) under the then international gold standard of the Bretton Woods era, it is widely considered to be relevant under the current international monetary system.

The degree of the internationalization of the RMB is also attested by figures provide by the Society for Worldwide Interbank Financial Telecommunication (SWIFT), the RMB has entered the top five of world payments currency by value in November 2014. Since then, the RMB has mostly retained the rank of the fifth most used world payments currency by value.[3]

In addition to pushing its currency to the rest of the world, China has stepped up its involvement in the international financial system. Working within the existing global monetary architecture, however, may not satisfy all the needs of a fast growing emerging economy. For historical reasons, the current international orders are mostly defined by the developed world. International financial organizations, including the World Bank and the IMF, are perceived to be US-centric, and to set rules that serve mainly the interests of major developed countries.

While there are agreements on changes to be made such that the fast-growing emerging market countries will have their fair representation in these institutions, the progress is deemed to be slow. A case in point is the reform within the IMF that involves its governance, quotas, and voting policy.[4] During their 2014 summit in Brazil, the BRICS (Brazil, Russia, India, China, and South Africa) countries expressed their disappointment at the IMF reform, and put their names on the dotted line to form the New Development Bank,[5] which represents an alternative funding source to the IMF. Besides the New Development Bank, China took the lead in

---

[3] See SWIFT (2015a, 2015b). In February 2015, the RMB fell back to position #7, and for the month of August 2015, it was the fourth most used one. China ranked number 13 in January 2013.

[4] The discussion of the current IMF reform started as early as 2006. See, for example, http://www.imf.org/external/np/fin/quotas/pubs/index.htm, for a collection of IMF related documents. The last Outcome of the Quota Formula Review was published in 2013 (International Monetary Fund, 2013); 2013, Outcome of the Quota Formula Review — Report of the Executive Board to the Board of Governors, http://www.imf.org/external/np/pp/eng/2013/013013.pdf)

[5] The New Development Bank BRICS, which was initially called the BRICS Development Bank, was officially launched in July 2015 in Shanghai as its headquarters. The five BRICS countries have equal voting rights. See http://ndbbrics.org/index.html for additional information.

establishing the Asian Infrastructure Investment Bank, the objective of which is to provide funding to infrastructure projects in the Asia region.[6,7]

It is quite obvious that the coming of China to the international monetary system has ripple effects on the current international monetary architecture. Its implication is likely to go beyond the geoeconomic landscape and affect geopolitics dynamics. Besides supporting the global use of the RMB, China's involvements in setting up these new supranational financial intuitions are perceived as evidence of China's intention to free itself from the incumbents by setting her own international rules and orders. The question is not only how China is going to flex her economic muscles; it is also a question of how do the traditional powers respond to China's rising roles in both the global financial market and the international political arena.

Circumstantial events indicate that the traditional powers have not been receptive to China's emerging role in the international economic (and political) arena. For instance, the US announced policy of a "pivot" or "rebalancing" in foreign policy toward Asia, which covers economic, political, and military elements and is widely seen as an attempt to contain China's growing influence in the region (CRS Report for Congress, 2012). The reluctance to embrace China is also indicated by the exclusion of China from the negotiation of the Trans-Pacific Partnership trade agreement and the non-supportive stance of the US for the Asian Infrastructure Investment Bank. While there are reasons behind the rivalry, the global economy will benefit from migrating toward an international structure that recognizes the fair representation of growing dynamic economies.

5.2 International Currency: Functionalities and Determinants

Before discussing the internationalization of the RMB, we overview the functionalities and determinants of an international currency. Literally speaking, an international currency is one that is used and held outside its

---

[6] AIIB was officially launched in June 2015 in Beijing. Mr. Jin Liqun has served as the President-designate since September 1, 2015. See the official AIIB website at http://www.aiibank.org/ for additional information.

[7] Also, in November 2014, a month after 21 countries signed a Memorandum of Understanding on the AIIB in Beijing, China pledged US$40 to set up the Silk Road Fund.

country of issuance. That is, it is a currency that can serve the three functions of money both within and outside the domestic economy. The three basic functions of money are medium of exchange, store of value, and unit of account, and these functions are interrelated. The role of an international currency in the global economy is closely related to these three basic functions.

The global dimension of an international currency enriches its functionality. Traditionally, the functions are discussed from the perspectives of public (government) and private (Cohen, 1971; Kenen, 1983; Krugman, 1984; Chinn and Frankel, 2007; Genberg, 2009). For instance, the public functions include facilitating foreign exchange market interventions, anchoring the value of a currency, and serving as international reserves. Private functions include facilitating international trade and investment, storing private wealth, and pricing globally traded commodities, including gold and oil. These functions are summarized in Table 5.1 and briefly discussed below.[8]

5.2.1 Functionalities

Since the 1950s, the US dollar has been the prominent international currency that is used in a large proportion of international transactions and accounts for a lion's share of global reserves. The discussion below thus from time to time makes references to the role of the US dollar in the global market.

Table 5.1   Roles of International Currency

Function of Money	Governments	Private Sectors
Medium of exchange	Vehicle currency for foreign exchange intervention	Invoicing trade and financial transactions
Store of value	International reserves	Currency substitution (private dollarization)
Unit of account	Anchor for pegging local currency	Denominating trade and financial transactions

Source: Chinn and Frankel (2007).

---

[8] See, for example, Cohen (1971), Kenen (1983), and Chinn and Frankel (2007).

(a) Medium of exchange

Medium of exchange is a primary function of a currency. It means that the currency can be used to facilitate exchange or trade of goods and services and enhance economic efficiency by minimizing transaction costs. Using a currency as a medium of exchange can avoid barter and minimize the time spent in exchanging goods and services.

There is a subtle difference between an invoicing and a settlement currency. A transaction invoiced in one currency can be settled with another currency. The medium of exchange function is more relevant for a settlement currency than an invoicing currency. The US dollar, which is the prominent international currency, is commonly used to both invoice and settle international trade and financial transactions.

A unique character of an international currency is its function as a vehicle currency. That is, the currency is not just for transactions between residents and nonresidents, it is also used for transactions between nonresidents outside the country of issuance.[9] Again, the US dollar is a common vehicle currency used in international trade and financial transactions (Goldberg and Tille, 2008).

Central banks can use an international currency to intervene in the foreign exchange market. Using the US dollar as an example, a central bank can use it to influence the dollar exchange rate of its currency, or use it as a vehicle currency to affect the cross-rate of its currency against the another currency.

(b) Store of value

The store of value function allows a currency to transfer purchasing power over time and across space; it improves economic efficiency by separating the timing and the location of receiving income and spending. For a central bank, it can denominate reserves in international currencies to preserve and manage its national wealth. Indeed, the US dollar accounts for a very large share of global reserves. For instance, the IMF Currency Composition of Official Foreign Exchange Reserves (COFER) reported in early 2015 affirms that the US dollar accounts for over 60% of the reported global

---

[9] See Yu and Gao (2011) for additional discussions.

reserve holdings.[10] For individuals, they can hold part of their wealth in international currencies either to diversify the currency composition of their wealth or to guide against local currency depreciation.

(c) Unit of account

Pricing different goods and services in a common currency facilitates the exchange of goods and services. For international transactions, pricing or invoicing in a common international currency reduces impediments to trade. Indeed, one global function of an international currency is its role in pricing internationally traded commodities including gold and oil. The common price denomination promotes trading of these commodities around the world and reflects status of the pricing currency. Again, commodities traded in the global market are commonly quoted in the US dollar.

When an economy would like to peg or anchor the value of its currency, it can use the unit of account function of an international currency. The US dollar is a common anchor used for this purpose. For example, Hong Kong adopts a currency board framework and pegs the value of Hong Kong dollar to the US dollar at the rate of one US dollar to 7.8 Hong Kong dollars.

5.2.2 Determinants

Basically, the international status of a currency depends on the supply provided by of the issuance country and the demand from the rest of the world and, thus, is ultimately determined by market forces. The extant studies identify a number of factors determining the global status of an international currency.[11] These factors are briefly discussed below.

(a) Size matters

The size of the domestic economy is one of the important factors affecting the international use of its currency. A common way to gauge the size of

---

[10] See the COFER website: http://data.imf.org/?sk=E6A5F467-C14B-4AA8-9F6D-5A09E C4E62A4

[11] See, for example, Cheung (2015), Chinn and Frankel (2007), Chen and Peng (2010), Eichengreen (2014), Lane and Burke (2001), and Prasad and Ye (2012, 2013).

an economy is its gross domestic product (GDP). The size effect mainly works through two channels: (i) trade channel and (ii) reserve channel.

The trade channel is typically based on the anecdotal observation that a large economy, such as the US, is usually engaged in large-scale trade activities. The import and export activities usually generate related foreign exchange transactions involving its currency. If the economy has extensive trade links with different countries, it benefits from network externalities that lower transaction costs, and its trading partners will be willing to use its currency to invoice and to settle their transactions. As a result, the global status of the currency is germinated and advanced. As affirmed in Chinn and Frankel (2007), the currency of a country that has a large share in international output and trade has a huge natural advantage to be an international currency.

The global status of a currency is sometimes assessed by its contribution to the composition of global reserves. For instance, the large proportion of global reserves held in the US dollar is a reflection of its supremacy in the world. Studies have found that there is a significant positive relationship between an economy's GDP share of world total and its share of global reserves (Chinn and Frankel, 2007). Eichengreen and Frankel (1996) shows that every one percentage point increase in the share of an economy's GDP in the world total, its currency experiences a 1.33 percentage point increase in its share of central bank reserve holdings. Since one of the motivations of holding reserves is to smooth out international trade activity, the link between the economy size and reserve currency may work indirectly through the trade channel.

(b) Financial sector

Both the depth and breadth of the financial sector of an economy have positive implications for the global status of its currency. A country that issues an international currency typically has an efficient domestic financial sector in which a wide variety of securities are traded in active and liquid primary and secondary markets. Similar to the one in international trade, a large and developed financial sector yields the network effect that lowers transaction costs, and attracts businesses from international investors and central banks. As a result, the currency is gaining popularity, and the world is willing to use it to conduct international transactions. Thus, when a country has an efficient and liquid financial sector, it promotes the international acceptance of its currency.

The international role of the US dollar, for example, is well served and supported by its sophisticated financial sector, including its large and deep government bond market.

In passing, we note that full convertibility is not a necessary precondition of an international currency. A case in point is that capital controls were commonplace in, say, the 1950s, and there were international currencies in that period. We will come back to the convertibility issue later.

(c) Confidence

To be a viable international currency, it has to be accepted by the rest of the world. If nonresidents do not have confidence in the currency, they will not hold it or use it to conduct transactions. Thus, confidence in a currency contributes to nonresidents' willingness to accept it as an international currency and hence is a critical factor that determines the global status.

Loosely speaking, the confidence in a currency is influenced by both economic and political factors. The economic well-being of an economy affects the value of its currency. A stable economic structure and a healthy fiscal system offer a favorable environment for economic activity. On the other hand, a nonsustainable economic path or a high level of debts are warning signs of economic ills down the road, which will hurt the currency's value. High exchange rate volatility and inflation rate are indicative of potential mishaps that have negative impacts on a currency's value. Large exchange rate volatility presents a high level of uncertainty about the relative purchasing power while a high inflation rate means a quick erosion of purchasing power.

Political factors refer to both domestic political stability and political relationship with the rest of the world. Under a politically stable economy with good governance and a sound legal and judicial system, nonresidents do not have to worry about abrupt policy changes that will trigger volatile variations in the currency value.

If a country is in (constant) political rows with other countries, it is hard to imagine that those countries are willing to accept its currency as an international currency and use it to conduct their international business.

That is, to convince the world to accept its currency as an international currency, the country has to consider its position in the global political structure and engage with the world in a politically responsive and responsible manner.

In passing, we note that the confidence of international investors is affected by the transparency of both economic and political policies.

(d) Network externalities

Network externality is an important factor influencing a currency's global status. When they are only a few participants, the market for the currency will be thin and the pricing will be inefficient. When there is a critical mass of participants, the market becomes liquid, has breadth and depth, supports efficient pricing mechanisms, and offers low transaction costs. These features will attract extra potential participants to the currency. An exporter, for instance, will find it convenient and cost-effective to use a currency for invoicing and settlement if everyone else is using it. There is hysteresis effect in the process of becoming an international currency.

The network effect draws on a large market base, and nurtures the global status of a currency. The supremacy of the US dollar, for instance, is sustained and reinforced by its extensive global trade and financial networks. The established network effect also gives rise to the strong inertia of an international currency; that is, the global status is unlikely to be drastically changed in a short run (Greenspan, 2001). As noted by Chinn and Frankel (2007), a widely accepted trade invoicing currency is likely to be used to invoice financial transactions. A widely accepted financial transaction invoicing currency is likely to be a vehicle currency in foreign exchange market and becomes an anchor currency pegged by small economies.

(e) Capital account convertibility

Capital account openness is a relevant factor that affects the international status of a currency. We expect an international currency to be accepted as payments to settle international trade and financial transactions. Tradability in global financial markets facilitates cross-country payment arrangements. If a country imposes restrictions on capital flows and controls over foreign currency exchanges, it will inconvenience other countries in using its currency or holding it as reserves. An open capital account supports the global status of a currency.

However, complete capital account openness is neither a necessary nor sufficient condition for a currency to be an international currency. The historical experiences of pound sterling and US dollar illustrate capital account openness is not necessarily a binding prerequisite. Both currencies obtained their prominent international currency status when capital controls were the norm. As recent as the 1970s, the US government had restrictions on dollar inflows from overseas. The experiences of pound sterling and US dollar undermine the view that capital account openness is an indispensable pre-condition of an international currency.

Nevertheless, we should recognize that, within the current international economic order, most international currencies are subject to limited capital controls imposed by their issuance countries. When capital controls are not necessary the norm, capital account openness can be a favorable factor that strengthens the global status of a currency.

5.3 Promoting the International Use of the RMB

Since the advent of the 2007–08 global financial crisis, the Chinese authorities have actively implemented a series of measures to promote the use of the RMB overseas. In this section, we recap some of these policy measures.[12]

5.3.1 Bilateral RMB currency swap agreements

The world experienced a rare and severe dollar liquidity shortage in the early phase of the global financial crisis. The sharp drop in global dollar liquidity brought down global trade volume and, hence, output. It also put the global financial system that relies on dollar funding and refinancing

---

[12] See, for example, Brummer (2015), Chen and Cheung (2011), Cheung (2015), Cheung and Miao (2014), Cheung, Ma and McCauley (2011a, b), Eichengreen (2013), Frankel (2012), Yu and Gao (2011), Lee (2010), Maziad and Kang (2012), McCauley (2011), Stier *et al.* (2010), and Yu (2012).

under critical stresses. The event vividly illustrates the fragility of the US dollar centric global financial arrangement. To minimize its dependence on US dollar financing, China began to negotiate bilateral local currency swap agreements with its selected trading partners. A unique feature of these agreements is that they involve the national currencies of the signing countries, and not the US dollar.[13] With these swap arrangements, China can foster the use of the RMB to conduct transactions with these partners, and overseas.

Table 5.2 lists the bilateral RMB currency swap agreements signed by China between 2008 and 2015. The bilateral agreement typically has a maturity of three years and is renewable. Through the agreement, China can swap the RMB into the counterparty's currency and put it into its own banking system. Similarly, the agreement partner, say, the Hong Kong Monetary Authority, can obtain RMB funding through the swap from the People's Bank of China and provide it as an emergency source of RMB liquidity to Hong Kong's banking system. The swap funding is expected to be used to finance, say, trade transactions. The implementation of these bilateral RMB currency swap arrangements could free these countries from the US dollar liquidity shortage experienced in the crisis. In doing so, the RMB has a role in the international stage.

Exercising these local currency agreements, overseas monetary authorities conducted a total of RMB1.03 trillion of currency swap transactions in 2013. In the first half of 2014, the currency swap transactions amounted to RMB511 billion. In the second quarter of 2014, People's Bank of China used KRW 400 million (equivalent to RMB2.4 million) under the China–Korea bilateral RMB currency swap arrangement to facilitate trade financing of the corporate sector. This was also the first time for the People's Bank of China to deploy foreign currency funds under the bilateral currency swap agreements (People's Bank of China; 2013, 2014).[14]

The network of bilateral RMB currency swap agreements provides a stable platform for using the RMB in designed transactions and mitigates

---

[13] The currency swap agreements signed by China in the past, say, under the Chiang Mai Initiative and the Multilateral Chiang Mai Initiative have the US dollar as the swap currency.

[14] According to the People's Bank of China (2015), the usage of these swap lines was amounted to RMB96.5 billion by the end of 2014.

Table 5.2   Bilateral RMB Currency Swap Agreements Signed by People's Bank of China

Signing Date	Counterparty	Swap Amount
December 12, 2008	Bank of Korea	RMB180 billion and KRW38 trillion
January 20, 2009	Hong Kong Monetary Authority	RMB200 billion and HK$227 billion
February 8, 2009	Bank Negara Malaysia	RMB80 billion and MYR40 billion
March 11, 2009	National Bank of the Republic of Belarus	RMB20 billion and BYR8000 billion
March 23, 2009	Bank Indonesia	RMB100 billion and IDR175 trillion
April 2, 2009	Central Bank of Argentina	RMB70 billion and ARS38 billion
June 9, 2010	The Central Bank of Iceland	RMB3.5 billion and ISK66 billion
July 23, 2010	Monetary Authority of Singapore	RMB150 billion and SG$30 billion
April 18, 2011	Reserve Bank of New Zealand	RMB25 billion and NZD5 billion
April 19, 2011	Central Bank of the Republic of Uzbekistan	RMB0.7 billion and UZS167 billion
May 6, 2011	Bank of Mongolia	RMB5 billion and MNT1 trillion
June 13, 2011	National Bank of Kazakhstan	RMB7 billion and KZT150 billion
October 26, 2011	Bank of Korea	RMB360 billion and KRW64 trillion

November 22, 2011	Hong Kong Monetary Authority	RMB400 billion and HK$490 billion
December 22, 2011	Bank of Thailand	RMB70 billion and THB320 billion
December 23, 2011	State Bank of Pakistan	RMB10 billion and PKR140 billion
January 17, 2012	Central Bank of the United Arab Emirates	RMB35 billion and AED20 billion
February 8, 2012	Bank Negara Malaysia	RMB180 billion and MYR90 billion
February 21, 2012	Central Bank of the Republic of Turkey	RMB10 billion and TRY3 billion
March 20, 2012	Bank of Mongolia	RMB10 billion and MNT2 trillion
March 22, 2012	Reserve Bank of Australia	RMB200 billion and AUD30 billion
June 26, 2012	National Bank of Ukraine	RMB15 billion and UAH19 billion
March 7, 2013	Monetary Authority of Singapore	RMB300 billion and SG$60 billion
March 26, 2013	Central Bank of Brazil	RMB190 billion and BRL60 billion
June 22, 2013	Bank of England	RMB200 billion and GBP20 billion
September 9, 2013	Hungarian National Bank	RMB10 billion and HUF375 billion
September 12, 2013	Bank of Albania	RMB2 billion and ALL35.8 billion

(Continued)

Table 5.2   (*Continued*)

Signing Date	Counterparty	Swap Amount
September 30, 2013	The Central Bank of Iceland	RMB3.5 billion and ISK66 billion
October 9, 2013	European Central Bank	RMB350 billion and EUR45 billion
April 25, 2014	Reserve Bank of New Zealand	RMB25 billion and NZD5 billion
July 18, 2014	Central Bank of Argentina	RMB70 billion and ARS90 billion
July 21, 2014	Swiss National Bank	RMB150 billion and CHF21 billion
August 21, 2014	Bank of Mongolia	RMB15 billion and MNT4.5 trillion
September 16, 2014	Central Bank of Sri Lanka	RMB10 billion and LKR225 billion
October 11, 2014	Bank of Korea	RMB360 billion and KRW64 trillion
October 13, 2014	The Central Bank of the Russian Federation	RMB150 billion and RUB815 billion
November 3, 2014	Qatar Central Bank	RMB35 billion and QAR20.8 billion
November 8, 2014	Bank of Canada	RMB200 billion and CAD30 billion
November 27, 2014	Hong Kong Monetary Authority	RMB400 billion and HK$505 billion

December 14, 2014	National Bank of Kazakhstan	RMB7 billion and KZT200 billion
December 22, 2014	Bank of Thailand	RMB70 billion and THB370 billion
December 23, 2014	State Bank of Pakistan	RMB10 billion and PKR165 billion
March 18, 2015	Central Bank of Suriname	RMB1 billion and SRD520 million
March 25, 2015	Central Bank of Armenia	RMB1 billion and AMD77 billion
April 10, 2015	South African Reserve Bank	RMB30 billion and ZAR54 billion
May 25, 2015	Central Bank of Chile	RMB22 billion and CLP2.2 trillion
September 3, 2015	National Bank of Tajikistan	RMB3 billion and TJS3 billion

Note: All agreements have a maturity of three years and are renewable.
Source: PBC website (http://www.pbc.gov.cn/huobizhengceersi/214481/214511/214541/2967384/2016072010054297624.pdf).

the potential danger of dollar shortage on China's trade activity. Some studies on the determinants of these bilateral swap agreements are Garcia-Herrero and Xia (2015), Liao and McDowell (2014), and Lin *et al.* (2016).

5.3.2 RMB trade settlement

Realizing the detrimental effect of the US dollar squeeze on its international trade, China launched its pilot scheme for RMB cross-border trade settlement in 2009. In using its own currency to settle trade with other economies, China does not have to rely on other vehicle currencies, including the US dollar, to conduct and complete international transactions. In fact, the bilateral RMB currency swap arrangement is a policy initiative to support the RMB trade settlement. For instance, through the swap arrangement, the partner country could obtain RMB to settle trade with China.

The use of RMB to settle cross-border trade, however, could be traced back to at least 2003. At that time, the practice of RMB trade settlement mainly took place along China's borders with, say, Cambodia, Mongolia, Russia, and Vietnam. An obvious reason is to free both sides from the burdens of using hard currencies such as the US dollar. The directives issued by China's State Administration of Foreign Exchange (2003a, 2003b), in Chinese, provide some hints on the use of RMB in settling cross-border trade back in the 2000s. As these cross-border RMB trade settlements are not directly relevant to the current policy on internationalizing the RMB, we focus only on the post-2009 arrangements.

In April 2009, China's State Council approved the cross-border trade settlement scheme that allowed Shanghai and other four cities in Guangdong Province to settle their trade with counterparts in Hong Kong in RMB. In 2010, the scheme was expanded to cities in 20 Chinese provinces. The counterpart of the RMB settlement scheme was also broadened to include all trading partners. In August 2011, the scheme was expanded again to cover the whole China.

By reducing the reliance on the US dollar, the RMB cross-border trade settlement helps Chinese companies to manage exchange rate risk and provides an incentive for these Chinese companies to convince their counterparts to adopt RMB to conduct trade with them. It has been reported that Chinese companies, possibly with support of Chinese authorities, offer price concessions to transactions settled in RMB rather than in, say, the US dollar.

In the beginning, the Chinese importers instead of exporters were the main users of the RMB cross-border settlement. It is probably due to the fact that the RMB is not freely available to nonresidents. The foreign importers of Chinese goods, thus, may not have the RMB to settle their purchases. Hence, it is not easy for Chinese exporters to arrange a RMB settlement. The Chinese importers, on the other hand, can settle their trades with the RMB as long as their trading partners agreed. As a result, the scheme becomes a source of the RMB to nonresidents, and supplies the currency to offshore markets. When the offshore RMB pool expands, foreign importers can acquire RMB to pay for their imports from China. Over time, we observe the RMB trade settlement scheme involves a more balanced of Chinese importers and exporters.[15]

With China's robust strength in international trade, the market in general anticipates the RMB will gain its position in the area of trade settlement. The adoption of RMB settlement is relatively easy for the Chinese corporations — it simplifies its funding process and facilitates exchange rate risk management. However, for foreign corporations, the use of the RMB presents a new chapter in their corporate finance operation. They have to, for example, establish the related funding or banking arrangements and set up their internal systems, including the legal and risk management procedures to handle transactions in the RMB. Due to inertia, the adaptation process may take some time to realize. When the network of RMB settlement grows over time, the network externality effect will encourage international corporations to implement the change and adopt the RMB to settle transactions. Then, we expect a sustainable growth of overseas use of the RMB.

Since the introduction of scheme in 2009, both the share and the volume of cross-border trade settled in the RMB have exhibited impressive growth. The share has substantially increased from 0.2% in 2009 to around 29% in 2015. The amount has also increased from a relatively

---

[15] The use of RMB settlement sometimes is affected by the difference in the onshore and offshore RMB exchange rates. We will discuss the phenomenon later in the chapter.

minute amount of RMB4 billion in 2009 to RMB7,234 billion in 2015. Despite the share of China's trade settled in the RMB is less than the one-third or 30% predicted by Chen *et al.* (2009) and Cui *et al.* (2009), the growth streak in five years is quite astonishing.[16]

Indeed, in August 2015, the RMB briefly overtook the Japanese yen and became the fourth most used world payments currency by value (SWIFT, 2015b). Back in August 2012, the RMB ranked 14. The strong trade settlement performance of the RMB affirms that the currency is progressing steadily to dominate China trade in a near future and become an international currency.

Nevertheless, we note that, even as the fourth most used currency, the RMB in August 2015 only settled 2.79% of global payments by value, which the US dollar accounted for 44.8%, followed by the euro at 27.2% and the British pound at 8.5%. Thus, the RMB still has a long way to challenge the US dollar in the global market.

5.3.3 Direct foreign exchange trading

The primacy of the US dollar in the global market is reflected by its prominent role in the international foreign exchange market. Literally, the US dollar could be directly traded and exchanged against any other currencies in the world — over 80% of bilateral currency trading in the global market are against the US dollar.[17] The euro — the second most active currency — accounts for less than 40% of the total global bilateral currency trading. The widespread use in the global foreign exchange market reflects and reinforces the global status of the US dollar.

The history of the direct foreign exchange trading of the RMB is quite short — the main exception is its trading against the US dollar. China has gradually begun the direct bilateral foreign exchange trading

---

[16] Japan settled about at most 40% of its trade in the Japanese yen (Goldberg and Tille, 2008; Ito *et al.*, 2010).

[17] The triennial market surveys conducted by the Bank for International Settlements show that the US dollar has consistently accounted for 80% to 90% of the global bilateral currency trade since the 1990s (Bank for International Settlements, 2013, 1995). Note that the total percentage share sums to 200% because two currencies are involved in one transaction.

of the RMB against other currencies beyond the US dollar since 2010. In August 2010, Malaysian Ringgit was the first developing country currency that is allowed to trade against the RMB directly in the China Foreign Exchange Trading Center.[18] Later in December of the same year, the Chinese RMB became directly exchangeable for Russian Ruble in the Moscow securities exchange — it was the first official arrangement that allows direct trading of the Chinese currency outside mainland China and Hong Kong.[19]

In the next few years, China signed a few other agreements and established direct trading of the RMB against the Japanese yen, the Australian dollar, the New Zealand dollar, the British pound, the euro, the Singaporean dollar, the Korean won, the Canadian dollar, and the Swiss Franc. Table 5.3 lists the currencies besides the Hong Kong and the US dollar that have official direct bilateral currency trading arrangements with the RMB. While the list is relatively short, it covers some of China's major trading partners.

Table 5.3 Direct Foreign Exchange Trading of Other Currencies

Starting Date	Currencies
August 2010	Malaysian ringgit
December 2010	Russian ruble
June 2012	Japanese yen
April 2013	Australian dollar
March 2014	New Zealand dollar
June 2014	British pound
September 2014	Euro
October 2014	Singapore dollar
December 2014	Korean won
March 2015	Canadian dollar
November 2015	Swiss franc

---

[18] Initially, the trading band was 5% above or below the central parity rate.

[19] The turnover volume grew 700% in 2014 to RMB48 billion (ruble 395 billion). In March 2015, the exchange started trading of cash-settled RMB–Ruble futures.

These RMB cross foreign exchange rates lower the currency conversion cost and promote the bilateral trade and investment between China and its counterparts. In the absence of the cross rates, the exchange of the RMB into, say, the Korean won has to be typically conducted via the US dollar exchange rates of the RMB and won. The cost of going through the triangular exchange is higher than the direct bilateral trade. Thus these RMB cross rates not only simplify the paperwork, they also improve price transparency and reduce the foreign exchange cost of China's cross-border trade and investment transactions. Importantly, the direct foreign exchange trading promotes the international use of the RMB (and the currencies of the counterparties), and reduces the world's reliance on the US dollar.

In sum, direct foreign exchange trading between the RMB and non-US currencies facilitates China's cross-border trade and investment and makes the Chinese currency appealing to international investors.

5.3.4 Offshore RMB markets

For the RMB to be a true contender in the global financial market, it has to be accepted for conducting business both within and outside China, and by residents and nonresidents. The establishment of offshore RMB markets is an obvious policy move to promote the international use of the RMB. With the existing capital control policy, China can experiment with various exchange rate liberalization measures in an offshore market and observe their economic implications and consequences. At the same time, nonresidents can experience the pros and cons of using the RMB to conduct trade and investment transactions without subject to the stringent rules and regulations prevailing in China.

An offshore RMB market allows both China and the rest of world to explore the opportunities and challenges of a globalizing Chinese currency. Anecdotal evidence indicates that China has been quite proactive in establishing offshore RMB centers since the 2008 global financial crisis. Beginning with Hong Kong, offshore RMB businesses have prosperously spread to other major international financial centers and contributes to the increasing acceptance of RMB in the global market.

Hong Kong is the first offshore RMB center designated by China. The development of its offshore RMB market could be traced back to 2003.

Given its unique political and financial status, Hong Kong has maintained a noticeable lead over other international financial centers, including London and New York, in the global offshore RMB business. Arguably, the market in Hong Kong reflects China's policy — both past and current — on offshore RMB centers. Thus, after a general discussion of offshore currency markets in the rest of this subsection, we will discuss the offshore RMB market in Hong Kong in the next subsection.

In general, an offshore currency market is a market that specializes in trade and financial transactions denominated in currencies not issued by the jurisdiction where the market is located. It usually serves a large proportion of nonresidents. For instance, as an offshore RMB market, Hong Kong with Hong Kong dollar as its legal tender facilitates a large share of global RMB transactions that cover trade settlements, foreign exchange transactions, currency deposits, loans, bond issuances, and equities.

One important feature of an offshore market is that it separates the currency risk from the country risk. The currency risk is then combined with the risk of the jurisdiction in which the offshore market is located. Usually, an offshore market is established in a jurisdiction with a good reputation of the rule of law, sound financial market infrastructure, and favorable regulatory and tax policies on offshore transactions.

An offshore market has to offer both convenience and confidence to attract offshore currency businesses. Convenience requires good trading capacity and settlement efficiency. Typically, it requires a deep and broad market with an established trading and clearance infrastructure. The convenience to market participants is further enhanced with a well-connected transactional network and a good set of investment and funding alternatives.

The confidence of international participants relies on the rule of law governing the offshore currency market. Before they enter the offshore market, they have to be sure if their money and investment are safe and protected by law. Of course, the government attitude toward offshore transactions could critically affect the confidence of international participants and the prospect of a market as an offshore currency center.

The business possibility of offshore currency activity can be affected by the policy stance of the country that issues the currency. While offshore currency transactions take place outside the currency issuance country, the money flows associated with these transactions at the end have to be cleared in the onshore banking system. The currency issuance country could thus manage offshore transactions via rules and regulations on clearing balances of foreign financial institutions being held with onshore banks. For instance, by imposing (or threatening to impose) stringent restrictions on these clearing balances, the onshore authorities can create prohibiting inconvenience for offshore transactions. The reluctance of the Bundesbank, for example, was perceived as a reason of the limited degree of the internationalization of the Deutsche mark before the euro era.[20]

The renowned offshore currency markets include London in Europe, New York in North America, and Tokyo in Asia. These markets support a wide range of products denominated in numerous currencies. In addition to these three, there are a few scattered around in the global economy and operate on a smaller scale; they include Hong Kong, Singapore, Dubai, Luxemburg, and Frankfurt.

The market for offshore dollar transactions is commonly called the Eurodollar market. The US dollar is the most predominant currency in offshore currency markets around the world, and, indeed, the global Eurodollar market constitutes the largest segment of the global financial market. The sprawling of these offshore dollar markets facilitates greatly the international use of the US dollar for trade and financial transactions across different time zones and geographic locations. On the one hand, the existence of these offshore markets is supported by the prominence of the US dollar in the international monetary system and, on the other hand, provides the network effect that reinforces the global status of the dollar.

Taking the hint from the US dollar, one expects China's drive to internationalize its currency will benefit from an effective network of offshore RMB markets.

5.3.5 The offshore RMB center in Hong Kong

As noted earlier, Hong Kong is the first offshore RMB center and accounts for a lion's share of the global offshore RMB business. Since 2004, China has been using Hong Kong as a laboratory to experiment with the use of the

---

[20] See, for example, Franke (1999).

RMB outside its own regulatory system. Thus, in the current subsection, we provide an overview of the evolution of the offshore RMB market in Hong Kong.[21]

During its British colony era, Hong Kong was already a renowned global financial center and a main *entrepôt* for China trade. Indeed, Hong Kong was widely considered as China's window to the rest of the world. After the sovereignty change in 1997, Hong Kong has become a special administrative region of China, and by most measures, has maintained its status of a renowned global financial center. Since then, the governance of Hong Kong is under the stipulation of The Basic Law of the Hong Kong Special Administrative Region, which, essentially, is a mini-constitution. The Hong Kong Basic Law embodies the spirit of the "one country, two systems" policy that was originally envisioned by the then paramount leader Xiaoping Deng and allows Hong Kong to maintain its own legal and financial systems. Specifically, Hong Kong retains its own currency, the Hong Kong dollar, and imposes no capital controls.

Because of its unique economic and political characteristics, Hong Kong was chosen as a testing ground for assessing the outcomes and implications of RMB convertibility and capital account liberalization. Although Hong Kong is legally an integral part of China, China has control measures that regulate its cross-border activities with Hong Kong. On financial transactions, for instance, Hong Kong is treated as an offshore instead of an onshore market. There are specific rules and procedures instituted to govern RMB movements between China and Hong Kong.

To prepare for the RMB business in Hong Kong, in 2003, China appointed the Bank of China Hong Kong as the local clearing bank for RMB transactions. It is the first local RMB clearing bank outside mainland China. The Hong Kong Interbank Clearing Limited provides the RMB real-time gross settlement system — an important infrastructure to support the RMB clearing services in Hong Kong and facilitate RMB transactions in other overseas financial centers.[22]

---

[21] See, for example, Cheung (2015).

[22] The Hong Kong Interbank Clearing Limited is a private company jointly owned by the HKMA and the Hong Kong Association of Banks, and provides real-time settlement services in Hong Kong dollar, RMB, euro, and US dollar. Hong Kong Monetary Authority (2015) offers some quick facts about the system including the list of participating banks.

Currently, the RMB settlement system in Hong Kong is directly connected with the China National Advanced Payment System (CNAPS) in China. The link facilitates the Hong Kong system to handle RMB transactions with mainland China. It operates from 8:30 a.m. to 5:00 a.m. the next day Hong Kong time, which overlaps with business hours in Europe and the Americas.[23] At the end of 2014, the Hong Kong RMB real-time gross settlement system served 225 banks around the world.

In February 2004, 32 banks in Hong Kong were allowed to conduct personal RMB businesses for Hong Kong residents including RMB deposit, currency exchange, credit card, and remittance services. Some specific measures are: (i) individuals are allowed to convert up to RMB20,000 daily in Hong Kong[24] and (ii) certain industries are allowed to conduct selected corresponding services. Since then, Hong Kong has introduced and developed various RMB-denominated investment products that promote the global use of the RMB. These products include Dim Sum bonds,[25] equity listings, insurance policies, and commodity contracts.

The progress of the RMB business in Hong Kong was slow before 2008. After the global financial crisis in 2008, China has intensified its efforts on broadening and deepening the offshore RMB market. In March 2011, the Beijing government announced its formal support in the National 12th Five-Year Plan (2011–2015) for Hong Kong to develop its role as an offshore RMB business center. In the following, we review a few aspects of the offshore market in Hong Kong.

(a) CNH, the offshore RMB

In July 2010, Hong Kong Monetary Authority and the People's Bank of China signed the Supplementary Memorandum of Co-operation on

---

[23] Since 2013, the Hong Kong system is connected to the Shenzhen Financial Settlement System to push the cross-border RMB payment services cut-off time to 11:00 p.m. Also, it is expected to be connected to the China International Payment System (CIPS), which was designed to facilitate international RMB settlements. The first phase of CIPS that includes 11 domestic and eight locally incorporated foreign banks was launched in October 2015.

[24] The RMB20,000 conversion limit was lifted before the launch of the Shanghai-Hong Kong Stock Connect scheme in November 2014.

[25] A Dim Sum bond refers to the bond denominated in the RMB and issued in Hong Kong (and other offshore markets).

RMB business, which allows the trading of spot and forward RMB and RMB-linked structural products in Hong Kong.[26] Prior to the signing of the memorandum, there was no officially endorsed FX market for the RMB in Hong Kong. Since then, the RMB transacted in Hong Kong has been essentially traded like a convertible currency. Because the currency is subject to different rules and regulations, market practitioners view the RMB traded in Hong Kong is different from the RMB in China. Instead of the usual RMB's trading symbol CNY, they label the RMB traded in Hong Kong as CNH and other offshore markets. CNY, nonetheless, retains its status as the only official ISO currency code used internationally (SWIFT, 2011).

The Hong Kong daily trading in spot RMB has grown from almost nothing in July 2010 to an estimated average volume of US$400 million by the end of 2010, and to US$4 billion by the end of 2013. At the end of April 2015, the daily turnover of RMB foreign exchange transactions in Hong Kong has reached US$93 billion equivalent (Hong Kong Monetary Authority, 2016, p. 13). Despite the rapid growth, the CNH trading in Hong Kong is quite small relative to the onshore market. Bank for International Settlements (2013), for instance, indicates that Hong Kong accounted for 16% of the total global RMB foreign exchange trading and the onshore market accounted for 59% of the trading volume.[27]

Due to the different supply and demand structures in Hong Kong and China and the presence of capital controls, the CNH in Hong Kong and the CNY in the onshore China market are usually traded at different prices. Figure 5.1 presents the premium of CNH over CNY.

When the CNH was introduced, its supply was limited. The demand for the RMB that is not subject to China's capital controls pushed the CNH price up. In the early months of its existence, CNH exhibited a premium up to 2.5%. The value of CNH relative to CNY experienced a sharp drop in September 2011, and almost reached a discount of 2%. There is a

---

[26] See Hong Kong Monetary Authority (2010a). Before July 2010, nondeliverable RMB forwards instead of deliverable forwards are commonly traded in the market.

[27] According to the triennial central bank surveys conducted the Bank for International Settlements, the average RMB daily forex turnover in the global market surged from US$1.7 billion in 2004, US$14.6 billion in 2007, US$29.2 billion in 2010 to reach US$119.6 billion in 2013 (Bank for International Settlements, 2004, 2007, 2010, 2013).

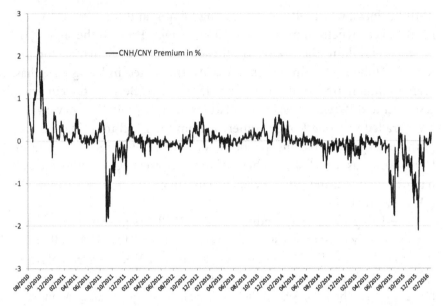

Figure 5.1   Premium of CNH over CNY (Aug 2010 to Mar 2016)

speculation that the drop is triggered by unwinding of CNH buying that was not backed by imports and exports trade activity and the possibility of the hard landing risk in China. After the second half of 2015, CNH has experienced a few instances of large discounts, which were attributed to uncertainties associated with the change of the RMB fixing mechanism introduced in August 2015 and the related concerns of China's inclination to depreciate RMB in face of tough economic conditions.

The CNH money market in Hong Kong is relatively small. On top of the net RMB trade settlement balance, the CNH FX rate can be swung by market expectations of the RMB appreciation potential and the global risk appetite. The onshore rate, on the other hand, mainly follows the officially guided market rate and the onshore demand and supply conditions. While China's capital control measures are not 100% water tight, the presence of CNH-CNY premiums attests to the effect of capital controls that segregate the Hong Kong from the Chinese financial market.[28]

---

[28] China's capital controls and their effectives are discussed in, for example, Chen (2013), Cheung and Herrala (2014), Cheung and Qian (2011), Ma and McCauley (2008), and Prasad and Wei, (2007).

(b) Offshore RMB deposits

The initial volume of RMB deposits in Hong Kong was minute when it was authorized to conduct deposit-taking. At the end of February 2004, the amount of CNH deposits was only RMB895 million. However, it grew rapidly and passed a historical level of RMB1.004 trillion by December 2014. The size of the CNH pool signifies the liquidity of the offshore RMB market. It has implications for both offshore and onshore markets because investors with CNH could access the growing universe of RMB-denominated products in offshore markets and in onshore financial markets, say, via the renminbi-qualified foreign institutional investor (RQFII) scheme.[29]

The evolution of CNH deposits is depicted in Figure 5.2. Its growth pattern mirrors China's efforts to promote the international use of its currency. The growth of the CNH deposit experienced a first surge in July 2007 — the first time bonds denominated in RMB were issued in Hong Kong. These bonds are dubbed "Dim Sum" bonds. The first Dim Sum bond was issued by the China Development Bank, a Chinese policy bank that is under the direct jurisdiction of China's State Council. An obvious implication of the issuance is the official endorsement of extending the scope of offshore RMB business to include investment products. Between July 2007 and May 2008, the CNH deposit increased over 100% in less than a year from RMB27.9 billion to RMB77.7 billion.

The scheme for cross-border trade settlement in RMB launched in 2009 and expanded in 2010 provides another impetus to the growth of the CNH market. The Supplementary Memorandum of Co-operation signed by the Hong Kong Monetary Authority and the People's Bank of China further encourages the growth of the CNH business.[30] The expansion of CNH deposits accelerated in mid-2010. For instance, during the period

---

[29] The scheme was introduced by China in December 2011. Authorized RQFII holders are institutions approved by China to channel RMB funds raised in Hong Kong (or offshore RMB markets) to invest into China's securities markets. In early 2012, Hong Kong's Securities and Futures Commission allowed the first group of companies to conduct their RQFII businesses.

[30] The Supplementary Memorandum (Hong Kong Monetary Authority, 2010) essentially allows a rich menu of RMB trading activities — including spot and forward RMB trading and RMB-linked structural products — in Hong Kong.

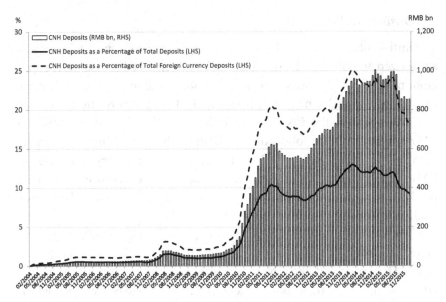

Figure 5.2   Offshore RMB Deposits in Hong Kong (Feb 2004–Jan 2016)

Note: CNH = Offshore RMB in Hong Kong.

Source: CEIC.

between July 2010 and November 2011, the CNH deposit grew by 500% from the amount of RMB103.4 billion to RMB627.3 billion. The phenomenal growth rate makes CNH the second most popular foreign currency after the US dollar in the Hong Kong market.

The decline of the CNH deposit in the first half of 2012 triggered the concern about the prospect of the offshore market. The concern, however, was dismissed in the mid-2012 when China reaffirmed the role of Hong Kong as a prime offshore RMB center. The volume of CNH deposit regained its upward trajectory and reached a historical level of RMB1.004 trillion in December 2014. The dips experienced in 2014 and 2015 were associated with the uncertainties triggered by the currency's downward movements, and the related concerns of the coming of a weak RMB policy.

Undeniably, the CNH deposit market has a relatively short history. Its growth is quite eye-opening: its size has increased from RMB895 million in February 2004 to the high mark of RMB1.004 trillion in December

2014, which is more than 1,000 times. Even with the noticeable decline in late 2015, the size of the CNH pool in Hong Kong is still above RMB800 billion.

The number of banks participating in the RMB clearing platform offered by Hong Kong has increased from 32 in February 2004 to 224 in December 2014; an increase of slightly over 600%.

By the end of 2014, the CNH deposits represent about 12.6% of the total deposits and 24.1% of the foreign currency deposits in Hong Kong.[31] It is noted that, despite its phenomenal growth, the total amount of RMB deposits in Hong Kong is less than 1% of China's RMB deposit balance, which stood at the level of RMB113.9 trillion as of December 2014. When the market was pulling money out of the Chinese currency market, the size of CNH deposits dropped below, respectively, 10% and 20% of the total deposits and the foreign currency deposits in Hong Kong. The swing high-lights the sensitivity of the CNH business to market sentiments toward China's economic policy.

(c) RMB trade settlement in Hong Kong

As discussed in the previous subsection, denominating and settling cross-border trade in the RMB is one of China's recent policies to pro-mote the international use of its currency. To recap, the Chinese State Council approved in April 2009 a pilot scheme for cross-border trade settlement in RMB. Five Chinese cities — Dongguan Guangzhou, Shenzhen, and Zhuhai — in the Guangdong Province and Shanghai were included in the pilot scheme when the scheme was launched in July 2009. Then, the scheme was expanded to cover 20 of the 31 mainland Chinese provinces in June 2010 and to cover the entire China in August 2011. Given its advanced financial infrastructure, experiences in trade financing, and traditional *entrepôt* role of China trade, Hong Kong was chosen as the location to experiment with the RMB trade settlement initiative.[32]

---

[31] The US dollar accounted for 31.4% — the highest percentage among all foreign curren-cies — of the total deposits in Hong Kong as of December 2014.

[32] Despite Hong Kong being the often talked-about RMB trade settlement center, the pilot scheme, in fact, covers Hong Kong, Macau, and the ASEAN member countries.

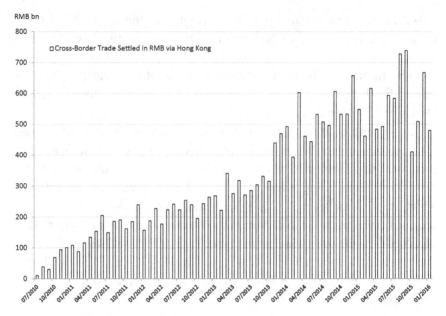

Figure 5.3   Volume of Cross-Border Trade Settled in RMB via Hong Kong (July 2010–Jan 2016)

Source: Hong Kong Monetary Authority, People's Bank of China.

Figure 5.3 presents the volume of trade settled in RMB conducted via Hong Kong. The value of RMB trade settlement has been growing strongly since 2010. The drastic increase in RMB trade settlement in the second half of 2010 was facilitated by China's policy of expanding Hong Kong's capacity to conduct offshore RMB transactions with the "Memorandum of Cooperation on Renminbi Business" signed on July 19, 2010. Indeed, the monthly RMB trade settlement volume jumped from the level of RMB10 billion in July 2010 to RMB480 billion in January 2016; an increase of more than 46 times in five years. In addition to its strong growth, Hong Kong conducts most of the cross-border RMB trade settlement; for example, the RMB6.8 trillion settled via institutions in Hong Kong in 2015 accounts for over 90% of China's trade settled in RMB (Hong Kong Monetary Authority, 2016).

It is perceived that the trade settlement figures are over-stated. For example, when the CNH in Hong Kong is traded at a premium to the CNY in China, the Chinese companies are willing to invoice their imports from their overseas associates in the RMB. Their overseas associates, in turn, convert the RMB into the US dollar in the CNH market at a better exchange rate to make the final payment. Thus, such an arbitrage activity inflates the actual level of trade settled in the RMB. Nevertheless, even allowing for possible misclassified transactions that are related to arbitrage between onshore and offshore markets via trade invoicing with associates, the growth of the volume of trade settled in RMB is still quite phenomenal.

(d) Dim sum bonds

A milestone of the offshore market experiment is the issuance of RMB-denominated bonds in Hong Kong. These bonds are commonly known as Dim Sum bonds, a nickname after a popular Cantonese cuisine.[33] The new chapter of the offshore RMB market started with the Dim Sum bonds issued by the China Development Bank in 2007.

Prior to the issuance of Dim Sum bonds, most local Hong Kong banks offered an interest rate of 0.4% for CNH deposits and these deposits are deposited back to the People's Bank of China at the interest rate of 0.72%. The investment returns from holding CNH deposits is very limited. Dim Sum bonds offer an alternative investment opportunity for the offshore RMB.

The issuances and outstanding amounts of Dim Sum bonds are plotted in Figures 5.4 and 5.5 respectively. Since the first issuance, there is a steady flow of Dim Sum bond offers in Hong Kong. The Dim Sum bond market has expanded quite quickly after the relaxation of rules on remitting offshore RMB back to China. The issuance volume in each year was over RMB100 billion between 2011 and 2014, but experienced a drop in 2015. The outstanding amount is increasing steadily until a slight decline is observed in 2015. By the end of 2014, the outstanding amount of Dim Sum bonds was RMB368 billion.[34]

---

[33] Following the emergence of other offshore RMB centers, RMB-denominated bonds issued outside mainland China are sometimes are called Formosa bonds (in Taiwan) and Lion City bonds (in Singapore).

[34] As of the end of 2015, the outstanding amount of HKD debt instruments (bonds issued by Exchange Fund, statutory bodies, government, multilateral development banks, non-MDB overseas borrowers, authorized institutions, and local corporates) was HK$1,525 billion (around RMB1,277 billion).

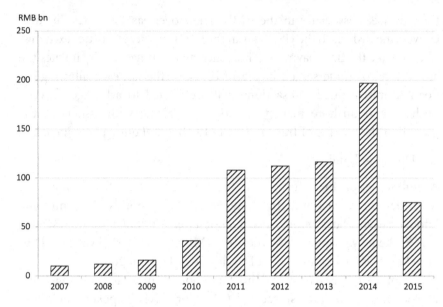

Figure 5.4   Dim Sum Bond Issuance in Hong Kong

Source: Hong Kong Monetary Authority.

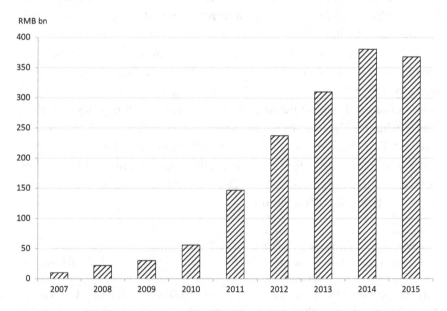

Figure 5.5   Outstanding Dim Sum Bonds in Hong Kong

Source: Hong Kong Monetary Authority.

In the beginning, Dim Sum bond issuances are dominated by institutions closely related to the Chinese government, including China's Ministry of Finance, China's policy banks (China Development Bank and Export–Import Bank of China), and state-owned banks (Bank of China and China Construction Bank). Gradually, the list of issuers is expanded to include (a) corporation issuers (e.g., Hopewell Highway Infrastructure Ltd.), multinational corporations (e.g., McDonald's and Caterpillar), and international institutions including the World Bank and the Asian Development Bank. By the end of 2015, the group of issuers has significantly broadened from Chinese sovereignty and bank issuers to financial institutions and corporations from different parts of the world account; those registered overseas represent 41% of the Dim Sum bond issuers.[35] The breakdown of the issuers is depicted in Figure 5.6.

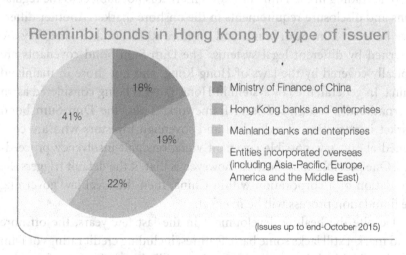

Renminbi bonds in Hong Kong by type of issuer

- 18%
- 41%
- 19%
- 22%

- Ministry of Finance of China
- Hong Kong banks and enterprises
- Mainland banks and enterprises
- Entities incorporated overseas (including Asia-Pacific, Europe, America and the Middle East)

(Issues up to end-October 2015)

Figure 5.6   Distribution of Dim Sum Bond Issuers in Hong Kong

Source: Hong Kong Monetary Authority.

---

[35] One noticeable issuer is the Malaysia's sovereign wealth fund, Khazanah Nasional Berhad, which issued the first sukuk in the Chinese currency RMB in Hong Kong in October 2011. The first Dim Sum sukuk issuance had a relatively small size of RMB500 million and a tenor of three years. For Hong Kong, the Khazanah Nasional Dim Sum sukuk issuance reassures its prominent status as an offshore RMB center and its potential role as an Islamic financing hub.

Among all the issues, the sovereign RMB bonds issued by China's Ministry of Finance have attracted considerable attention from the market. Every year since 2009, the Ministry of Finance has issued its RMB sovereign bonds in Hong Kong. The sizes of issuances are usually large, and they range from the RMB6 billion offer in 2009 to the RMB28 billion offered in 2014. In 2015, the Ministry of Finance also offered in two slots with a total amount of RMB28 billion Dim Sum bonds in Hong Kong — these bonds were offered to institutional investors, foreign central banks and regional monetary authorities, and retail investors.

Different from other Dim Sum bond issues, the Ministry of Finance sovereign bonds cover long tenors up to the maturity of 30 years. The issuance of long-term RMB-denominated bonds is seen as an effort to set up an offshore market yield curve, which is essential for the operation of a full-fledged offshore RMB bond market.

The trading in the Dim Sum bond market is not subject to the regulations and disclosure requirements in the onshore market. Another difference between Dim Sum bonds and onshore RMB bonds is that they are governed by different legal systems. The Dim Sum bond covenants are typically covered by the laws of Hong Kong, and not those in mainland China. In general, the law system in Hong Kong is being considered as an internationally recognized legal framework. Thus, the Dim Sum bond market is attractive to individual and sovereign investors who are concerned about, say, possible covenant violations and insolvency proceedings. One possible complication, however, is that, if the default triggers the liquidation of a corporation within China, then the local law governing the liquidation process will be in effect.

Despite the healthy development in the last few years, the offshore bond market still lacks some basic features, including credit ratings of Dim Sum bonds, which have expanded quite rapidly but at the cost of diluting issuer's quality. The presence of low-quality issuers raises concern about Dim Sum bonds that are without explicit clauses in their covenants to protect the investors. Naturally, the availability of objective credit ratings and improved investor protection will nurture the dynamic growth of the Dim Sum bond market.

During its rapid growth phase, the Dim Sum bond has gone beyond the plain vanilla version that is denominated and traded in RMB. Shui On Land

Ltd., a Hong Kong based property developer, issued a synthetic Dim Sum bond in December 2010, denominated in RMB but traded in the US dollar. Indeed, the bonds are sold in US dollars, will be redeemed for US dollars at maturity, and the coupons are paid in US dollars at the prevailing exchange rates. In essence, a synthetic Dim Sum bond issuer transfers the exchange rate risk to the buyer. A synthetic bond will appeal to investors who expect the RMB will appreciate against the US dollar during the holding period.

For Chinese corporations, China's regulatory approval has to be obtained before issuing Dim Sum bonds in Hong Kong. However, no regulatory approval is required for synthetic Dim Sum bonds. Also, the US dollar proceeds from bond issuance could be remitted back to China following the existing procedure and thus, the uncertainty associated with RMB remittance, which has to be approved on a case-by-case basis, is avoided.

(e) RMB-denominated equity

The prospect of the offshore RMB market in Hong Kong depends on the menu of RMB-denominated assets and liabilities. On the one hand, Hong Kong has to accumulate a sizable pool of offshore RMB to support and sustain an active offshore market. On the other hand, the creation of offshore RMB-denominated investment products enhance the acceptability and demand for the CNH. In the last few years, several investment opportunities, beyond bank deposits and bonds, were introduced to expand the class of CNH assets.

The Hong Kong Exchanges and Clearing Limited is quite progressive in promoting the listing of RMB-denominated products. The first RMB-denominated initial public offering in Hong Kong was issued by the Hui Xian REIT in April 2011. Hui Xian is a real-estate investment trust backed by a real-estate property in Beijing. In the beginning, retail investors are not too enthusiastic in trading of RMB-denominated equities. The lack of liquidity is cited as a concern.

Despite its lukewarm start, the Stock Exchange of Hong Kong rolled out the RMB Equity Trading Support Facility on October 24, 2011, to facilitate RMB-denominated equity trading. In essence, the facility was established to ensure that investors have sufficient and reliable RMB liquidity for trading RMB denominated equity shares in the secondary market in Hong Kong.[36] By March 2015, there were 18 RMB-denominated stocks covered by the Trading Support Facility.[37]

Since 2011, the Chinese regulators have revised rules on overseas listing and on investing offshore RMB in the domestic capital markets. One "new" product is the dual currency (Hong Kong dollar and Chinese renminbi) share. The first dual currency share was listed by Hopewell Highway Infrastructure Limited on October 29, 2012, with 0737 as the Hong Kong dollar-denominated stock code and 80737 the RMB-denominated stock code.[38] According to the local trading rules about dual-currency listings, Hopewell Highway Infrastructure shares can be traded interchangeably between Hong Kong dollar and RMB.

In December 2011, the China Securities Regulatory Commission, the People's Bank of China, and the State Administration of Foreign Exchange jointly announced the launch of the RMB-qualified foreign institutional investor (RQFII) scheme. The RQFII scheme is an expansion of the original qualified foreign institutional investor (QFII) scheme, which allows authorized foreign entities to invest in China using foreign currencies — mainly the US dollar — converted into the RMB. The RQFII program, on the other hand, allows nonresidents in offshore markets using offshore RMB to purchase approved funds denominated in RMB in China's domestic market.

The RQFII scheme underscores the fast growth of RMB-denominated exchange trade funds. Initially, the China Securities Regulatory

---

[36] The facility is operated by the Hong Kong Securities Clearing Company Limited, which is a wholly owned subsidy of the Hong Kong Exchanges and Clearing Limited. For additional information on the Facility, see the website http://www.hkex.com.hk/eng/market/sec_tradinfra/tsf/tsf.htm.

[37] The codes and short names of these 18 stocks are 80737 (HOPEWELL INFR-R), 82811 (HT CSI300 ETF-R), 82822 (CSOP A50 ETF-R), 82832 (BOSERA FA50-R), 3008 (C-SHS CSI 300-R), 83095 (VALUE A SHARE-R), 83100 (EFUND CSI100-R), 83107 (C-SHS CSI STA-R), 83118 (HGI MSCI CN A-R), 83120 (EFUND CES 120-R), 83127 (HZ CSI300-R), 83128 (HS AINDTOPETF-R), 83132 (C-SHS CSI HLC-R), 83136 (HGI MSCIA50-R), 83137 (CSOP CES A80-R), 83180 (CAM CES A80-R), 83188 (CAM CSI300-R), and 87001 (HUI XIAN REIT).

[38] Officially, the dual-currency share is dubbed a "dual counter" trade equity by the Stock Exchange.

Commission only approved Hong Kong subsidiaries of China's fund management companies and securities companies to participate in the pilot RQFII scheme, and the investment funds were mainly restricted to fixed income products. Then, the scheme has become inclusive and opened to foreign financial institutions and asset managers, and the class of allowable assets is extended beyond fixed income products.

The liberalization of the RQFII program offers international investors a wide range of exchange-traded RMB-denominated funds that cover different investment options and styles of securities in China, and enhances the level of foreign participation in the Chinese capital market.[39] Indeed, a good number of stocks under the RMB Equity Trading Support Facility are these RMB-denominated funds.

(f) Other RMB-denominated products

Since the official endorsement of CNH in 2010, both the public and private sectors have introduced investment products for the RMB accumulated outside mainland China. In addition to those discussed in the previous subsections, we briefly describe a few more here. One type of these products is RMB-denominated gold contracts. The century-old bullion house in Hong Kong, the Chinese Gold & Silver Exchange Society, has started trading a new product called "Renminbi Kilobar Gold" since October 2011. The Renminbi Kilobar Gold is quoted in RMB for one kilogram of gold. It requires settlement in RMB and physical delivery of specified gold bars.[40] In February 2012, Hang Seng Bank offered the first RMB Gold ETF. Both products offer choices to investors to deploy their offshore RMB holdings and promote the global status of the RMB as a commodity pricing currency.

Besides RMB spot trading, a number of exchange traded and over-the-counter RMB derivative products are available in Hong Kong. In September 2012, Hong Kong Exchanges and Clearing Limited introduced

---

[39] After Hong Kong, China has granted RQFII quotas to financial institutions in other countries, including Germany, Korea, Great Britain, France, Luxemburg, and Singapore.
[40] In September 2014, the Hong Kong Bullion Society became the first exchange outside mainland China to secure the approval to set up a precious metals vault in the Qianhai special economic zone.

the first deliverable RMB futures contract — USD/CNH futures.[41] The trading volume has picked up quite impressively since its inception. The average daily volume increased from 568 contracts in 2013 to 830 contracts in 2014 and 1062 in 2015.[42]

The trading volume growth has been benefited from China's policy of widening the trading band of the RMB, and the heightened level of uncertainty about China's economic policy. The Hong Kong deliverable contract is now the most well-transacted one in the global offshore RMB market.

The unexpected decline of the RMB value in the first quarter of 2014 brings one of the popular over-the-counter products — the RMB Target Redemption Forward (TRF) — to media attention. It is perceived that the RMB TRF is a popular derivative product for directional bet on RMB movement. Some market commentators argued that the decline was engineered by the Chinese authorities to bring in two-way RMB fluctuations, and end the expectations of a one-way bet on RMB appreciation. The prolonged decline and the associated volatility inflicted huge losses to these adopted directional hedging strategies, and holders of TRFs that are established for directional bet on the RMB.

A RMB TRF contract is a leveraged structured product that allows its holder to buy the RMB against a foreign currency (usually the US dollar) following a prefixed schedule (say, monthly) at a predetermined rate. It generates limited profits but incurs significant potential losses when the RMB is weakening. Until 2014, the popularity of TRF contracts was supported by the strong market view on the RMB appreciation trend since the 2005 exchange rate reform. It is estimated that, between the start of 2013 and February 2014, the total value of TRF leveraged positions was around $350 billion, and the losses triggered by the 2014 RMB decline amounted to billions.[43]

---

[41] The Chicago Mercantile Exchange (CME) launched on February 25, 2013, its own version of deliverable RMB futures settled in Hong Kong bank accounts. CME introduced cash-settled RMB futures in 2006.

[42] The trend is quite encouraging: the average daily volume was 2,071 contracts in December 2015 and over 3,000 contracts in the first few months of 2016. The trading volume information is available from the HKEx website.

[43] Banks in Taiwan at that time were believed to account for a quarter of the RMB TRF market. After the episodes, TRF contracts were banned for two to three months, and eight banks were fined by the Financial Supervisory Commission.

The episode highlights the level of product sophistication available in the nascent CNH market. See, for example, Hong Kong Monetary Authority (2015) for additional information on RMB-denominated products offered in Hong Kong.

5.3.6 A global offshore RMB network

The growth potential of the offshore RMB business has not gone unnoticed. The nascent offshore RMB in Hong Kong has attracted widespread interest from various financial cities. These cities are eager to explore the possibility of setting up the infrastructure to compete for a share of the global offshore RMB business. At the same time, to promote the use of the RMB, China has been progressively guided the establishment of offshore RMB centers in different geographic regions. The presence of efficient and effective offshore RMB centers across different geographic locations and time zones will enhance the global RMB liquidity and business opportunities, and these developments help to increase the acceptance of the RMB in the global market. Thus, it is in China's interest to support additional RMB trading markets and work with other financial centers to develop offshore RMB business.

(a) Local offshore RMB clearing

Since 2010, offshore RMB businesses in various forms have been proliferated across continents. Given the onshore capital control policy, financial centers find it hard to expand their RMB activities without China's endorsement and support. One sought after endorsement is the assignment of an authorized local RMB clearing institution.[44]

The presence of a local clearing bank has both symbolic and practical elements. It could be symbolic in the sense that, since 2004, foreign banks and corporations already have had access to the offshore RMB clearing through the RMB real-time gross settlement system in Hong Kong, which is linked to China's National Advanced Payment System in China.

---

[44] Other endorsement actions including the signing of bilateral currency swap arrangement and the offer of RQFII quotas that provide the needed RMB liquidity and investment opportunities to operate and expand the offshore market smoothly.

London, for example, has established itself as a prime offshore RMB center in Europe and, excluding China and Hong Kong, accounted for over 50% of RMB foreign exchange transactions (SWIFT, 2013) before housing a RMB clearing bank of its own in 2014. On the practical side, the presence of a local RMB clearing channel opens up business opportunities, reduces transaction costs, and offers liquidity in case of a RMB squeeze.

By July 2015, China authorized local offshore RMB clearing banks in 18 financial cities; they are listed in Table 5.4. Out of the 18 cities, seven are located in the Asia-Pacific region. The ones in Hong Kong and Macau are quite natural. Indeed, Hong Kong literally monopolized the offshore RMB settlement and clearing infrastructure until Taiwan and Singapore had their local RMB clearing services authorized in early 2013. The offshore

Table 5.4   Local Offshore RMB Clearing Banks

Offshore RMB Center	Authorized in	Authorized Bank
Hong Kong, China	December 2003	Bank of China, Hong Kong
Macau, China	August 2004	Bank of China
Taiwan	February 2013	Bank of China
Singapore	May 2013	Industrial and Commercial Bank of China
London, UK	June 18, 2014	China Construction Bank
Frankfurt, Germany	June 18, 2014	Bank of China
Seoul, South Korea	July 2014	Bank of Communications
Paris, France	September 2014	Bank of China
Luxembourg	September 2014	Industrial and Commercial Bank of China
Doha, Qatar	November 2014	Industrial and Commercial Bank of China
Toronto, Canada	November 2014	Industrial and Commercial Bank of China
Sydney, Australia	November 2014	Bank of China
Bangkok, Thailand	January 2015	Industrial and Commercial Bank of China
Kuala Lumpur, Malaysia	January 2015	Bank of China
Santiago, Chile	May 2015	China Construction Bank
Budapest, Hungary	June 2015	Bank of China
Johannesburg, South Africa	July 2015	Bank of China
Zurich, Switzerland	November 2015	China Construction Bank

business in Taiwan is underpinned by its special political relationship and economic ties with mainland China. Singapore leverages its role as a major financial hub in South East Asia to develop its offshore RMB business. Korea, Malaysia, and Thailand all have close trade ties with China. The heavy focus on Asian Pacific is in accordance with the idea of pushing the RMB to Asia before the rest of the world.

Six clearing banks were appointed in Europe. A foothold in Europe is a necessary step to globalize the RMB. The case for London is quite compelling. Undeniably, London is a formidable global financial center with the largest foreign exchange market and extensive networks of multinational corporations. It is hard to underestimate the potential of London in the global network of offshore RMB markets, and it can act as the western hub of Chinese finance and provide a full host of RMB business services in the Western Hemisphere and beyond.

The UK is quite progressive in seeking the opportunities to develop its offshore RMB business — it was the first G7 country that signed a bilateral currency swap line with China (RMB200 billion, 2013), the first western country to issue sovereign debt denominated in RMB (October 2014),[45] and the first foreign market in which China's central bank made its first overseas debt offering of 5 billion RMB one-year bills in October 2015.[46]

Before 2014, relying on clearing and settlement infrastructure for RMB trading in Hong Kong, London was a leading center of RMB transactions with Hong Kong and China. The appointment of China Construction Bank in London as the first offshore RMB clearing bank authorized outside Asia further affirms and strengthens the city's role in global offshore RMB business.

---

[45] British Columbia was the first foreign regional government to issue Dim Sum bonds, which are listed in Luxembourg. After the UK move, countries including France, Luxembourg, and Sri Lanka are planning for their own sovereign Dim Sum bond issuances. In passing, we note that the UK is the first western country recognized the People's Republic of China.

[46] The debt sale coincided with the high profile state visit to Britain by the Chinese President Xi Jinping. During the same visit, the RMB200 billion bilateral local currency swap agreement was extended for a further three years, and enlarged to the amount of RMB350 billion.

Of the other five centers in the continental Europe, Luxembourg is a leading financial center in Europe with established asset management, international bond listings, and private banking businesses, and has a strong presence in the RMB business in the Eurozone. France and Germany, on the other hand, have deep and broad economic links with China. Hungary has a long-established relationship with China. And Zurich has its special role in the global financial market. The inclusion of these key European cities to the core offshore RMB network facilitates the use and acceptance of the RMB in the Western world.

With the addition of Doha, Sydney, Santiago, and Toronto, the core network of offshore RMB centers with clearing facilities covers the global financial world and makes 24-hour round-the-clock RMB trading possible. In sum, the globalizing RMB policy is panning out gradually from developing cross-border transactions, to establishing regional, international, and global networks.

(b) Not invited

New York is one noticeable global financial center missing from Table 5.4. China began trading of its currency in the US in January 2011. At that time, for a US individual customer, the daily purchase amount is limited to the equivalent of $4,000 a day, and there is no limit on converting RMB back into dollars. For businesses that are engaged in international trading, there are no conversion limits. However, New York, compared with say, London, seldom publicly expresses its interest in establishing an offshore RMB market.[47] Growth of its RMB activity is mainly driven by private sector initiatives for settlement of RMB-denominated trade transactions, which often enjoy discounts offered by the Chinese counterparts.

Apparently, New York is behind in the game of securing offshore RMB business; its share of global RMB business is smaller than, for example, the UK. For instance, according to SWIFT (2015b), the UK market accounts for more 50% of the RMB foreign exchange trading activity outside China and Hong Kong, and the US market accounts for 11.9%.[48]

---

[47] San Francisco city, the third largest financial center in the US, on the other hand, was reported on planning to be a center for offshore RMB trading (Ross, 2013).
[48] The UK is also ahead of the US in term of handling global payments in the RMB (SWIFT, 2015b).

From an economic point of view, New York can be a very promising offshore RMB center in Americas. It has one of the most, if not the most, sophisticated financial markets in the world. And the US is both China's main trade partner and FDI provider. The US corporations including McDonald's and Caterpillar are noticeable foreign corporate issuers of Dim Sum bonds. It also commands an excellent geographic location that serves the time zone after London, and the South American countries that have extensive trade with China.

The underlying reason why China assigned offshore RMB clearing banks to Toronto in North America and Santiago in South America but not to New York or any US city is likely to be politically driven. The implicit (and explicit) rivalry between China and US is quite well documented. Despite the extensive private economic links, the political rhetoric, which is at times bellicose, against China does not help New York to gain endorsement to be a prime offshore RMB center.

In addition to berating its exchange rate and trade policies, the US does not hide its efforts of containing China through, say, its policy of rebalancing toward Asia, failed attempt to discourage allies to sign up the China-led Asian Infrastructure Investment Bank, and the formulation of the Trans-Pacific Partnership trade agreement.[49] These bellicose actions — mostly from officials and some from private sector — drive China to alternative financial centers to promote its RMB business network.[50]

Evidently, China has strategically guided the development of the offshore RMB market in Hong Kong and the global offshore RMB network. In addition to economic efficiency, diplomatic and political considerations affect China's choices of offshore RMB centers. Circumstantial evidence from Table 5.4 suggests that countries, especially the large developed countries that express interest and adopt "deferential" tactics, are more likely to get China's endorsement and support.

In the case of London, both the public and private sectors were quite conscientious in soliciting global offshore RMB business. It takes a

---

[49] The US, Japan, and 10 other countries signed in October 2015 the Trans-Pacific Partnership agreement, which is subject to ratification and final approval of individual national legislations.

[50] Japan, which has engaged in on and off political rows and territorial disputes with China, is another obvious omission from Table 5.4.

respectful approach to China, and collaborates with, say, Hong Kong and Singapore to build up its offshore RMB capacity. Toronto is another case in point. Arguably, its financial and trade sectors are not as prominent as the US ones in the Americas time zone. Nevertheless, Canada has a relative cozy relationship with China. The proactive public and private sector initiatives, including the issuance of Dim Sum bonds by the regional government in British Columbia, have paid off. By 2015, Canada became the first country in the North America to host an offshore RMB trading hub that has a local RMB clearing bank, RQFII quota, and swap line arrangement, which are the main elements for developing RMB businesses.

(c) Where does Hong Kong stand?

Despite the proliferation of financial centers engaged in offshore RMB activities, Hong Kong is still a major player — a status that Hong Kong might be able to keep in the near foreseeable future. Hong Kong in the 2010s has withstood the challenges from the formidable competitors including London, Singapore, Taiwan, and New York that have relentlessly beefed up their capacities to compete for offshore RMB businesses, and maintained its leading position in processing global RMB payment activity and accounted for 70.4% of RMB payments (SWIFT, 2015b). In addition to the first-mover advantage, China's policy support including, for instance, the explicit policy statement in China's 12th Five-Year (2011–2015) Plan to develop Hong Kong into a prime offshore RMB center contributes to Hong Kong's success.

Conceivably, Hong Kong plays a very unique role in China's game plan to establish its offshore RMB network. The development of an offshore market has both its pros and cons for the currency and its home country. In general, offshore markets offer a number of advantages. They can (a) enhance the currency's liquidity and allow nonresidents to gain access to the currency, (b) allow market participants to bypass and evade rules and regulations in the onshore market, (c) provide nonresidents a convenient business environment with local operating hours, location, and language, and (d) offer diversification and management advantages.

Even with these advantages, offshore currency markets can yield adverse effects. For instance, the usual concern is the monetary and financial instability induced by a loosely regulated offshore market that amplifies market risk and undermines authorities' ability to conduct domestic policy and manage capital flows.[51] China indeed is quite concerned about unregulated massive capital movements that can destabilize its under-developed financial sector and domestic economy. In the process of promoting the use of the RMB overseas, China is unlikely to remove all capital controls, which have been proved essential to manage its economy and insulate it from adverse global capital flows.

Thus, in addition to the usual economic considerations, China would like to find offshore RMB centers that are amenable to regulatory cooperation, which allows China to manage the effect of RMB flows on its economy. Through regulatory cooperation arrangements, China can assess the implications of intermediating international transactions in the RMB. For instance, by regulating the pace, the amount, and the channel through which offshore RMB capital is remitted back to the domestic market, China can evaluate the effectiveness of its capital control measures and its ability to manage the Chinese economy. Such a measured strategy to experiment with offshore RMB transactions is in accordance with China's revealed preference for gradual reform approach.

Against this backdrop, it is easy to infer that Hong Kong commands an insurmountable advantage over other offshore financial centers: it offers the offshore market regulatory cooperation China would like to have. China has sovereignty over Hong Kong, even though the territory has a legal and financial system different from China's. Hong Kong's unique conditions make it an ideal testing ground for offshore RMB business; it is an offshore market in which China can dictate both the growth and the evolution of the offshore RMB business via fiat and legislation.

Compared with other financial centers that have different political and market structures, Hong Kong is relatively pliable and can work out the nitty-gritty of regulatory cooperation that China would like to have for its offshore RMB experiment. With its advanced financial market infrastructure and excellent track record on implementing offshore RMB strategies, Hong Kong is likely to maintain a considerable lead in the global offshore RMB business in the near future.

---

[51] A different view on the cost is that the global status facilitated by offshore currency markets promotes the exorbitant privilege — the US dollar is commonly referred to as the global currency that enjoys the exorbitant privilege and imposes costs to other economies (Eichengreen, 2011).

Of course, the primacy of Hong Kong is not a foregone conclusion. Developments both inside and outside China can affect Hong Kong's role in the global offshore RMB arena. For instance, the launch of the China International Payment System (CIPS) in October 2015 will undermine Hong Kong's role in settling international RMB transactions. Before CIPS, cross-border RMB payments are routed through offshore RMB clearing banks, including the one in Hong Kong. These designated banks connect the global payment system and the domestic China National Advanced Payment System (CNAPS), which supports Chinese characters but not all non-Chinese-based international payment instructions.[52] The first phase of CIPS encompasses 19 core domestic financial institutions. It is a cross-border RMB payments infrastructure designed to integrate global RMB transactions into CNAPS. Eventually, CIPS will operate independently and handle directly offshore and onshore RMB payments into and out of China. The middleman role of offshore RMB clearing banks will then be minimized. Despite its head start over other offshore RMB centers, Hong Kong has to be vigilant in developing its offshore RMB business in response to developments both inside and outside of China.

The prospect of global RMB business is quite promising, though. When the currency has gained global acceptance, and is increasingly used overseas, the demand for RMB will go beyond the traditional area of trade invoicing and settlement. The experiences of other global currencies suggest that, when the RMB realizes its potential as a global currency, it can support multiple active offshore RMB markets around the world. Indeed, multiple centers are required to facilitate its use overseas. When the overall offshore RMB business is growing, it will benefit Hong Kong and other financial centers. At that time, the relative share of Hong Kong in the global offshore RMB market is likely to be lower than the current level, but its absolute size will be larger.

5.3.7 Other measures

In addition to the policy measures described above, China has promoted the use of the RMB overseas via various channels, both direct and indirect

---

[52] According to SWIFT (2015b), the SWIFT network supports Chinese Characters via Chinese Commercial Code or via Chinese characters in MX (ISO 20022 messages).

ones. For example, in September 2009, China agreed to purchase up to 32 billion SDR-denominated notes from the IMF and to pay for these with RMB (People's Bank of China and the International Monetary Fund, 2009).

The transaction has the dual effect of denominating its official claims on the rest of the world in RMB and diversifying into the SDR component currencies: the US dollar, the euro, the yen, and the pound sterling. Even though it is symbolic, the actual implications in terms of the international use of the RMB illustrated by Cheung, Ma and McCauley (2011a, 2011b), who label the strategy of denominating China's claims on the rest of the world in RMB as the "renminbization" of China's foreign assets. Also, from the perspective of the currency composition of international assets and liabilities, China can promote the use of its currency overseas by denominating its official aid programs in Asia, Africa, and Latin America in the RMB (Cheung , Ma and McCauley, 2011a, 2011b), and through its RMB Settlement of Outward Direct Investment (ODI) program introduced in January 2011. These measures improve RMB's liquidity and enhance the scope of deploying RMB around the world. The RMB Qualified Foreign Institutional Investor (RQFII) scheme introduced in late 2011, on the other hand, offers offshore RMB the opportunities to be invested back in the onshore market.

(a) RMB qualified foreign institutional investor initiative

While the market was contemplating different investment opportunities for CNH holders, the China Securities Regulatory Commission, the People's Bank of China, and the State Administration of Foreign Exchange introduced the RMB Qualified Foreign Institutional Investor (RQFII) pilot scheme on December 16, 2011. The RQFII is a variation of the QFII program that China has had since 2002. The main difference is that investors pay offshore RMB for the former program but a foreign currency — usually the US dollar for the latter one.[53]

---

[53] The two schemes are for managing inflows into China's capital market. The Qualified Domestic Investor (QDII) scheme, on the other hand, is for Chinese residents to invest in overseas markets. There are corresponding programs for hedge fund and private equity investments; namely, the qualified domestic limited partner (QDLP) program, the Renminbi Qualified Foreign Limited Partner (RQFLP) program, and Qualified Foreign Limited Partner (QFLP) program.

The RQFII pilot scheme essentially allows nonresidents to deploy their CNH — offshore RMB — holdings to purchase Chinese securities via authorized RMB-denominated funds established in Hong Kong and other designed foreign markets. It is a major policy initiative following the issuance of Dim Sum bonds to offer nonresidents another class of RMB-denominated assets. While the investment in Dim Sum bonds is typically governed by laws in Hong Kong, products underlying RQFII are governed by laws in China.

Initially, the pilot scheme had a quota of RMB20 billion and only allowed authorized subsidiaries of China's brokerage houses and fund managers in Hong Kong to these China-focused funds, which are geared toward fixed income products instead of equities. Since then, the RQFII program has been expanded to different offshore RMB centers including Australia, Germany, Korea, Great Britain, France, Qatar, Luxemburg, Singapore, Switzerland, and Taiwan[54] (Table 5.5), opened to foreign financial institutions and asset managers, and covered asset classes beyond fixed income products. The liberalization of the RQFII program leads to a wide range of RMB denominated funds that offer different investment styles and securities in China. The presence of this class of RMB assets shores up the demand for offshore RMB, and provides foreign investors direct exposure to the Chinese capital market.

(b) Shanghai–Hong Kong stock connect

After the historic memorandum of understanding signed by the China Securities Regulatory Commission and the Securities and Futures Commission of Hong Kong on October 17, 2014 that defines the cooperation framework of the two regulators, the pilot program Shanghai–Hong Kong Stock Connect was officially launched on November 17 the same year.[55]

---

[54] In a summit meeting with Taiwan's Financial Supervisory Commission (FSC) officials in 2013, China Securities Regulatory Commission consented to Taiwan's participation in the RQFII program with a quota of 100 billion yuan. The program was included in the cross-strait service trade pact, which has not been launched yet.

[55] The implementation of the pilot Connect program involved the two securities regulators (China Securities Regulatory Commission and the Securities and Futures Commission of Hong Kong), the two exchanges (the Hong Kong Stock Exchange and Shanghai Stock Exchange), and the clearing affiliates.

Table 5.5   RQFII Quota (RMB Billion, as of December 28, 2015)

Location	Authorized Quota Limit	Aggregated Approved Quota
Hong Kong	270	270
Singapore	50	31.5
UK	80	25.8
France	80	19.8
South Korea	80	71
Germany	80	6
Qatar	30	0
Canada	50	0.2
Australia	50	10
Switzerland	50	5
Luxembourg	50	5
Taiwan	100 (expected)	0
Total	970	444.3

Source: Bloomberg, State Administration of Foreign Exchange (SAFE).

The Stock Connect program represents an ongoing effort in liberalizing China's capital market. Prior to the introduction of the connect initiative, individual investors can gain exposure to China's securities market through funds and products offered by selected financial institutions and institutional investors that are authorized to invest in China's capital market under the QFII and RQFII schemes. The former scheme settles in the US dollar or a major foreign currency, and the latter settles in offshore RMB. The Stock Connect, on the other hand, allows individual and institutional investors to purchase designated Chinese (Hong Kong) stocks through their brokerage accounts in Shanghai (Hong Kong).

The Shanghai–Hong Kong Stock Connect is lauded as a big step toward liberalizing the Chinese capital market and integrating the largest Asian capital market into the global capital world. Under the program, Hong Kong and Shanghai investors are allowed to trade a specified list of stocks in each other's market.[56] Specifically, all Hong Kong and overseas

---

[56] http://www.hkex.com.hk/eng/csm/chinaConnect.asp, for example, posts some detailed information about the Stock Connect program.

individual investors, through their authorized brokerage accounts in Hong Kong, can trade eligible Shanghai-listed A-shares directly. Mainland individual investors who hold an aggregate balance of not less than RMB500,000 in their securities and cash accounts and institutional investors can participate in the programme to purchase Hong Kong-listed stocks directly.

To manage money flows, the cross-exchange trading is subject both aggregate cross-boundary investment quota and daily quota. For Hong Kong investors investing in China, or so-called Northbound trading, the aggregate quota is RMB300 billion with a daily quota of RMB13 billion. For mainland investors investing in Hong Kong stocks, or so-called Southbound trading, the aggregate quota is RMB250 billion with a daily quota of RMB10.5 billion.[57]

Again, the liberalization policy follows the usual protocol of gradual reform. The Chinese stock is opened to the rest of the world in a defined manner; the flow with specific caps has to be through Hong Kong. If things work smoothly, then the experiment will be expanded. Indeed, it is reported that the Shanghai–Hong Kong Stock Connect will be followed by a similar Shenzhen–Hong Kong Stock Connect program. In September 2015, it is also reported that China and Britain agreed to conduct a feasibility study for a stock exchange connect scheme between London and Shanghai.

Figures 5.7 and 5.8 plot the end-of-the-month total (buys and sells) turnover values and the corresponding daily turnover averages for the Northbound and Southbound trading, respectively. By the end of February 2016, the Northbound trading had a total turnover value of RMB1,746 billion, and an average daily turnover of around

---

[57] On eligible stocks, Northbound trading covers the constituent stocks of SSE 180 Index and SSE 380 Index, and the SSE-listed A shares, which have corresponding H shares listed on SEHK, but not SSE-listed shares, which are not traded in RMB or are under risk alert. Southbound trading covers the constituent stocks of Hang Seng Composite LargeCap Index and Hang Seng Composite MidCap Index, and the H-shares, which are simultaneously listed and traded on SSE, but not those stocks not traded in HK dollar, H-shares which have corresponding A-shares listed and traded on a mainland exchange other than SSE, and H-shares which have corresponding SSE-listed shares placed under risk alert.

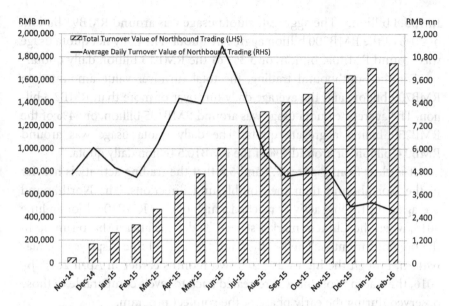

Figure 5.7   Total Turnover and Average Daily Turnover Values of Northbound Trading

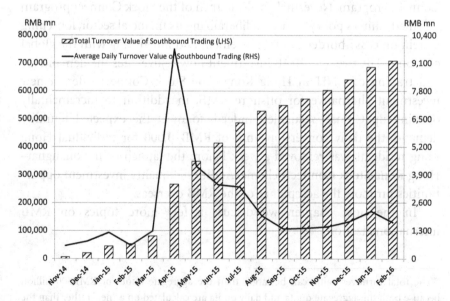

Figure 5.8   Total Turnover and Average Daily Turnover Values of Southbound Trading

RMB5.8 billion.[58] The aggregate quota usage was around RMB91 billion, or 30% of the RMB300 billion aggregate quota. The daily net quota usage was around RMB0.4 billion, or 3.3% of the RMB13 billion daily quota.

For the Southbound trading, the total turnover value amounted to RMB709 billion, and the average daily turnover of more than RMB2.3 billion. The aggregate quota usage was around RMB135 billion, or 54% of the RMB250 billion aggregate quota. The daily quota usage was around RMB0.4 billion, or around 4% of the RMB10.5 billion daily quota.

It is clear from Figures 5.7 and 5.8 that the trading activity is heavier in the Northbound than the Southbound directions. The Northbound average daily trading activity reached a high of over RMB10 billion in June 2015, when the Chinese market started its decline after a sharp run up in the previous months. The Southbound trading volume displays a similar pattern, though the high was reach two months earlier in April 2015. By 2016, the trading volume was retreated back to levels comparable to those observed during the early phase of the connect program.

It is perceived that the sensational equity market roller-coaster and the resulting chaos have dampened the momentum of the Stock Connect initiative, and delayed the launch of the Shenzhen–Hong Kong Stock Connect program. Nevertheless, the launch of the Stock Connect program affirmed China's policy stance on liberalizing its financial sector, loosening its rein on cross-border capital movement and integrating with the global economy. The two-way RMB investment flow rejuvenates the demand for and trading of CNH in Hong Kong. The Stock Connect offers a new investment alternative for offshore RMB, in addition to incrementally opening up China's securities. Indeed, to meet the expected liquidity demand, the daily conversion limit of RMB20,000 for individual Hong Kong residents was removed a week before the launch of the Shanghai–Hong Kong Stock Connect scheme. Additional quality investment opportunities promote the acceptance of the RMB overseas.

In the next chapter, we discuss a few more topics on RMB internationalization.

---

[58] The total turnover value can be larger than the aggregate quota of RMB300 billion because both the aggregate quota and daily quota are calculated on a "net" rather than the "gross" basis.

Chapter 6
RMB Internationalization: II

As discussed in the previous chapter, the cross-border use of the RMB, especially in the trade area has been expanding quite briskly in recent years. However, if China maintains its *status quo* and does not have complementary changes in its domestic market, the offshore experiences will have only limited implications for the overall acceptance of the RMB by the international community.

Circumstantial evidence affirms that China, albeit in a gradual manner, continuously introduces policies to liberalize its financial markets, trade flows, and investment environments. An example is interest rate liberalization that is a crucial component of China's financial reform. It has taken place incrementally over time. For instance, on July 19, 2013, official restrictions on lending rates were removed. Three months later, on October 25, the benchmark loan prime rate, which is based on lending rates of selected banks, was launched to affirm the role of market forces in the loan market. Then the ceiling on deposit rates has been raised gradually. The lifting of the ceiling to 1.5 times the official benchmark rate in May 2015 was considered a sign that interest rate liberalization is near completion and controls on domestic interest rates will be removed in 2015. Indeed, the deposit ceiling was removed in October 2015.[1]

In this chapter, we continue our discussion on the global role of the RMB. First, we consider a few developments in China that have implications for promoting the cross-border use of the currency. These developments are related to China's continuous efforts to enhance its economy, in general, and financial system, in particular. They have both direct and indirect effects on the acceptance of the RMB in the international market. Then, we assess the motivation behind the RMB internationalization policy, the accomplishments so far, and the future prospect.

6.1 Developments in the Onshore Market

In the following subsections, we briefly discuss a few reform initiatives related to RMB internationalization; they are the experimental Qianhai special economic zone, the free trade zones in Shanghai and other locations, Panda bonds, and the domestic bond market.

6.1.1 The Qianhai project

On June 27, 2012, China unveiled a bold economic reform initiative to create a special economic zone within the first special economic zone Shenzhen in China. The zone is known as the Qianhai Shenzhen–Hong Kong Modern Service Industry Cooperation Zone. Essentially, the central government approved the plan to develop Qianhai, a port district of Shenzhen, into a high-level, high-quality, and high value-added modern service industry cooperation zone that enjoys pilot policy preferences beyond those available to Shenzhen. The initiative received praise and is viewed as a confirmation of China's commitment to capital account liberalization and determination to boost the international use of the RMB.

---

[1] The ceiling removal completed official interest rate liberalization process, which provides suitable conditions for currency convertibility. Nevertheless, China is perceived to assert its influences and to manage the rates and volume of credits, if necessary, via moral suasion and, possibly, other administrative means.

Hong Kong and international banks are encouraged to establish offices in Qianhai and build up Qianhai's financial industry. To foster the business link between Hong Kong and Shenzhen, the Chinese government announced that at least one-third of the zone's land will be reserved for Hong Kong companies to build facilities for banks, securities brokers, insurers, and mutual funds. Several large banks, including HSBC and the Standard Chartered Bank, have set up their offices in Qianhai by December 2014.

To be sure, the Qianhai area is not set for completion until 2020, and the reform initiative goes beyond the financial sector. Nonetheless, the hype surrounds the provisions related to offshore RMB business. One key theme of the experimental zone is that offshore RMB capital could be sent back to Qianhai. Possible arrangements include eligible enterprises and banks in Qianhai could conduct cross-border renminbi loan businesses that include borrowing RMB loans from banks in Hong Kong, issuing Dim Sum bonds, and extending offshore RMB loans. These arrangements will convert Qianhai into an offshore RMB center within China.

An offshore RMB center within China offers some benefits. For instance, it provides a platform to develop sophisticated financial operations in the domestic market and to enrich the investment opportunities of offshore RMB by recycling it back to China. However, there may be some unintended consequences. Currently, China employs capital control measures to manage its economy. One concern is the possible adverse effect of leaking offshore RMB capital back into the domestic Chinese economy. If offshore RMB could be loaned to enterprises in Qianhai, then should China institute some regulatory oversight of Qianhai to preserve the existing capital controls for the rest of China?

In principle, the influence of offshore transactions on the domestic offshore market could be contained. A good example is the US International Banking Facilities (IBFs) set up in December 1981. By requiring banks to keep different books for onshore and offshore transactions that are subject to different regulations, IBF creates an offshore market setting that is physically located within the US (Dufey and Giddy, 1994; He and McCauley, 2013). A well-functioning domestic offshore market such as the IBF could create a symbiotic relationship between onshore and offshore markets. Similarly, Japan established the Japan Offshore Market in Tokyo in December 1985 to accommodate offshore yen transactions within Japan.

Policy measures designed to establish an onshore offshore market may not have the designated effects. For instance, the Japan Offshore Market that was established in respond to foreign pressure did not contribute significantly to the liberalization of Japan's capital account and the international use of the Japanese yen (Osugi, 1990; Takagi, 2011). Indeed, an onshore offshore market could backfire. Krongkaew (1999), for instance, asserted that the Bangkok International Banking Facility established in 1993 that allowed enormous capital inflows is one of the causes of the 1997 crisis in Thailand.

The real issue is, of course, the cost for China to implement a set of operationally efficient regulations to insulate the domestic sector from possible adverse impacts of offshore RMB capital. Some related issues are the implications of the presence of segregated onshore and offshore accounts for tax, regulatory, and risk management policies. Given China's relatively unsophisticated financial system, the administrative and operative costs of setting up and maintaining effective barriers to contain the spillovers from an offshore market that is physically located within China can be quite high.

The financial innovation of recycling offshore RMB capital could give a short-term boost to the offshore RMB markets, but at the risk of impeding the long-term growth potential of the international use of the RMB. Along the path to become an international currency, the RMB should evolve to be a vehicle currency that facilitates transactions among nonresidents. Consider the prime global currency the US dollar, a large proportion of international transactions denominated in the US dollar do not involve US entities. Currently, the liquidity in the offshore RMB market is still quite low on the international scale. If the RMB recycle program works too well, it will constrain the offshore RMB liquidity available to nonresidents and, thus, stifle the use of the RMB as a vehicle currency. This will, in turn, inhibit the growth of the offshore RMB market. Thus, be careful what you ask for, you just might get it — in the absence of a progressive scheme to provide RMB to nonresidents, an RMB recycle program may work against the objective of promoting the overseas use of the currency.

6.1.2 The Shanghai free trade zone

Shanghai has played a unique role in the modern Chinese history. It is widely believed that the city is designated to be a global center for onshore

RMB business. The anointment of Qianhai to be the hub connecting the offshore market in Hong Kong and the domestic market raised the question of the role of Shanghai in promoting the RMB. However, China's State Council reassured the role of Shanghai in China's reform agenda in July 2013 with the approval of the establishment of the China (Shanghai) Pilot Free Trade Zone, which is commonly known as the Shanghai Free Trade Zone. The zone was officially inaugurated on September 29 the same year.[2]

Initially, the Shanghai Free Trade Zone spanned an area of 28.78 square kilometers in the city's Pudong New Area and comprised four bonded zones, namely Waigaoqiao Free Trade Zone, Waigaoqiao Free Trade Logistics Park, Yangshan Free Trade Port Area, and Pudong Airport Comprehensive Free Trade Zone. On December 28, 2014, the Standing Committee of the National People's Congress announced that the zone will be expanded almost four times and cover a total area of 120.72 square kilometers by including the Jinqiao Export Processing Zone, the Zhangjiang High-Tech Park, and the financial center Lujiazui. At the time of writing, the expansion makes Shanghai the largest free trade zone among the four established zones — the other three zones are discussed in the next subsection.

Similar to the Qianhai initiative, the official plan of the Shanghai Free Trade Zone encompassed reform measures in several service industries. The official document stated that the Shanghai Free Trade Zone, under the presumption of risk controllability, can be the testing ground of capital account RMB convertibility, market-determined interest rates, and cross-border RMB transactions. When the specifics of reform measures are introduced over time, we observe that the implemented new policies go beyond the financial industry and cover a broad market reform program. These specifics include regulatory and operating rules introduced to promote capital market development, facilitate trade, and enhance cross-border investment.

One example is the introduction of the negative-list management mode for foreign investment. On September 30, 2013 — one day after its official inauguration — the Shanghai Municipal People's Government released the "Special Administrative Measures on the Entry of Foreign Investment into China (Shanghai) Free Trade Zone (2013 Negative List)," which essentially specifies foreign investment projects that are restricted or banned in the Shanghai Free Trade Zone.

---

[2] The zone's official website is http://en.shftz.gov.cn/.

The negative-list approach lessens the burden of foreign investors. For new investments not on the negative list, foreign investors only have to complete the relevant official record-filing procedure, instead of seeking approval, and are subject to the same rules and regulations that govern domestic firms. The initial negative list is considered quite long — it covers a total of 190 industries and activities.[3] Then it was trimmed to 139 in 2014 and 122 in 2015.[4] The negative list approach provides a fresh impetus to foreign investors to invest in the Shanghai Free Trade Zone.

Financial market reform is an ongoing task in the free trade zone under the stipulation of currency convertibility and interest rate liberalization to facilitate cross-border capital and commodity flows. By early 2015, one achievement for the banking sector is cash pooling, which allows companies to move their working capital freely in and out of the country, without applying for a foreign debt quota. Further, foreign corporations registered in the zone are allowed to borrow up to twice the value of their registered capital without seeking prior approval as in the past. The data available in February 2015 shows that companies in the zone have borrowed RMB19.7 billion from offshore banks in total. It is also reported that two-way renminbi flows arising from the cross-border two-way sweeping program, which effectively allows corporate fund mobility, have grown substantially to a level of more than RMB27.2 billion between January and August, 2014.[5] We believe that the offshore borrowing for firms in the Shanghai Free Trade Zone will be relaxed further, and that the new regulation that includes banks will be a significant breakthrough.

In addition to revamping the efficiency of the operating environment in the free trade zone, China has flexed its muscles in commodity markets to enhance the international appeal of the RMB. As one of the leading producers and consumers, China opened its gold bullion trading to foreign investors on September 18, 2014. The Shanghai Gold Exchange, the largest gold exchange platform in China, launched in the free trade zone

---

[3] In 2014, the Ministry of Commerce said that the negative list approach for foreign investment is not allowed outside the designated free trade zone.

[4] The 2014 negative list was released by the Shanghai Municipal Government. The 2015 list was announced by the China's State Council on April 20, 2015 and was applicable to the four free trade zones in operation then.

[5] See, for example, the reports by Wildau (2015) and Wong (2015).

the international board that allows global investors to trade RMB-denominated gold contracts.

The opening of the gold market helps the free trade zone (and Shanghai) to develop a multidimensional financial sector, integrates China's gold trading with the global gold market, and strengthens China's pricing power. The currency denomination reduces exchange rate risk for both domestic producers and foreign suppliers, and offers a means to hedge gold denominated in, say, the US dollar again the RMB.

The trading volume in the international board has picked up quite quickly. By April 2015, it was reported that the trading volume in the "free trade zone" international board exceeded the one in the formerly dominant Shanghai Gold Exchange for domestic contracts.

Before the Shanghai Gold Exchange launched its international board, international investors have access to exchange trading of gold in RMB via the century-old bullion house Chinese Gold & Silver Exchange Society in Hong Kong.[6] Since October 2011, the Hong Kong trading platform has offered its product "Renminbi Kilobar Gold" that requires settlement in RMB and physical delivery.[7] The role of the Hong Kong gold market in fostering the globalization of China's gold market and the international use of the RMB was further enhanced with the launch of the Shanghai-Hong Kong Gold Connection program in July 2015. The spirit of the gold connect arrangement is similar to the stock connect program discussed in the previous chapter.[8] Under the gold connect program, investors in Hong Kong can participate in trading on both the main board and international board of the Shanghai Gold Exchange.

---

[6] The Chinese Gold and Silver Exchange Society began its operations back in the Qing dynasty in 1910 under the name of the "Gold and Silver Exchange Company." The current name was formally registered in 1918. The Hong Kong gold market that opens for both international and local investors is one of the major global gold trading centers.

[7] The Hong Kong Stock Exchange in December 2014 introduced three RMB-priced metal mini futures, namely London aluminium mini futures, London zinc mini futures, and London copper mini futures. In October 2015, it announced the plan to introduce three other RMB-priced metal mini futures — London Nickel mini futures, London tin mini futures, and London lead mini futures.

[8] In 2015, China was reported to explore the feasibility of cooperating with, respectively, the London Stock Exchange and the Deutsche Boerse. Incidentally, the Deutsche Boerse agreed to acquire the London Stock Exchange in March 2016.

To assert its roles and pricing power in the global gold market, it was reported in early 2015 that China is preparing the launch of a gold denominated in RMB. The fixing is based on trading with Shanghai Gold Exchange as the central counterparty and the participation is open to members of the international board.[9] A RMB-denominated gold fix offers both practical and symbolic benefits. It reduces currency risk for local traders and suppliers, and promotes the development of related derivatives products. Symbolically, the role of a gold price benchmark raises the currency's status to a global commodity currency — a role that is currently enjoyed by the US dollar. The gold fix, thus, can be seen a significant step in promoting the global image of the RMB.[10]

6.1.3 Other free trade zones

A signature of China's reform policy is to replicate a successful experimental measure. An early example is the launch of the Shenzhen Special Economic Zone in the 1980s, and the subsequent establishments of special economic zones that have underscored China's economic development. A recent example is the Shanghai Free Trade Zone initiative. In early 2014, it was reported that 12 free trade zones, in addition to the Shanghai one, were approved by the central government. Nevertheless, it was not until December 12, 2014, that the State Council announced the establishment of free trade zones in Fujian, Guangdong, and Tianjin — these three zones have been officially in operation since April 2015.

There are a few common features of these free trade zones. For instance, all the four free trade zones have to follow the negative list issued by the State Council that lists prohibited or restricted areas for foreign

---

[9] The London fixing is based on an over-the-counter system and was alleged price manipulation in the early 2010s. For a long time, the London fixing is considered the global benchmark for spot gold while the New York market provides the benchmark for gold futures prices. In June 2015, Bank of China joined the London Bullion Market Association gold price auction that determines the fixings.

[10] After the final draft was completed, the Shanghai Gold Exchange indeed lunched the gold fixing in RMB on April 19, 2016. The morning fix was set at RMB256.92 per gram (~$1,234.50 an ounce).

investment.[11] Another commonality is that these zones are designated to explore streamlined administrative procedures that promote international transactions and enhance efficiency and competitiveness.

While they share some similarities, these free trade zones have their own economic and geographic characteristics. The Shanghai Free Trade Zone enjoys the first mover advantage and the prosperous Shanghai economy, and is expected to continue the liberalization process to strengthen its positions in international trade and investment, and in financial market development including RMB internationalization.

The other three zones are strategically located along the east coast. Geographically speaking, Fujian is close to Taiwan. Its free trade zone focuses on strengthening economic and social links with Taiwan. Indeed, the Fujian Free Trade Zone initiated policies for cross-Strait cooperation and hiring Taiwan nationals. The Guangdong Free Trade Zone covers districts in the cities of Guangzhou, Shenzhen, and Zhuhai. The districts in Shenzhen and Zhuhai are believed to be devoted to deepen the connection and cooperation between the Guangdong province and the two special administrative regions, namely Hong Kong and Macao. Tianjin, the main city on the northeast coast will serve the free trade zone testing ground of the North-East China, including the capital city Beijing and the Hebei province. In addition to fostering modern financial and service industries, these free trade zones serve to prove the benefits of the reform and liberalization policies on promoting economic growth via rejuvenating trade and investment.

6.1.4 The domestic bond market

Capital market liberalization has substantial implications for China's ability to sustain its growth momentum. A vibrant and efficient financial sector is deemed essential for supporting the Chinese advances in the manufacturing and trade sectors. On the one hand, a well-functioning financial sector facilitates the matching of savings and investment, and

---

[11] The negative-list management mode for foreign investment was introduced in Shanghai in 2013. The State Council issued the negative list starting 2015, the year the other free trade zones began their operations.

offers a viable funding alternative to bank loans. On the other hand, it is conducive to managing the economy via effective uses of monetary policies. Besides domestic considerations, a deep and liquid financial sector promotes the global status of the RMB and strengthens China's capacity to withstand adverse international capital flow effects. The advanced US financial sector is a case in point.[12]

The bond market is one of the main vehicles in modern finance to mobilize savings and to fund investment. Size-wise, China has the world's third largest domestic bond market after the US and Japan.[13] Domestic bonds are traded in two markets — one is the interbank bond market that is regulated by the People's Bank of China, and the other is the exchange bond market comprises the Shanghai and Shenzhen stock exchanges that are regulated by the China Securities Regulatory Commission. The interbank bond trading dominates the Chinese domestic bond market, and accounts for over 90% of the total trading volume.

Despite its sheer size, the Chinese bond market is a targeted area of ongoing liberalization efforts.[14] Besides gradual changes in regulatory environment to enhance liquidity and efficiency, China strategically opens up its domestic bond market to foreign investors. The opening up of the domestic debt market is seen as part of overall policy to promote the international use of the RMB and expand investment choices for foreign investors.

Before 2016, there are three main ways foreign investors can access the market. The qualified foreign institutional investor (QFII) scheme introduced in 2002 allows authorized foreign investors to participate in the exchange bond market. In July 2012, China Securities Regulatory Commission relaxed the rule and allowed licensed QFIIs to access the

---

[12] Ma and Yao (2015) discuss the link between China's bond market and RMB globalization. Bai *et al.* (2013) examine the microstructure of China's bond market.

[13] The value of bonds outstanding was RMB48.8 trillion as of December 2015.

[14] For example, starting from 2012, nonfinancial companies are approved by the National Association of Financial Market Institutional Investors to sell bonds through private placements. At the time of writing, all companies listed on the Shanghai or Shenzhen stock exchanges, subject to the verification and approval from the China Securities Regulatory Commission could issue corporate bonds that are traded in these exchanges.

interbank bond market. The US dollar is the typical currency QFIIs converted into RMB to invest in the local market.[15,16]

In December 2011, the RMB qualified foreign institutional investor (RQFII) scheme was launched to expand the scope of the foreign institutional investor program. In essence, authorized RQFIIs are allowed to invest in China with offshore RMB balances. Hong Kong is the first jurisdiction received RQFII quotas (see also Sections 5.3.5e and 5.3.7a).

The People's Bank of China, in 2010, introduced a program that allows foreign central banks, RMB clearing banks located outside mainland China, and overseas banks that help settle cross-border trade in RMB to participate in the local interbank bond market. Later the group of participants was extended to include sovereign wealth funds, supranationals, and insurance companies.[17] It is commonly perceived that the interbank bond scheme targets heavyweights in global finance, including supranational and governmental institutions, and is an official effort and gesture to support the overall policy of enhancing the global acceptance of the RMB.

In July 2015, China lifted the quotas that limit the investments of central banks, sovereign-wealth funds, and international financial institutions including the World Bank in the bond market. For these designated institutions, they do not have to go through the lengthy process of obtaining quotas and approvals for investing in China's bond market.

On a public note posted on its website in February 2016,[18] the People's Bank of China announced a policy that allow most types of overseas institutional investors to invest in the Chinese interbank bond market without

---

[15] The US dollar is put under a custodian account and converted to the RMB subject to supervision of the State Administration of Foreign Exchange.

[16] In addition to domestic bonds, licensed QFIIs are allowed to invest in equities, funds, and other investment vehicles approved by the China Securities Regulatory Commission.

[17] The details of the approval, especially the one that is pertaining a foreign central bank from the People's Bank of China, are seldom released. The identities of commercial agents that received approvals are, however, announced.

[18] See People's Bank of China (2016; Public Notice No. 3 [2016], posted on February 24, 2016 and was dated in Chinese February 17); http://www.pbc.gov.cn/english/130721/3037272/index.html.

the previous prior approval and quota requirements.[19] Essentially, the new policy extends trading arrangements to central banks in July 2015 to a wide set of foreign financial institutions, and opens up the third largest bond market in the world to most foreign institutional investors. The expanded access to foreign investors is in accordance with China's ongoing policies of liberalizing financial markets and integrating into the global financial market.[20]

Both the foreign institutional investor and People's Bank of China programs entice foreign investors to store their savings in the RMB. An unintended consequence is that these programs will further increase China's net foreign currency exposure by piling its RMB liabilities. Since the 1990s, China has gradually built up it net international investment (NIIP) position and became a large creditor in the global market. China's net long foreign currency position is a result of its strong trade account performance and inflows of direct and portfolio investments, and the limited amount of RMB liabilities held by foreigners.

Figure 6.1 shows that China's NIIP is increasing steadily in the 21st century; from below US$ 500 billion in 2004 to almost US$ 2 trillion in 2013 before backing down a bit in 2014. As a percentage of GDP, however, NIIP has started to drift down after reaching the 33% mark in 2007. The decline reflects the economic growth is stronger than the growth of the NIIP position.

The issuance of Panda bonds — bonds denominated in RMB and issued by foreigners in China — helps reduce China's overall exposure to foreign currencies. By denominating its claims on foreign issuers in RMB, China mitigates the risk of, say, the weakness of the US dollar that it has a net long position.

---

[19] The mentioned financial institutions include commercial banks, insurance companies, securities companies, fund management companies, other asset management institutions, pension funds, charity funds, and endowment funds. Hedge funds and individual investors are not included.

[20] Some commentators note that the policy change offers support to the RMB by encouraging capital inflows and, thus, can be a calculated response to large capital outflows and pressures on RMB followed the 2015 summer market turmoil.

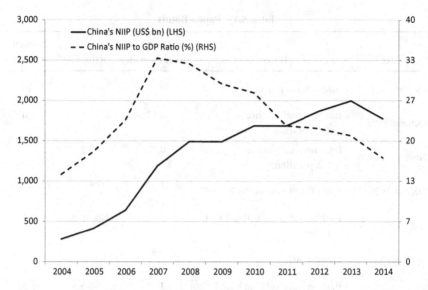

Figure 6.1   Net International Investment Positions of China and its GDP Ratio

Source: International Monetary Fund, National Bureau of Statistics.

Panda bonds were initially issued by two supranational institutions, namely the Asian Development Bank and the International Finance Corporation.[21] In October 2005, both institutions issued Panda bonds that have a maturity of 10 years (Table 6.1). Then, they individually offered a second round of Panda bonds in 2006 and 2009.

In May 2010, the Bank of Tokyo-Mitsubishi UFJ Ltd. became the first foreign commercial bank to sell Panda bonds via its subsidiary in China. In April 2014, the German carmaker Daimler AG became the first foreign nonfinancial corporate to issue panda bonds. The proceeds are used to fund its operation in China.

Evidently, the issuance of Panda bonds is quite sporadic. One reason behind the anemic interest is the onerous regulatory framework that includes rules governing the use of proceeds and the accounting standards. On September 16, 2010, People's Bank of China, the Ministry of Finance,

---

[21] There were five years of preparatory work before the inaugural Panda bond issue (Wolfowitz, 2005).

Table 6.1   Panda Bonds

Issue Date	Issuers	Size (billions, yuan)	Rates (%)	Maturity (year)
October 2005	Asian Development Bank	1	3.34	10
October 2005	International Finance Corporation	1.13	3.4	10
November 2006	International Finance Corporation	0.87	3.2	7
December 2009	Asian Development Bank	1	4.2	10
May 2010	Bank of Tokyo-Mitsubishi UFJ (China)	1	Negotiated	2
April 2014	Daimler AG	0.5	5.2	1
September 2015	Bank of China (Hong Kong) Limited	1	3.5	3
September 2015	HSBC Holdings Plc	1	3.5	3
October 2015	China Merchants Holdings (Hong Kong)	0.5	3.03	1
December 2015	Standard Chartered Bank	1	3.5	3
December 2015	The Republic of Korea	3	3	3
January 2016	The Canadian province of British Columbia	3	2.95	3

Note: The Panda bonds that have been issued as of February 2015 are presented. The information is compiled by the authors.

the National Development and Reform Commission, and the China Securities Regulatory Commission (2010) revised the rules governing panda bonds.[22] Since then, international institutions, upon the approval of the State Administration of Foreign Exchange, could remit their proceeds

---

[22] The initial document that governs Panda Bond 《国际开发机构人民币债券发行管理暂行办法》 was announced on February 18, 2005 by People's Bank of China, the Ministry of Finance, the National Development and Reform Commission, and the China Securities Regulatory Commission. The 2010 revised version was available on http://www.mof.gov.cn/mofhome/jinrongsi/zhengwuxinxi/zhengcefabu/201009/t20100930_341568.html.

from Panda bond sales overseas, either in RMB or foreign currencies. The rule change, nevertheless, does not jump-start the Panda bond market noticeably.

To further signal its willingness to open up its capital market, China, in September 2015, approved two international commercial banks — Bank of China (Hong Kong) and HSBC — to issue Panda bonds. These two financial institutions each sold RMB one billion of panda bonds with a tenor of three-years in the same month they received the approval.[23] Both banks indicated that they will use the proceeds outside China. The potential of using the proceeds to support offshore business is quite attractive to international commercial banks that are interested in offshore RMB business. Later in the same year, the Standard Chartered Bank became the first foreign bank to issue Panda bonds after the RMB was admitted to the SDR currency basket, and South Korea became the first country to sell sovereign panda bonds in China's interbank bond market. Apparently, global issuers are looking into Panda bonds.[24]

As evidenced in Table 6.1, 2015 is a banner year for the issuance of Panda bonds; both the amount of issuance and the number of issuing entities in 2015 are larger than the corresponding figures from 2005 to 2014 combined.

The establishment of the Shanghai and other free trade zones has further rekindled the interest in panda bonds. Panda bonds diversify and deepen the local bond market and add a new landscape to the domestic market. To guide against regulatory risks, market participants contemplate that the Free Trade Zone is a good location to adopt usual accounting standards and flexible conditions for the use of proceeds. With appropriate changes that reduce the gap between the regulatory framework and the usual international practice, the foreign companies, especially those with operations in China, will be inclined to issue Panda bonds that help manage their exchange rate risk.

---

[23] Bank of China (Hong Kong) claimed the first international commercial bank to issue panda bonds, though some consider HSBC is the first foreign bank to issue panda bonds.
[24] It was reported in the news that there are countries and corporations are planned for sales of Panda bonds in the near future.

6.1.5 Implications for offshore markets

The global acceptance of the RMB depends not only on what the currency can do offshore but also on the conditions in the domestic markets. Currency internationalization is not an event, but is a process. Despite the circumstances under which the US dollar gained its prominent global currency status in the 1950s are different from those faced by China now, its acceptance by international investors is enforced by the progressive development in, say, the US treasury market then (Eichengreen and Flandreau, 2012). Along the path to become a full-fledged global currency, a deep and vibrant domestic financial market is a big plus that boosts the confidence of international investors.

Given its growing economic strength, especially in the trade area, China's upcoming role in the global economy and the international monetary architecture are highly anticipated; it is only a matter of when it is going to happen. Nevertheless, it is well perceived that financial liberalization is a key element of promoting the RMB to the global stage. In addition to establish versatile offshore RMB centers, China has to offer the rest of the world a domestic financial sector with sufficient depth and breadth that can efficiently process massive capital movements. A healthy interplay and feedback between the offshore and onshore markets provides organic growth of the currency in the global market.

Currently, China's financial sector is quite underdeveloped with nontrivial restrictions on markets and foreign participation. The positive is that, as the anecdotal evidence suggests, the government is determined to transform the economy, in general, and the financial sector, in particular. Among the "ubiquitous" spread of reform measures, the few mentioned in the previous and current chapters assert the veracity of China's policy intentions.

Will the development in the domestic market including the removal of capital controls suffocate the growth of the nascent offshore markets? For instance, will the Panda bond market drive out the Dim Sum bonds overseas? Will the Qianhai project and the free trade zones undermine the future role of the offshore RMB market, say, in Hong Kong?

The proliferation of Dim Sum bonds definitely benefits from the stern regulatory rules on Panda bonds, in addition to the usual gap between the domestic and offshore RMB interest rates. Overseas issuers appear to be more comfortable with the regulatory regime in Hong Kong or other offshore RMB centers than the one in mainland China. With its usual gradual reform mandate, we could expect the ongoing effort to liberalize and relax the restrictions on Panda bonds will be introduced in measured steps and in designated locations before applying to the whole country. That is, the "Panda" has to take some time to catch up with the "Dim Sum." Even when China is fully opened up, which could be a distant goal, it does not necessary spell the death of Dim Sum bonds.[25] Again, using the US dollar as an example, both the euro-bond and Yankee bond markets have coexisted in the last few decades.

The launch of the Qianhai project and free trade zone initiative has revived the discussion on the implicit rivalry between Hong Kong and the other Chinese cities to be China's financial center. While Hong Kong has its first mover advantage and is a recognized international financial center, cities like Shenzhen and Shanghai have their own respective advantages in developing their financial markets. Under the presumption that the two reform experiments conducted in limited physical areas would trigger and speed up financial reforms at the national level, Hong Kong will be marginalized and lose out in the process. While the construction of the Qianhai region will be completed in 2020, the Shanghai Free Trade Zone was officially in operation in September 2013 and the other three were in business in April 2015. Additional free trade zones are expected in the near future. Will, say, Shanghai — China's commercial heavyweight and designated international financial market — with the free trade zone provision undermine its archetypical competitor Hong Kong?

The consequences of the (implicit) rivalry and competition between Hong Kong and, say, Shanghai depend crucially on how fast China could revamp its financial market regulations, tax policies, and the related governance practices. The history of international finance shows that the process of capital account liberalization is usually laden with financial and economic crises. Bayoumi and Ohnsorge (2013), for example, show that the capital account liberalization in China may trigger net portfolio

---

[25] The growth of the Dim Sum bond market, similar to other offshore RMB assets, is affected by China's economic environment. For instance, the declined in the Dim Sum bond activity was coincided with the heightened uncertainty triggered by the market turmoil experienced by China in 2015 (Figures 5.4 and 5.5, Chapter 5).

outflows. Indeed, China is quite concerned about the adverse effects of capital flight,[26] and capital flight can slow China's financial reform drive. Thus, it is reasonable to assume that China maintains its gradual approach, and adopts the "feel the rock, wade across the river" strategy to navigate carefully through the minefield of capital account liberalization.

In such a case, Hong Kong is likely to maintain its comparative advantages in brokering financial transactions for the time being. Even though Hong Kong is the designated offshore RMB market,[27] it has to compete and, more importantly, cooperate with other overseas international finance centers and onshore financial centers to promote the international use of the RMB. With its first mover advantages, Hong Kong is well positioned to meet the challenge of increased competition. Compared with other Chinese cities, Hong Kong has the ingredients of a full-scale international finance center, including established financial market infrastructure, well-regarded legal system, and extensive international network. Barred from some unexpected developments, China can use it as a testing ground for further financial reforms.[28] China, in promoting onshore financial centers, could diversify its financial business within and outside the country.

A relevant question is: what is the role of offshore RMB centers when China has removed capital controls and instituted capital account convertibility? When China achieves full financial liberalization, the global offshore RMB market will be much larger than its existing size. At that time, an offshore center like Hong Kong can be dwarfed by, say, Shanghai, though it will enjoy a health volume of offshore RMB activity but not its current large share. The experiences of the US dollar, for example, suggest that the growing global RMB activity can support multiple offshore and onshore financial centers. Thus, offshore RMB centers will still play their role in supporting the global uses of the RMB. The anecdotal evidence

---

[26] Some studies on China's capital flight are Cheung, Steinkamp and Westermann (2016), Cheung and Qian (2010), Gunter (1996, 2004), Kar and Freitas (2012), and Wu and Tang (2000). A recent example is China's efforts to stem capital outflows in the second half of 2015.

[27] The National 12th Five-Year Plan (2011–2015) stated China's formal support for Hong Kong's role as an offshore RMB business center.

[28] Some commentators noted that the 2014 Occupying Central movement and the related rows on electoral reform package could dent China's confidence in Hong Kong.

indicates that China is still quite enthusiastically promoting offshore RMB business around the global.

In the last few decades, China has implemented reform measures to transform itself into a modern and wealthy economy. With successes in manufactures and trade, it is moving along to revamp its financial markets. There are feedbacks between policies of RMB internationalization policy and financial sector liberalization. As usual, we observe China is taking the gradual and trial-and-error approach, and following a two-pronged strategy that involves both offshore and onshore markets to promote the international use of the RMB and to implement its financial liberalization agenda.

6.2 Why Internationalize the RMB?

In the 1980s and early 1990s, China's efforts on revitalizing its economy were not uncommonly met with skepticism. The perception has changed quite drastically since the turn of the 21st century. China, despite its relative rigid economy system, has established itself as a major player in the global economy, especially in manufactures and trade. China's push to join the WTO was a watershed event. It asserts China's determination to modernize its economy. To complement and strengthen its own policies for upgrading its manufacturing sector and international trade, the accession to the WTO forces changes from outside and reaffirms the transition away from a planned toward a market-based economy and the willingness to abide by rules on international trade practices.

In the wake of China's aggressive policy to promote the international use of its currency, the world has to reassess the landscape of the international monetary architecture, and the related geoeconomics and geopolitics. It is hard to underestimate the global impact of liberalizing the financial sector of China, which is the largest trade nation and second largest economy of the world.[29]

Indeed, an International Monetary Fund (2010a) study by its Strategy, Policy and Review Department anoints the RMB as one of the three

---

[29] See, for example, Chen and Cheung (2011), Cheung, Ma and McCauley (2011a, 2011b), Eichengreen (2013), Frankel (2012), Yu and Gao (2011), McCauley (2011), and Yu (2012) for early discussions on RMB internationalization.

national currencies that could compete with the US dollar in the global market. The other two currencies are the euro and the Japanese yen. The international acceptance of the RMB is partly supported by China's growing economic prowess and extensive production chain and trade networks, and is partially benefited from demise performance of the US dollar during the crisis, the euro due to the European sovereign debt crisis, and Japanese yen because of Japan's two lost decades.

The implications for the global economy, to a great extent, depend on China's motivation. For instance, it is one story if China would like to be a responsible "stakeholder" of the international monetary system. The scenario, especially for the incumbent powers, will be quite different if China plans to establish its own global monetary architecture. Obviously, it is hard to speculate China's motivation because the motivation is likely to be of multitude nature and evolves over time. Nevertheless, we outline a few reasons why China is promoting RMB in the remaining part of the section.

One of the suggested motivations is economic pragmatism in the midst of a dollar shortage crisis. The speech by the then governor of the People's Bank of China (Zhou, 2009) highlights the concern of relying on one super-sovereign reserve currency. The dollar squeeze did not only curtail trade with the US; it also restricted trade between other countries as the US dollar is the main vehicle currency for international trade. To reduce its reliance on the US dollar for international transactions, China advocates the use of currencies of trade partners to settle trade and encourages cross-border trade settlement in RMB. In the process, China signs various RMB bilateral swap line facilities with its trading partners. As discussed in Section 5.3.2, the RMB trade settlement scheme has progressed quite well and, in a few years, achieved a very respective volume.

Besides economic pragmatism, the use of RMB overseas helps China to rebalance the currency composition of its international balance sheet. With its strong trade surplus, foreign direct investment, and inward portfolio flow, China has established a large short position in its own currency and the corresponding long position in other currencies; especially the US dollar.

The foreign currency exposure reflects China's asymmetric policy on capital flow. It is open to foreign direct investment but imposes capital controls to manage RMB borrowings by nonresidents. Only until recently, the RMB is essentially restricted to circulate in China; outflow of RMB capital is subject to severe management measures. A result is that China has an acutely skewed international balance sheet: long foreign currency, mostly the dollar, and short domestic currency.[30] The lack of internationalization of the RMB hinders the prospect of alleviating the China's foreign currency exposure.

Through promoting the international use of the RMB, China could denominate some of its external claims in RMB. It can be achieved for example when foreigners are willing to issue RMB-denominated debt obligations including Dim Sum and Panda bonds, Chinese companies are allowed to use the RMB for overseas projects, and China's foreign aids are in the RMB. Cheung, Ma and McCauley (2011a, 2011b), for instance, label the process of denominating China's claims on the rest of the world in RMB the process of "renminbizing" China's international assets.

Note that RMB internationalization requires nonresidents retain the RMB as either asset or liability. The renminbization focuses on nonresidents acquiring RMB liabilities. As a result, China could alleviate, if not normalize, its skewed currency composition of its international assets, and share the foreign exchange risk embedded in its international balance with nonresidents. The implied risk management effect is a benefit provided by the general process of internationalizing the RMB.

The initiative of making the RMB a prominent global currency carries certain nationalistic pride elements. A big role of RMB in the world certainly lifts up China's global prestige and reaffirms its role in the world. The idea is in accordance with the "China Dream" slogan popularized by Jinping Xi in 2013. Circumstantial evidence points to the observation that, after XiaoChuan Zhou delivered his famous speech in 2009 that implicitly challenges the US dollar and implies an international role of RMB, the State Council approved the RMB cross-border trade settlement program that promotes the use of RMB overseas. Since then, there is a steady flow of policy measures on internationalizing RMB.

It is almost an open secret that different constituencies in China do not have the same view on the relative role of the state in managing the economy, or the appropriate pace of liberalizing the (financial) market.

---

[30] In fact, China has allowed the rest of the world to invest in it than, say, Japan has. In particular, nonresidents have a stake in China's equities (direct investment and portfolio) equivalent to 24 percent of China's gross domestic product (GDP), while nonresidents of Japan have a stake in Japan's equities of only 17 percent of Japan's GDP (Ma and Zhou, 2009).

To ensure a steady reform momentum, external constraints are brought into the picture from time to time. The accession to the WTO is an often cited example — an arrangement with an external party to reinforce and strengthen the domestic reform policy.

The promotion of the global status of the RMB, in this sense, can be interpreted as a disguised component of China's financial liberalization policy. To make the RMB an international standard accepted by the rest of the world, China has to loosen its grip on the currency and allow market forces to play their roles. The internationalization objective is in line with nationalistic sentiments and thus is relatively easy to gain traction. The efforts to promote the currency's international status in turn provide the support of the financial reform agenda.

Even in the early stage, some market participants questioned if China's policy to create a global RMB is aimed at under-cutting the US dollar global supremacy. The general view, at least in the early 2010s, is that the Chinese effort cannot challenge the dollar's prime position in the international monetary architecture. In the medium to long term, a possible scenario is that the RMB is one of the multiple global currencies.

The developments under President Xi's leadership, however, suggest that, moving forward, China is not content with being a "stakeholder" of the existing global financial system which is dominated by the US. The recently launched Belt and Road initiative,[31] the BRICS New Development Bank, and the Asian Infrastructure Investment Bank exemplify China's intention to create its own international economic and financial network. A global RMB will be a key element of the sino-centric world order. For incumbents, the question is: what are the implications of these new sino-centric supranational organizations for the existing international order? A related question is: is the RMB internationalization policy a stepping stone to establish China's capacity to dethrone the US dollar?

6.3 The Level of International Use of the RMB

In the last few years, the RMB has made much headway into the global market. To what extent has the RMB become an international currency?

---

[31] It is initially called "one belt, one road" initiative.

In this section, we do a simple stocktaking of RMB's accomplishments in being used in the international arena. Specifically, we assess the trading volume in the global foreign exchange market, the volume of international trade settled in RMB, the membership of the Special Drawing Right basket, the role of a reserve currency, and a few other features. We wrap up the section with the discussion of a RMB globalization index.

6.3.1 Global foreign exchange market

The global foreign exchange market is the world's largest financial market. The roles of national currencies in international transactions are reflected by their trading activities in the global foreign exchange market. According to the triennial central bank surveys published by the Bank for International Settlements, the US dollar has been the most transacted currency and involved in more than 80% of the total number of transactions in the global market since the 1990s. The finding essentially attests the prominent role of the US dollar in the global financial system.

The growth of the Chinese currency transaction volume has benefited from China's efforts to promote the international use of the RMB. The Bank for International Settlements (2013) triennial central bank survey shows that the RMB is among the emerging market currencies that experienced significant increases in their trading volumes. The growth was mainly driven by the expansion of RMB trading in offshore markets. According to the Bank for International Settlements triennial central bank surveys, the average RMB daily forex turnover in the global market surged from 1.7 billion in 2004, 14.6 billion in 2007, 29.2 billion in 2010 to reach 119.6 billion in 2013 (Bank for International Settlements, 2004, 2007, 2010, 2013).

The rapid growth makes the RMB the ninth most actively traded currency in 2013. Its share of global foreign exchange trading increased to 2.2% in 2013, compared with 0.9% in 2010, 0.5% in 2007, and 0.1% in 2004. Even the 2013 share is small compared with the top currencies, namely the US dollar (87.0%), the euro (33.4%), the Japanese yen (23.0%), and the British pound (11.8%), the improvement is quite good. Note that because two currencies are involved in each foreign exchange transaction, the sum of the percentage shares of individual currencies totals 200% instead of 100%.

While its growth is quite respectable, the RMB trading turnover is quite small compared with the size of the Chinese economy. China in 2013 is the second largest economy in the world in terms of nominal GDP. However, the RMB only accounts for 2.2% of the global foreign exchange trading in the 2013 BIS Survey. Relatively, the US dollar, euro, Japanese yen, and British pound account for, respectively, 87.0%, 33.4%, 23.0%, and 11.8% of the global foreign exchange trading turnover in the 2013 survey. The Hong Kong dollar — the currency of China's special administrative region — accounts for 1.4% of the global turnover, considering that the GDP of Hong Kong was only 3% of that of China.

Table 6.2, for comparison purposes, lists the top 10 mostly traded currencies in the 2013 BIS Survey and their GDP and trade figures. Clearly, China has the smallest average daily turnover to GDP ratio among these countries. Relative to the size of its economy, the New Zealand dollar is the most heavily traded currency.

Table 6.2   Daily Average Turnover of Top 10 Currencies (USD billion) in 2013

	Daily Turnover (USD bn)	GDP (USD bn)	Daily Turnover to GDP Ratio (%)	Daily Turnover Percentage Share (%)*	Merchandize Trade (USD bn)	Daily Turnover to Trade Ratio (%)
USD	4,652	16,663	27.9	87.0	3,908	119.03
EUR	1,786	13,219	13.5	33.4	4,832	36.96
JPY	1,231	4,920	25.0	23.0	1,547	79.57
GBP	631	2,678	23.6	11.8	1,122	56.22
AUD	462	1,497	30.9	8.6	495	93.31
CHF	275	685	40.1	5.2	409	67.27
CAD	244	1,839	13.3	4.6	934	26.12
MXN	135	1,262	10.7	2.5	780	17.30
CNY	120	9,491	1.3	2.2	4,160	2.88
NZD	105	185	56.8	2.0	81	128.95

*Note: As two currencies are involved in each transaction, the sum of shares in all individual currencies will total 200%.

Source: BIS Triennial Central Bank Survey, Global foreign exchange market turnover in 2013. IMF WEO Database October 2015. IMF IFS Database.

Further, the RMB turnover volume is relatively small compared with China's import and export activities. When normalized by annual trade volume (exports plus imports), China's 2013 average daily foreign exchange turnover to international trade ratio is 2.8%, again the smallest in the table. New Zealand has the largest ratio followed by the US.[32] Taking its huge trade sector into consideration, China still has a long way to go in promoting the use of the RMB in the global economy. Despite the rapid turnover growth in the last few years, the use of RMB in the global foreign exchange market is still quite small.

One limitation of the BIS survey is that it is only updated once every three years. To obtain up-to-date information about the RMB usage, we examine the statistics provided by SWIFT. According to the SWIFT RMB Monthly Tracker, both the ranking of RMB and its share in world payments have been steadily increased in the past few years (Figure 6.2). Since

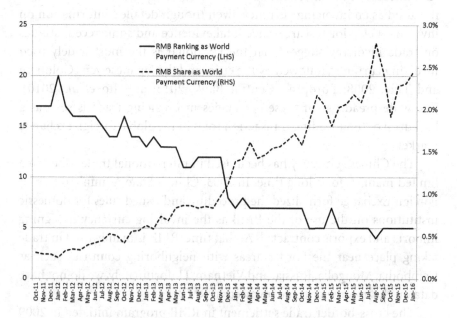

Figure 6.2   RMB Ranking and Share as a World Payment Currency

Source: SWIFT.

---

[32] The average daily foreign exchange turnover to international trade ratio of Hong Kong, a special administrative region of China, is 7.8% in 2013.

2012, the rank of RMB has gradually increased before taking a pause at the seventh position in 2014. Then, the RMB mostly occupied the position of the fifth most used world payments currency that accounted for slightly between 2% to 3% of the transacted value. In August 2015, it briefly bumped the Japanese yen off the fourth position.

Despite the high ranking, the share percentage accounted for by the RMB is relatively small. The phenomenon reflects the network externalities in selecting a payment currency. Because of the endogenous cost reduction mechanism, the payment currency choice tends to congregate to a few ones such that the top ranked currencies will account for a large share. In general, the SWIFT record is comparable to that of the 2013 BIS survey.

6.3.2 Invoicing/settlement/pricing currency

An indicator of the international role of a currency is the extent to which it is used as an invoicing currency. Even though detailed information on invoicing behavior is scarce, anecdotal evidence and some recent studies on trade invoicing suggest that the US dollar is the most widely used invoicing currency, followed by the euro, and the Japanese yen (Goldberg and Tille, 2008; European Central Bank, 2013; and Ito *et al.*, 2010). The widespread use of these currencies in invoicing trade is seen as a backdrop of their leading transaction roles in the global foreign exchange market.

The Chinese currency has been used in international trade, albeit in a limited manner, for a long time. In 2003, China's State Administration of Foreign Exchange formalized the procedure and issued rules for domestic institutions on the use of the RMB as the invoicing currency in signing imports and exports contracts.[33] At that time, RMB is mainly used in trade taking place near the border areas with neighboring countries such as Cambodia, Mongolia, Russia, and Vietnam. Unfortunately, we do not have data on the volume of trade invoiced in RMB.

The cross-border trade settlement in RMB program initiated in 2009 has opened a new chapter on the RMB's role in trade settlement. Besides official endorsement, it is reported that companies are offering price

---

[33] See State Administration of Foreign Exchange (2003a, 2003b).

incentives to their overseas trading partners for settling transactions in RMB. As a result, the volume of cross-border trade settled in RMB has grown steadily since then. The cumulative volume of trade settled in RMB has increased from less than RMB4 billion at the end of 2009, to RMB290 billion by November 2010. The trade settled in RMB amounted to RMB6,550 billion in 2014 and RMB7,234 billion in 2015, which are around 24% and 29% of China's total trade, respectively, in 2014 and 2015. The percentage is getting close to the prediction that one-third of China's exports could be invoiced in the RMB (Chen *et al.*, 2009). Of course, whether the one-third stipulation is achievable or not depends on economic and political developments in both China and the global economy.

A point seldom discussed is on the use of the RMB as a vehicle currency. Relatively speaking, it is easy for Chinese companies to convince and entice their trade partners to adopt RMB as either an invoicing or a settlement currency. The use of the RMB for transactions between non-residents outside China is not that obvious. The paucity of off-shore RMB presents one difficulty. The vehicle currency role of the RMB is also hindered by the presence of capital controls onshore and the lack of a full-fledged board and deep offshore RMB market. It is fair to say that China has some additional work to do to make the RMB a common vehicle currency used in international trade and financial transactions.

The RMB plays a very limited role in pricing commodities in the global market. Nevertheless, China is quite conscientious in establishing its influences in the global commodity markets. The evolution of the Shanghai Gold Exchange is a good example. Being a major consumer and producer of gold, China has gradually developed its domestic gold market, and then introduced the international segment, and launched its own gold fixing in RMB.

Similarly, as a main oil consumer, China is laying its game plan of playing a role in the global crude oil market. Specifically, it set up the infrastructure to launch in late 2015 crude futures contract that will be priced and settled in the RMB. International investors will be allowed to directly participate the trading of the RMB-priced crude futures that will be housed by the Shanghai Futures Exchange. China is reported to consider the expansion of the RMB pricing practice to other commodity futures such as copper, which China is a big consumer.[34]

6.3.3 Global reserve currency

A global currency provides the store of value service both at home and in markets overseas. Countries keep their foreign exchange reserves in global currencies for both facilitating international transactions and bolstering confidence in their economies. The share of global reserve holdings is an indicator of the preference for and the primacy of a global currency.

Since the US dollar was officially designated the global reserve currency in the 1944 Bretton Woods Conference, it has enjoyed the privileges including the seigniorage of a global reserve currency. The role of global reserve currency is reinforced with the US strong economic, military, and political strengths, and the fact that the US dollar is extensively used in setting global commodity prices and settling global trade and financial transactions.[35] As the most prominent reserve currency, the US dollar enjoys the lion's share of exorbitant privileges.

The global financial crisis exposed the fragility of the international monetary system that is built around a single pre-eminent global reserve currency, and triggered the debate on the role of the US dollar in the world market. Zhou (2009) presents the first official view directly on the issue and proposes the use of a super-sovereign reserve currency such as the special drawing right (SDR) managed by IMF. A provision in Zhou's elaboration is that the said super-sovereign reserve currency should include currencies of all major economies. The Chinese proposal is explicit on the prospect of other currencies, including the RMB, to be a reserve current and, implicit on diminishing the prominence of the US dollar.

The progress of promoting the international use of the RMB since Zhou's speech has been quite remarkable. With its steep and quick pene-

---

[34] According to the Word Bureau of Metals Statistics (http://www.world-bureau.com/), China accounts for slightly less than half of global copper demand.
[35] According to COFER (http://data.imf.org/?sk=E6A5F467-C14B-4AA8-9F6D-5A09EC-4E62A4), the US dollar typically accounts for over 60% of the reported/allocated global reserve holdings.

tration into the global market, will the RMB encroach on the US dollar global reserve currency status?

(a) RMB as a reserve currency

There is a temptation to draw a lesson from the history of the US dollar displacing the British pound as the prime global reserve currency in the first few decades of the 20th century.[36] Nevertheless, both the domestic and global situations faced by the US dollar then are quite different from those faced by the RMB now. For instance, before, say, the 1970s, exchange rates were essentially fixed, and cross-border capital flows were controlled. In the modern financial world, however, exchange rate flexibility and capital mobility are perceived virtues. The RMB managed trading band, and China's capital control measures, thus, become the two main deterrents for the RMB to be a reserve currency.

Besides differences in initial market conditions, the world does not have a similar precedent for integrating an economy of China's characteristics including its relative size, relative stage of development, and societal and political structure into the its global system. We have to be cautious in drawing historical lessons.

Foreign sovereign investors could access the RMB-denominated assets in three different ways. First, they can acquire RMB assets, say, Dim Sum bonds in offshore RMB markets. Note that China's Ministry of Finance, policy banks, and state-owned banks are active issuers in Hong Kong, a main offshore RMB center. Second, they can participate in the local equity and bond markets via the QFII and RQFII programs. Third, they can invest in the local interbank market through the special quota program for foreign central banks and sovereign wealth funds introduced by China's central bank in 2010. As noted earlier in the chapter, China scrapped the quota limit in July 2015. The program is believed to have minimum restrictions on fund movement and the RMB is effectively convertible for transactions under this program.

Before discussing factors that determine the global reserve currency stature, what do we know about the extent of the RMB being used as a

---

[36] See, for example, Eichengreen (2011, 2014), Eichengreen and Flandreau (2012), Prasad and Ye (2012), Schenk (2009), and Subramanian (2011a, 2011b).

reserve asset? Despite the often mentioned restrictions on capital movement, some central banks have included the RMB in their reserve portfolios. The publicly available information about these reserve holdings of RMB, however, is limited. The Chinese authorities typically do not publicize foreign central banks and sovereign wealth funds that are invested in the RMB market. Individual central banks, even if they admit including the RMB to their foreign exchange reserves, seldom provide detailed information about the composition of their reserves.[37]

According to press releases and news, the publicly known central banks that have the RMB in their foreign reserve holdings are, at the end of 2014, (a) 11 from Asia: Australia, Hong Kong, Indonesia, Japan, South Korea, Macau, Malaysia, Nepal, Pakistan, Singapore and Thailand, (b) six from Europe: Austria, Belarus, France, the Great Britain, Lithuania, and Norway, and (c) seven from South America or Africa: Bolivia, Chile, Ghana, Kenya, Nigeria, South Africa, and Tanzania. These economies typically have trade links with China. Market participants believe that there are central banks not declaring their RMB reserve holdings. Thus, the actual number is large than the 24 named above. Also, some central banks are considering the possibility of adding RMB to their portfolios.[38]

The information on the amount of reserves held in RMB is hard to come by. For instance, the IMF Currency Composition of Official Foreign Exchange Reserves (COFER) database — the common data source of global reserves — does not separately disclose the share of global reserves held in RMB.[39] Table 6.3 presents some data from the COFER database. It breaks down the total reported data into allocated and unallocated reserve holdings. The shares of seven global reserve currencies, namely the US dollar, the euro, Japanese yen, British pound, Canadian dollar, Australian dollar, and Swiss franc of the allocated reserve holdings are

---

[37] There are a few exceptions. For instance Chile, Malaysia, and Nigeria publically confirmed their RMB holdings. Australia publicly declared a 3% of its foreign exchange reserves were allocated to the RMB. The Great Britain kept the proceeds from its sovereign offshore RMB issuance in the RMB.

[38] For instance, the Reserve Bank of New Zealand and European Central Bank in 2014 were reported to consider the RMB as one of their global reserve currencies.

[39] IMF said it will separately identify the RMB in its COFER database starting October 2016.

Table 6.3   Global Foreign Exchange Reserve Holdings: Selected Data

	Q1 2014	Q2 2014	Q3 2014	Q4 2014	Q1 2015	Q2 2015	Q3 2015
Total foreign exchange holdings	11,854.97	11,989.50	11,766.20	11,591.13	11,435.22	11,459.72	11,203.36
Allocated reserves	6,246.89	6,312.10	6,183.94	6,084.98	6,062.94	6,662.60	6,605.69
Claims in US dollars	3,798.15	3,833.10	3,857.21	3,839.12	3,890.40	4,248.83	4,226.01
Claims in pound sterling	241.34	244.69	238.06	230.55	236.92	312.77	311.53
Claims in Japanese yen	245.49	254.11	244.62	237.09	254.69	253.89	249.17
Claims in Swiss francs	16.53	17.01	16.46	16.35	17.77	19.78	18.68
Claims in Canadian dollars	117.06	125.81	119.45	115.05	111.37	127.67	124.74
Claims in Australian dollars	118.26	121.02	116.45	108.23	104.83	126.76	121.26
Claims in euros	1,519.58	1,520.71	1,397.28	1,346.88	1,261.08	1,365.65	1,343.70
Claims in other currencies	190.48	195.65	194.41	191.72	185.89	207.26	210.58
Unallocated reserves	5,608.08	5,677.40	5,582.26	5,506.14	5,372.28	4,797.13	4,597.67

Note: The data on global foreign exchange reserve holdings in billions of US dollar reported in the IMF Currency Composition of Official Foreign Exchange Reserves (COFER) database; http://data.imf.org/?sk=E6A5F467-C14B-4AA8-9F6D-5A09EC4E62A4.

reported.[40] Among these currencies, the US dollar usually accounts for more than 60% of the allocated holdings, followed by the euro with over 20%.[41]

In October 2014, a deputy governor of the People's Bank of China, Hu Xiaolian, was quoted to assert that the RMB is the seventh largest global reserve currency.[42] If it is the case, then according the 2015Q3 COFER data (Table 6.3), the share of global reserves in RMB is between 0.28% (Swiss franc) and 1.84% (Australian dollar).

In its report on RMB Internationalization, People's Bank of China (2015) estimates that, at the end of April 2015, the foreign central banks hold approximately RMB666.7 billion. Using the 2015 Q1 COFER data, it amounts to 1.8% of the total allocated global reserves (or, 0.9% of the total; that is the sum of allocated and unallocated, global reserves).

Forecasts abound about the future RMB share of global reserves. For instance, a survey conducted by the Economist Intelligence Unit suggests a majority of institutional investors; especially those within China think the RMB will overtake the US dollar as the foremost global reserve currency.[43] Global reserve managers responded to surveys by HSBC believed the RMB can account for 10% of global reserves by 2025, and 12.5% by 2030.[44] Research studies such as Chen and Peng (2010), Hu (2008), and Lee (2010) suggest that, in the next 10 to 15 years, the RMB could account for 3% to 20% of global international reserves. The wide range of predictions, of course, reflects the sensitivity of the analysis to assumptions and methods used in these studies.

To make sense of these diverse guesstimates, it is instrumental to look at the factors that affect the future stature of the RMB as a global currency. Conceptually speaking, RMB's stature depends on both domestic and international conditions, and the convenience and confidence in using the

---

[40] China's official reserves were reported on a partial basis to the IMF and included in the 2015 Q2 figures. However, it is hard to extract information from these data about China's exact holding portfolio.
[41] These seven currencies account for more than 90% of allocated holdings — the data that have currency destination.
[42] Ren (2014).
[43] Economist Intelligence Unit (2014).
[44] These survey results are cited in, for example, Chan (2014) and Chen (2014).

currency.[45] The typical economic determinants focus on the size of the economy, the size of the trade sector, the presence of an open, well-regulated, and deep financial sector, and the ability to implement sound and sustainable economic policies. China does well on the first two counts and is making progress on financial reforms and macro management.

An issue that has not received much discussion is how to fund the RMB global reserve currency position. To buttress a world class reserve currency, China has to make the RMB available in a quantity much larger than the current level that it has permitted the rest of world to hold. In the past few decades, the US has conveniently offered global US dollar liquidity via its balance of payments deficit. China, however, has enjoyed huge trade surpluses and large foreign direct investment and portfolio inflows. The surplus and inflow do not provide RMB liquidity to the world. China has to find ways to send RMB abroad.[46] Of course, when the world abounds with RMB, then one has to worry about the Triffin dilemma and China's commitment to maintain a sound RMB policy.

Besides pure economic considerations, there are non-economic factors to consider. Are countries confident in RMB-denominated assets? Could countries entrust China's legal and regulatory system with their national savings? In addition, the choice of a reserve currency is affected by concerns about political uncertainty and corporate governance culture issues.

No less is the implications of political and military powers. The anecdotal evidence suggests that a prominent global currency usually goes with the political and military powers of the issuing country — it is true for the US dollar in the current time, the British pound in the 19th and early 20th centuries, and the Dutch guilder in the 17th and 18th centuries. These non-economic factors put China in a less favorable position to compete with, say, the US dollar for a global reserve currency title.

---

[45] Studies discuss the factors determine the RMB's global reserve currency status include Aizenman and Marion (2003, 2004), Aizenman, Cheung and Ito (2015), Chen and Peng (2010), Cheung and Qian (2009b), Cheung and Wong (2008), Cheung and Ito (2008, 2009), Eichengreen (2011, 2013), Lee (2014), Prasad (2014), Prasad and Ye (2012), and Subramanian (2011a, 2011b).

[46] Note that the bilateral RMB swap line agreements implicitly enhance the global RMB liquidity.

China is making progress in deepening its financial reforms and, to a less extent, political reforms. The slow progress in institutional and political reforms, coupled with its communist history, is an obstacle that impedes China's efforts to internationalize its currency and realize the preeminence of RMB globally. The territorial rows with its Asian neighbors do not help the situation. In the meanwhile, the US is unlikely to give up its role in the existing international monetary system — the non-economic factors are in its favor to maintain the US dollar as the foremost global reserve currency.

One development that could speed up the process of the RMB to gain the global reserve currency stature is the admission to the IMF's Special Drawing Right club.

(b) The special drawing right (SDR) club

The SDR is a supplementary reserve asset created by the IMF under the Bretton Woods regime in 1969.[47] The shift of the fixed rate regime to the post-Bretton Woods floating rate era, in principle, should have reduced the need for global reserves. The reality is that countries have not cut back their demand for international reserves. In 2009, SDR 182.7 billion was created to enhance global liquidity and global reserve holding. The 2009 allocation brought the total cumulative SDR allocations to SDR 204 billion.[48]

SDR is neither a currency nor a claim against the IMF. In addition to its role as a reserve asset, IMF and other institutions use SDR as a unit of account. Under the Bretton Woods setting, initially the value of the SDR was set to be one US dollar (initially, it is the value of 0.888671 grams of fine gold). After the Bretton Woods system, its value is defined by a basket of currencies. The size of the basket was shrunk from 16 to five currencies in 1981. The five-currency (the US dollar, the German mark, the Japanese yen, the French franc, and the British pound) basket was replaced with a four-currency basket in 1999, when the euro replaced the German mark and French franc.

---

[47] See the SDR factsheet (International Monetary Fund, 2015).
[48] There are in total four allocations: SDR 9.3 billion (1970–72), SDR 12.1 billion (1979–81), SDR 21.5 billion (August 10, 2009, and SDR 161.2 billion (August 28, 2009). The third allocation is a special one-time allocation targeting countries joined IMF after 1981.

The membership of the SDR appears to have implication for the global stature of a currency. For instance, the four member currencies are the top four global reserve currencies and the top four most actively traded currencies according the COFER data and the BIS 2013 report. The obvious question is a causality one — does the SDR select a top currency to the basket? Or, does the SDR membership make a currency a premier global currency?

The SDR is not a real physical asset — it is bookkeeping claim created to boost the total amount of global reserves under the fix rate period. Its role as a reserve asset is actually minor; as of 2014, the SDR account for only 2.5% of the global reserves reported to the IMF.[49] Virtually, there is no significant financial market that operates in the SDR and trades SDR-denominated assets or commodities. Despite its relatively minor role in the global market, the SDR membership is generally viewed with an elite status and as IMF's official recognition of a currency's role in the international economy. The composition of the SDR basket is usually reviewed every five years.

The discussion of including the RMB into the SDR was not that enthusiastic during the last review of SDR composition in 2010. The SDR currencies were selected based on (a) the size of the exports sector and (b) the "freely usable" criterion, and the weights are based on the scale of exports of goods and services, and the share of global reserves in the currency held by other IMF member economies. Despite a few vocal advocates including the then French president Nicolas Sarkozy, the general opinion was that it is premature to grant the RMB the SDR status.[50] At the end, the IMF executive board in November 2010 determined that the basket comprises four currencies, namely, the U.S. dollar, euro, pound sterling, and Japanese yen and their weights are, respectively, 41.9, 37.4, 11.3, and 9.4

---

[49] The total amount of 2014 Q4 global reserves reported by COFER are US$11,591.13 billion (Table 6.3). Using the dollar exchange of the SDR as of December 31, 2014 (US$1.44881) and the outstanding SDR 204 billion, the SDR accounts for 2.5% of the reported global reserves.

[50] For example, Gauthier-Villars (2011), McMahon (2010), and Yang (2010) expressed support for the RMB to be included in the SDR basket in 2010.

(International Monetary Fund, 2010b). Indeed, the SDR basket has been composed of these four currencies since January 1999.[51]

Essentially, the RMB satisfied the large exporter criterion in 2010 — it was turned away because it was not "free enough" to be a SDR currency.[52] Since 2010, China has greatly enhanced the currency's usability character and made the RMB a serious contender for the SDR status with its remarkable accomplishments in pushing the RMB overseas.

As the largest trade economy, there is no doubt that China meets the trade criterion of the SDR selection process. The discussion is on whether the RMB meets the freely usable criterion. Note that, in principle, a freely usable currency is not necessarily a convertible currency. The freely usable criterion was formally adopted in 2000 for SDR valuation.

The concept of a freely usable currency was established for IMF's operation and is based on two properties of "widely used" and "widely traded." The operational concept does not require the convertibility condition.[53] Finance and Strategy, Policy, and Review Departments, IMF (2011) presents alternative indicators and selection criteria for the SDR basket. For instance, it suggests using the currency composition of foreign exchange reserves, international debt securities, and international bank liabilities as indicators for "wide use," and foreign exchange spot market turnover as the indicator for "wide trading."[54] The main point is that it is the IMF who determines whether a currency is freely usable or not; and full convertibility is not a prerequisite.

---

[51] Since 1999, the weight assigned to the Japanese yen has drifted lower from 18% in 1999 to 9.4% in the 2010 review cycle.

[52] Back in 2009, China was already the second largest trade country after the US.

[53] Note that in the sixth edition of *Balance of Payments and International Investment Position Manual*, IMF (2009, paragraph 6.72), it states that "... reserve assets must be denominated and settled in convertible foreign currencies, that is, currencies that are freely usable for settlements of international transactions." And "(I)n addition, assets denominated in gold and SDRs may qualify as reserve assets." Also, see International Monetary Fund (2010c).

[54] It also proposes a new reserve asset criterion that is based on three key characteristics: liquidity in foreign exchange markets; hedgeability; and availability of appropriate interest rate instruments and the corresponding four indicators: currency composition of foreign exchange reserves, spot and derivatives market turnover, and an appropriate market-based interest rate instrument. See Finance and Strategy, Policy, and Review Departments, IMF (2011) for additional discussions.

The IMF's managing director Christine Lagarde pointed out that the SDR status of the RMB is a question of "when" not "if." Thus, we do not drill on whether the RMB has met the freely usable criterion. Instead, an interesting question is the potential benefit of having the RMB in the group of currencies that determine the value of the SDR? Since the SDR is not actively used in the international monetary system and global financial markets, its membership may carry more a symbolism value than a practical one. For China, the admission to the selective group of currencies represents the IMF recognition and endorsement of China's importance in the global economy and its continuous reform efforts. It is a symbolic boost to China's image on credibility in general, and on its currency in particular.

Will it catapult the RMB forward to be, say, the foremost reserve currency? Some commentators argue that the SDR status will affirm the RMB's official global reserve role and, thus, increase the demand by central banks for RMB reserve assets. The view, however, is oversimplified. Indeed, even without the SDR status, central banks acquire assets denominated in the RMB. The level of acceptance is likely driven by practical considerations. Holding RMB reserves represents a good gesture to China, and an endorsement of China's stature in the global market.

The management of reserves, which comprise a country's precautionary foreign exchange savings, calls for a deep and trustworthy financial market. A case in point is that the preeminent reserve currency role of the US dollar greatly benefits from the strong support offered by the US advanced financial sector and its deep and mature treasury market. Without the accompanying liberalization policy to develop and support a deep, open, and efficient financial sector, and a liquid and robust government bond market, the admission to the SDR club does not necessarily catalyze the central banks' demand for RMB reserves. The SDR status recognizes the RMB's international role, but it does not push it beyond the level justified by economic (and political) factors.

The inclusion of the RMB to the SDR basket echoes Zhou's (2009) message of promoting a multipolar international monetary system. When the reserve currency system is dominated by one currency, the hegemonic country can abuse the privileges of a reserve provider. A system of checks and balances is likely to exist in a multipolar world such that individual and competing reserve issuers push each other toward internationally responsible behaviors.

The Chinese authorities are quite expressive in 2015 to push the RMB to the SDR basket. The SDR status of the RMB is a good political gesture though it has limited direct material impact on the currency's role in the global market. The national pride and prestige associated with the SDR membership can provide a fresh impetus for China to implement tough structural reforms to strengthen its domestic economic health and the global economic structural balance. Thus, anointing the RMB a SDR member can trigger changes that lead to a sound international economic and political ecology that is good for both China and the world.

6.3.4 Other functions

In addition to the functions discussed in the previous subsections, an international currency can provide the services of an international cash currency, an anchoring currency of a pegged exchange arrangement, and a pricing currency of globally traded commodities. Not surprisingly, the RMB plays quite a minor role in these capacities.

China has strict rules on carrying RMB cash in and out of the country. Starting from 2005, individuals are allowed to take a maximum of RMB20,000 across the border. In 2007, People's Bank of China (PBoC) appointed the Bank of China, Hong Kong, as the custody institute of the RMB cash in circulation overseas. The custody institute also manages the supply and demand of RMB cash overseas.

Anecdotal evidence suggests that the Chinese currency is used in bordering countries including Russia, Mongolia, Kazakhstan, Kyrgyzstan, Tajikistan, and Vietnam. The strengthening of RMB and the growing trade ties with these countries in the first decade of the 21st century are driving the foreign accumulation of RMB banknotes. Further, the RMB banknote is gaining popularity, not only in Asia-Pacific economies including Macao, Hong Kong, Korea, Taiwan, and Singapore, but also in some European cities.

The data on the amount of RMB cash in circulation overseas are hard to come by. People's Bank of China (2015) reports that, in 2014, the cash flows in and out China are, respectively, RMB39.9 billion and 11.7 billion. Both figures are small compared with the total RMB cash in domestic circulation.[55]

At the time of writing, we are not aware of the use of RMB as an anchoring currency. The use of the RMB as a pricing currency is still at the early stage of development. While China denominates domestic commodity trading in RMB, the local market is mostly off-limits to foreigners. The International Board of the Shanghai Gold Exchange established in the Shanghai Free Trade Zone in 2014 is the first attempt to bring gold trading in RMB to international investors (Section 6.1.2). The official introduction of the RMB gold price fixing in April 2016 is a watershed event of the commodity price role of the RMB. Further, the planned trading of the RMB-priced crude futures represents another effort to enhance the global role of the RMB (Section 6.3.2).

6.3.5 Renminbi globalization index

How to assess the progress in these offshore RMB centers? The Standard Chartered Bank in November 2012 launched the Standard Chartered Renminbi Globalization Index (RGI) to gauge the development in offshore RMB centers. By measuring the overall growth in offshore RMB usage, the index is the first industry benchmark that assesses the progress of offshore RMB business activity and the implied degree of RMB internationalization.

The RGI is computed on a monthly basis based on four offshore RMB market components: (1) CNH deposits (denoting store of wealth), (2) trade settlement and other international payments (unit of international commerce), (3) Dim Sum bonds and certificates of deposit (CDs) issued (as vehicles for capital raising), and (4) foreign exchange turnover (unit of exchange), all from an offshore perspective and denominated in RMB. The weights of these components are inversely proportional to their 24-month normalized standard deviations.

Location-specific data for each component is used to compute a corresponding global aggregate. The index initially covered only Hong Kong;

---

[55] These figures are less than one percentage of the RMB6.03 trillion in circulation in 2014.

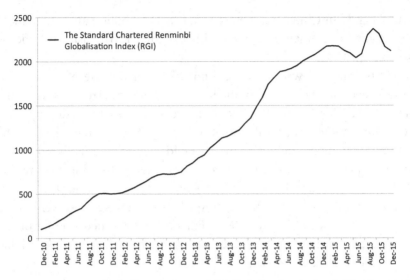

Figure 6.3   The Standard Chartered Renminbi Globalization Index (RGI) (Dec 2010– Dec 2015)

Source: Bloomberg.

Singapore and London were added in August 2011, Taiwan was added in July 2013, New York in January 2014, and Paris and Seoul were added in August 2014. As the offshore RMB activity expands, the bank will include additional parameters and markets.

The evolution of the RGI is depicted in Figure 6.3. The index started in December 2010 with a base value of 100. It grew steadily from 100 in December 2010 to 2,089 in December 2014; reflecting the growth in individual offshore RMB businesses, and in the number of offshore RMB centers. Clearly, there is steady growth momentum behind the offshore RMB activities. In particular, the index rose by 53% in 2014, mainly driven by the RMB trade settlement and the contributions of newly included offshore centers. In 2015, the index displayed an unusual bumpy ride following the volatile movements in the RMB market and domestic equity prices.

6.4 Looking Forward

China has systematically promoted the international use of the RMB in recent years. The result, especially in the trade arena, is quite noticeable.

There is little doubt that the RMB is on the path to become a global currency. The question is the pace at which the RMB is penetrating the international financial market, and the global status of the RMB relative to other incumbent global currencies. In the following, we consider some issues on furthering the global role of the RMB.

6.4.1 Offshore RMB markets

In the foreseeable future, we anticipate that both the scope and the scale of the global offshore RMB market will continue to grow. The pace is likely to be directed and dictated by the Chinese authorities and developments in the domestic economy. With the emphasis on stability, China will assume an active role in guiding the offshore market development and be very conscientious about the adverse feedback on its under-developed financial sector.

While the offshore markets play a constructive role and offer a scope for corporations and governments to work together to explore opportunities of using the Chinese currency in an efficient manner, we should not overplay the contribution of offshore RMB markets. On the one hand, with improved liquidity and enhanced investment opportunities, offshore markets offer opportunities to nonresidents to experience business dealings using the RMB and the Chinese authorities to assess the implications of intermediating international transactions without eradicating capital controls. On the other hand, as in the past, China maintains its usual gradual approach to liberalizing its economy including its financial sector, retains its grip on critical policy matters, and responds mainly to domestic rather than foreign considerations.

The offshore market policy is used to improve the RMB's overseas acceptance and is subordinate to the overall financial liberalization policy. It generates information for making changes but does not force domestic regulatory reform. That is, the role of offshore markets is complementary in the sense that it helps to achieve the RMB potential as a global currency but not to force changes in domestic policies to further the role of the RMB in the global market.

A well-designed network of offshore markets will advance the overseas acceptance and solidify the international status of the RMB. However, the ultimate acceptance of and demand for the RMB as a global currency are determined by the underlying economic forces shaped by China's economic fundamentals, and the global political dynamics. Offshore RMB markets themselves could not raise the RMB's status beyond what is justified by its economic and political attributes.

One shall not, however, underestimate China's determination to manage its economy according to its own terms. China's abrupt interventions of the stock market in July 2015 and the currency market in the subsequent months remind the world that China still tightly controls its economy. Indeed, the intervention instances stirred some concerns in the international community. China did not only intervene in the domestic stock and currency markets, it surprised the financial market by reportedly intervening in the offshore RMB market. International investors were confounded by the implications of these events for China's liberalization policy and for their investments in both the domestic and offshore RMB markets.

While the market turmoil of the 2015 summer may only be a hiccup of China's overall financial liberalization process, it highlights the path of the RMB to become a global currency that is laid with different types of hurdles.

6.4.2 Domestic market reforms

The prospect of the offshore RMB market and the RMB internationalization hinges upon China's overall reform policy in general and its capital controls and exchange rate policy in particular. As repeated quite often in official statements, reform is China's predetermined policy. The doubts are about the speed and the extent of the reform.

In February 2012, the Financial Survey and Statistics Department headed by SongCheng Sheng at the People's Bank of China issued a report in Chinese that outlines the process for opening up China's capital account and promoting the international use of the RMB.[56] The report outlines a three-stage approach. Specifically, the government can in one to three years relax restrictions on outward direct investments and promote the

---

[56] The report in Chinese "我国加快资本账户开放的条件基本成熟" was published in the *China Securities Journal* online and is available at http://www.cs.com.cn/xwzx/07/201202/t20120223_3253890.html.

"Going Global" policy; in three to five years to relax controls on trade and commercial credits and to promote the international use of the RMB, and in five to 10 years build up and strengthen financial markets and liberalize real estate, stock, and bond transactions.

While the outlined reform schedule is quite aggressive and is not in line with the usual gradual reform approach undertook by China in the last few decades, it reflects the desire to continue the financial market reform and the RMB internationalization process. Anecdotal evidence indicates that China has experimented with alternative means to push the liberalization process. The initiative of setting up free trade zones is a recent example (see Sections 6.1.2 and 6.1.3). The reform initiatives usually give the impression of piecemeal approach. Nevertheless, China's strategy is to transplant the tried and tested financial reform practice to other parts of the country so as to broaden the financial account liberalization policy to the national level.

To become a full-fledged international currency, China has to develop a deep and efficient financial sector and government bond market with prudent governance. Despite the usual hyperbolic rhetoric on how far and how fast China could liberalize its capital account and transform its financial sector, China has to take the time to put in place the hardware and, more importantly, the software that are required to establish and maintain a robust financial sector and the related regulatory framework.

6.4.3 Economic factors against political considerations

Notwithstanding official policies and good intentions, the economic quality of the currency itself is not the sole factor determining the acceptance of the RMB in the global market. Beyond some fundamental structural changes in its financial sector, China has to convince other countries to conduct international trade and financial transactions in its currency. The persuasion, as attested by Japan's attempt to internationalize its currency in the late 20th century (Ministry of Finance, Japan, 2003; Takagi, 2011), goes beyond economic reasoning. Political considerations, especially in East Asia, play a non-negligible role in adopting an international currency.

With the region's predominant antagonism toward hegemony, China's communist political structure, military buildup, and recent territorial rows with its neighboring countries including the announced China's East

China Sea Air Defense Identification Zone can seriously impede the acceptance of the RMB abroad and be a drag of its efforts to promote the international use of the RMB.

China has often reaffirmed its commitment to peaceful development, the non-interference foreign policy, and the five principles of peaceful coexistence.[57] Nevertheless, for its neighboring countries, these reassurances may not be completely convincing, especially when China is expanding its military capacity and continuing its territorial disputes with countries including Japan, Vietnam, and Philippines.[58] All these considerations would require China to make some extra efforts to promote the acceptance of the RMB in Asia and in the global market.

Recently, there are some apparent international efforts to contain China's influences. The US is the quite open in its intention to counter China's growing global influences. The pronounced foreign policy of "rebalancing" toward Asia (CRS Report for Congress, 2012) and the Trans-Pacific Partnership trade agreement exemplify the US determination to assert its value system and define the economic orders according to its own values.[59] The efforts go beyond economic one and extend to military elements. The US, for example, in October 2015 sent its naval force to the South China Sea to challenge China's territorial claims.

These non-economic developments have direct and indirect implications for the perspective of the RMB to become a global currency. Overall, to facilitate the global use of the RMB, China has to overcome limits defined by both economic and political factors.

---

[57] The Five Principles are: mutual respect for sovereignty and territorial integrity, mutual nonaggression, noninterference in each other's internal affairs, equality and mutual benefit, and peaceful coexistence. They were results of negotiations between China and India and formally included in the "Agreement between the People's Republic of China and the Republic of India on Trade and Intercourse between the Tibet Region of China and India" in 1956. See, for example, http://www.fmprc.gov.cn/eng/topics/seminaronfiveprinciples/t140777.htm.

[58] See, for example, Huang and Billo (2015) for discussions of these territorial disputes.

[59] On the benefits of the agreement, President Obama was quoted to say that "… we can't let countries like China write the rules of the global economy. We should write those rules." The full text of the agreement is available on https://ustr.gov/trade-agreements/free-trade-agreements/trans-pacific-partnership/tpp-full-text. The US official website is http://www.ustr.gov/tpp. For alternative views, see http://wikileaks.org/tpp/.

Chapter 7
Concluding Remarks

The reform championed by the modern reformist Deng Xiaoping has broad and far-reaching implications for China and the rest of the world. Since 1978, China has implemented various experimental economic reform initiatives at various levels and domains of its economy. In addition to China's size, the economic reform program is further complicated by the notion of bringing in market forces to enhance economic efficiency within the communist structure and to build a socialist market economy with Chinese characteristics. The mandate, arguably, predicates that China's reform journey does not have a historical precedent.

The experimental nature of reforms is often described by the old Chinese adage "feel the rock, wade across the river." In the last few decades, reform policies that are not necessarily in conformance to orthodox economics theory were implemented. The reform in terms of both its pace and economic results has not been progressed in a linear manner, depending on your view, it is a "two steps forward, one step back" or "one step back, two steps forward" process. Nevertheless, the ebb and flow of reform measures on average have delivered well and pushed the Chinese economy to the league of global economic powers.

Among various areas of reform, the previous chapters zoom in on the exchange rate policy. There is a strong feedback loop between China's exchange rate arrangement and its economy. Exchange rate is one of the key economic variables that determine the international flows of goods, services, and capital. Thus, the effects of China's exchange rate policy reforms can reverberate within China and across the global economy. The global interest in the RMB has intensified over time — with an early focus on its level of misalignment — even before China unveiled its intention to promote its currency's global status.

In this chapter, we recap a few main observations on China's exchange rate policy. Then we offer some general discussions on roles of the RMB from the domestic and international perspectives.

7.1 Experiences

The evolution of China's exchange rate policy aptly illustrates the inextricable link of economic policy and political ideology in China. Before the reform period, political considerations played an overwhelmingly important role in designing the exchange rate policy. The 1978 reform initiative swayed the balance toward economic incentives and efficiencies, albeit in a gradual manner. Pursuing economic development, instead of political movement and class struggle, became the primary endeavor. The re-pivot on economic prosperity has shaped the basic tune of reform in the subsequent years.

The important point to realize is that China is not in a rush to adopt a freely flexible exchange rate arrangement. Historical episodes have showed that China has managed its reform program in general and financial liberalization process in particular at its own pace. And it does not hesitate to resort to administrative measures and control policies to rein in market volatility.

On liberalizing exchange rate, if the pace is too fast relatively to reforms in, say, fragile financial markets, it can end in devastating financial instability. Comparable to its gradual reform tune, China takes a prudent attitude in liberalizing the exchange rate. Measured changes that bring in market mechanisms are sequentially introduced in accordance with the pace of reforms in real and financial sectors.

China's policymaking has, in general, adhered to its principle of independence, controllability, and practicality, and is ready to interrupt the process whenever it deems necessary. On exchange rate policy, a few examples are (a) during the 2007–08 global financial crisis, the policy was reverted back to a stability exchange rate arrangement and (b) in the aftermath of the 2015 summer turmoil, the authorities intervened in both the onshore and offshore RMB markets to restore market stability.

Despite repeated re-assurances, there are concerns about the scope and the pace of exchange rate reforms, and their implications for the global economy. The furious debate on RMB misalignment in the early 21st century reflects China's tensions with trading partners that are translated to complaints of China's unfair advantages from an artificially engineered cheap currency. The event provides a good case study on how difficult it is to determine the degree of misalignment of a currency. Circumstantial evidence usually suggests that currency management and currency misalignment are closely related. China's record of keeping a tight rein on its exchange rate does not help to dispel the accusation of RMB undervaluation. Even though the accusation is politically sensible, we showed in Chapter 4 that it can be hard to be substantiated by vigorous empirical evidence.

China's efforts to develop the global status of the RMB further arouse attention on its currency. A broader concern is how to integrate China into the international monetary system and its implications. It is hard to underestimate the implication of a global RMB coupled with China's prominent position in the trade arena for the global economic and political ecology. While there are skeptics on how far the Chinese currency can go under capital controls, there are hyperbolic rhetoric on the imminence of the RMB to dethrone the US dollar in the international monetary system.

Even though China has followed non-traditional approaches to seek the global use of its currency, the results are quite admirable. In contrast with the experiences of other global currencies, China has relied more on its own policy initiatives than market forces to promote the use of RMB overseas. For instance, it has strategically developed the offshore market in Hong Kong to conduct offshore RMB activities. Then, it sequentially endorsed other offshore RMB markets, and established local RMB clearing facilities in selected offshore centers in financial hubs around the world. Instead of full capital account convertibility, China manages possible effects of offshore activities by promoting the overseas use of its currency in defined areas, and with designated channels and links to the domestic market.

China first established the RMB's foothold in the global trade arena. It has incrementally modified its policy to promote the use of RMB in settling cross-border trade. The experiment began with Hong Kong as the middleman and a few designated Chinese cities. Then, the RMB cross-border settlement scheme was extended to cover other geographical areas. The scheme, which has benefited from China's extensive trade network and preferential policy encouragement, has progressed quite well since it was introduced in 2009. The RMB has become the fifth most used world payments currency since the end of 2014. It is quite an accomplishment as the RMB was only sparsely used in the global market back in 2009.

China has made some serious efforts to enhance its exchange rate formation procedure and, at the same time, reformed its economy. The culmination of years of reform endeavors has underscored IMF's momentous decision to admit the RMB to the SDR currency basket in November 2015. No matter whether the decision is politically motivated or a formal recognition of China's reform accomplishment, the SDR status that is symbolic of a global reserve currency is an open endorsement of the RMB and is quite positive for its future role in the global financial market.

7.2 Domestic Challenges

As noted in early parts of the book, liberalizing the exchange rate arrangement for a large country like China can be a complex undertaking. The task is further complicated by the fact that changes have to be made in the midst of transiting from a planned economy that is arguably quite under-developed in most if not all sectors to a market-based one overlaid with the superstructure of socialism with Chinese characteristics. There are important connections between reforms in the real and financial sectors. China has taken up substantial efforts in revamping its production structure and trade capacity in the early years of the reform period. The results are quite phenomenal — China has rapidly ascended to the leagues of largest economies and trading countries. While the transition to a modern economy is still a work in progress, these accomplishments so far suffice for China to push for the international recognition of its currency, the RMB.

To build up the RMB's potential to be a prominent global currency, China has to maintain and enhance its economic strength and establish a modern efficient financial sector. A strong global currency requires backing of a sound and powerful local economy. What it means is that China has to follow through its announced policy of reforms. After growing relentlessly in the last three and half decades, China has showed signs of slowing down. For instance, China's growth rate of 6.9% in 2015 is lowest in 25 years. The traditional industrial sector that supported growth in the past few decades declined while the services sector gained; but the gain does not completely offset the decline. The 2015 figure has extended the trend of slowing growth observed in the last few years.

During the high growth period, the government was praised for its competence in managing the economy through economic tough times. The slowdown has raised the concern of China's ability to manage its increasingly complex economy. Competition from other emerging economies and the projected dwindling of work population for instance, present headwinds for the Chinese economy going forward. The decline in population takes away the so-called demographic dividend from China's growth equation.[1] Also, a drop in population will cause in drop in demand.

Productivity improvement can alleviate the drop in labor force and enhance competitiveness. The ambitious "Made in China, 2025" initiative launched in 2015 represents a government-led concerted effort to upgrade the industrial base and prepare China to fend off low-end competition and compete in advanced manufacturing sectors. In addition to technology know-hows, the success of the transformation into advanced manufacturing requires reforms in corporate structures including management efficiency and governance.

China's future growth prospects can be enhanced by improving labor mobility and income inequality. The economic reform has induced a large scale of rural to urban migration and created a huge population of migrant workers. However, labor mobility is still bounded by the Hukou

---

[1] World Bank (2016) projects China's population of people between the ages of 15 and 64 will fall more than 10% by 2040. The projection has accounted for the lifting of the one-child policy. The *Wall Street Journal* reported on January 2016 that, figures from China's National Bureau of Statistics, the Chinese workers aged 16–59 showed a record drop of 4.87 million in 2015.

(household registration) system that was introduced back in 1958 to separate rural and urban residency and control migration within China. Restricted labor mobility is a form of market distortions that impedes economic development. China is rolling out Hukow reform in 2016 that allows migrant workers to settle in urban areas under some prespecified conditions. The move is deemed to be a step in the right direction of improving labor mobility. If the Hukow reform delivers the expected results, and labor can respond to market forces, then it will remove one impediment to economic development.

One cherished accomplishment of the economic reform is that it has lifted the standing of living of a vast China's populace. For instance, a study by the Asian Development Bank indicates that China reduced the size of its absolute poor population from 520 million in the 1990s to 230 million in the 2000s.[2] The dramatic decline of poor population, however, is overshadowed by the increase in income inequality. The rising economic tide does not benefit everyone equally, and income inequality has been worsened. Even according to the official Gini coefficient index — which some believe is too conservative — shows that China's income inequality is above the warning mark of 0.4 set by the United Nations, and is worse than, say, the G7 countries. The large Gini coefficient index reflects the income gap between those living in urban and those in rural areas, and between coastal and inland areas.

An equitable society offers a good social environment for sustainable economic growth, and is less prone to social dissatisfaction and unrest. The Chinese authorities have repeatedly emphasized the importance of social stability, and implemented social and industrial policies to narrow the income gap, say, between the urban and rural areas, and between the coastal and inland regions. Given the current wealth gap, China has some serious work to do to reduce inequality and build an equitable country.

Alongside the success story of economic reform, there are reforms in financial markets. The general impression is that financial reform has lagged behind economic reform. While the manufacturing sector has caught up with the rest of world and is quite competitive in the world

---

[2] See Asian Development Bank (2014, p. 7). The absolute poor population refers to those living on $1.25 or less a day.

market, the Chinese financial sector is still being viewed as underdeveloped and repressed, and lacking a strong regulatory supervision. Further, the currency is current account convertible but not capital account convertible. One possible reason behind China's resolutely cautious approach to financial reform are the crises experienced by other developing economies in their processes of liberalizing and opening up their underdeveloped and fragile financial systems, and the devastating economic impacts of volatile capital flows during these crises.

With the impressive stride in economic reform, China has to establish a modern financial system that matches advances in the rest of the economy to support the economic development, and to gain the utmost economic efficiency. Besides its international trade network, China has to further integrate into the global financial system to enhance its interactions with the rest of the world. Indeed, after the 2007–08 global financial crisis, China has stepped up the pace of financial reform and hinted the intention to get out of the shadow of the US-dominated international financial system (Zhou, 2009).

A modern and efficient financial sector provides support not just for the real economy, but also for the international status of the currency. It is perceived that the global role of a currency is greatly facilitated by a domestic bond market with sufficient breadth and depth.[3] In this regard, the Chinese domestic bond market has noticeably developed and liberalized in recent years. In July 2015, China essentially opened its domestic interbank bond market to overseas central banks and other designated public sector and supranational institutions by scrapping and streamlining quota requirement and application procedures. Further liberalization took place in February 2016 when the Central Bank allowed a wide set of overseas financial institutions to participate in the bond market.[4] In September 2015, China widened the foreign participation in its Panda bond market by expanding the group of approved issuers to include offshore financial institutions.

---

[3] See, for example, Ma and Yao (2016).
[4] See People's Bank of China (2016). The operational detail, however, was not announced at that time.

These liberalization measures are taken as a policy signal of affirming China's commitment to further integrate its economy into the global financial market and support the global role of its currency.

For the exchange rate, China reformed in August 2015 its mechanism of setting the daily central parity (fixing) rate of the RMB. In essence, the new fixing formation mechanism takes into consideration the previous closing rate, in addition to other factors that include demand and supply factors. The idea is to explicitly allow for market forces in determining the daily fixing. In November 2015, the domestic interbank foreign exchange market was opened to overseas central banks, supranational institutions, and sovereign wealth funds.[5] Last but not the least, in December 2015, China reiterated the practice and desirability of referencing the value of the RMB against a basket of currencies instead of just the US dollar. The reference to a basket of currencies was mentioned in 2005 when the grip on the RMB against the US dollar rate was loosened. Nevertheless, the bilateral RMB–US dollar rate has remained the market focus.

China officially completed the interest rate deregulation process in October 2015 by removing the deposit-rate ceiling rule. In addition, China has continued its programs to open up its domestic financial markets and allow its residence to invest overseas via, say, QFII, RQFII, QDII, Stock Connect, and free trade zone arrangements. The conversion between offshore and onshore RMBs is typically conducted via designated channels including free trade zone, RQFII, authorized RMB clearing bank overseas, and the bilateral local currency swap line agreements.

Despite all these financial liberalization measures, international access to domestic financial markets is still not completely free from administrative restrictions and quotas. And the RMB was neither fully

---

[5] The first batch of foreign institutions allowed to participate in the massive domestic interbank foreign exchange market includes three overseas central banks (Hong Kong Monetary Authority, Reserve Bank of Australia, and National Bank of Hungary), and four other international financial institutions (The International Bank for Reconstruction and Development, International Development Association, Trust Funds of World Bank Group, and Government of Singapore Investment Corp). On May 20, 2016, the first batch of foreign commercial banks were approved to directly trade in the Chinese foreign exchange market.

capital account convertible nor freely floated by the end of 2015.[6] In implementing these progressive policy changes, there are signs that financial reform has encountered speed bumps in 2015.

The authorities' handling of the 2015 summer financial market fiasco has triggered some serious concerns about China's ability and determination to strengthen market-based mechanisms for pricing capital and risks in financial markets. After the Shanghai benchmark stock index doubled in less than a year, it started its steep decline on June 15, 2015.

In response, the authorities implemented several intervention measures that include calling on state-owned institutions to buy up their stock holdings, prohibiting senior company officials and major shareholders from selling their stocks, suspending initial public offerings, and banning short selling in spot and futures markets. The unorthodox bailout measures were officially adopted to arrest the "unreasonable" drop in share prices; these measures, at the same time, rekindled the concerns over risks of investing in a command-style market. Foreign investors, especially those who cannot divest their investment in China, perceived these bailout measures with great skepticism.

The market sentiment got worse when China switched to a new RMB daily fixing mechanism and, simultaneously devalued the RMB on August 11, 2015. The policy shift was asserted to be an enhancement that expands the role of market forces in determining the RMB value. Pessimism about the RMB deepened and triggered capital flow out of the Chinese currency, which added pressure on its exchange rate. In the hope of stabilizing the market sentiment, the authorities intervened directly in the onshore and offshore markets, imposed reserved requirements on offshore RMB deposits, and tightened up capital flow management. Nevertheless, the authorities failed to convince the market participants, who interpreted the cumulated depreciation in the first few days of the policy change as a sign of currency war to shore up the lethargic Chinese economy. Foreign investors were caught off-guard by these intervention activities; especially those took place in offshore markets.

---

[6] The RMB is technically convertible for overseas central banks and public sector institutions that are allowed to participate in the domestic bond market.

China has undoubtedly underestimated the world response to its policy on the RMB. The market reaction was exacerbated by China's inability to dispel the pessimistic sentiment and claim the market; especially in the aftermath of the rogue stock market bailout attempt.

China's reactions to the summer turmoil that reverberated around the world offer some hints about the difficulties lying ahead of its financial reforms.

The inability to stem market volatility and soothe adverse sentiment raises the question of whether China's leaders can competently manage its financial sector that is growing more and more sophisticated over time. The intervention and control measures, the way they were deployed, and their muted effects smacked of mismanagement and desperation. These measures are contradictory to reform messages about enhancing the role of market forces the authorities reiterated in the past years. Do the authorities have a full grip on the country? Or, the era of China's market authoritarianism is over?

Poor communication strategy and inadequate coordination between agencies amplified the negative market sentiment. A case in point is the market reaction to change in the RMB policy in August 2015. Apparently, the decision of including market elements in the daily fixing mechanism is in line with China's push to join the SDR currency basket at that time, and is likely to have communicated with the IMF.[7] Nevertheless, the explanations and assurances offered by Chinese officials after the global market's wild responses failed to erase the skepticism about the motivation behind the drop in the RMB exchange rate. Interventions in the domestic and, especially, offshore markets have shocked global investors, renewed concerns about China's commitment to a market-based economy, and added yet another layer of uncertainty about the RMB reform policy.

The dramatic market response can be partially attributed to China's success in increasing the international use of its currency. Not to mention that the culmination of years of growth and integrating into the global system has transformed China into a systemic important economy in the world. Thus, fluctuations in the Chinese economy have rippling effects

---

[7] IMF issued positive press release http://www.imf.org/external/country/CHN/rr/2015/0811.pdf on China's change to the fixing mechanism.

on other economies.[8] With the increasing stakes, the world has paid greater attention to Chinese policies, in general, and its RMB policy, in particular. When China is in the limelight and being closely scrutinized, the adverse effect of policy opacity and obfuscation will be amplified in the market.

The failure to communicate is attributable to the intricate web of China's high power structure. The People's Bank of China[9] neither is independent nor has the power like the US central bank to set its own policy. The main government bodies and regulatory commissions governing the Chinese financial system, including the People's Bank of China, are under the jurisdiction of the State Council. Financial policymaking involves various constituents in the government and is influenced by leaders at the top.[10] The lack of well-defined authorities and accountabilities makes it difficult to carry out effective crisis management, especially when there is subpar coordination among agencies. The situation is further complicated by the silence of two recognized financial reformers; namely Premier Li Keqiang and central bank governor Zhou Xiaochuan, during the fiasco — is it emblematic of disagreements among top leaders on reform strategies and policies?

To complete its historic financial reform agenda, China has to re-assert its commitment and ability to carry out policies to establish a market-based financial system with prudential regulatory mechanisms that can support and promote sustainable economic growth. It is a huge task that requires concerted efforts to broaden and deepen domestic financial markets, to build a streamlined regulatory supervision framework for coordinating and governing economic and financial

---

[8] International Monetary Fund (2016), for instance, notes that financial spillover effects from China are growing.

[9] The bank was established on December 1, 1948. The central bank status was conferred on the Bank by the State Council in September 1983, and legally confirmed when the Law of the People's Republic of China on the People's Bank of China was adopted on March 18, 1995 by the 3rd Plenum of the 8th National People's Congress. See http://www.pbc.gov.cn/english/130712/index.html for additional information.

[10] The Central Leading Group for Financial and Economic Affairs under the Central Committee of the Communist Party of China, and led by President XI JinPing is considered the highest decision-making body for economic issues.

affairs,[11] and to establish a transparent protocol that facilitates communication with the market on government policies. Advances in these areas help improve efficiency, rebuild China's credibility, and investor confidence.

A related issue for China to consider is to reassess the sequence of liberalizing its capital account and developing its domestic financial markets. The typically recommended sequence is to develop domestic financial markets, liberalize the exchange rate, and open up the capital account. That is, domestic financial liberalization should precede external financial liberalization. The sequence adopted by China, however, is different from the usual recommended course — it has sought the international recognition of its currency while implementing measured financial reforms along the way. That is, China is proceeding with external financial liberalization before first accomplished domestic financial liberalization and related regulatory supervision framework. The history of international finance suggests that such a reversed sequence or can be a root cause of financial instability.[12]

Apparently, the strategy of globalizing the RMB is modeled after the successful WTO accession experience. The 2001 WTO accession provided a fresh impetus for reformers to push forward economic reforms and open up China. The culminated achievement in the subsequent years is admirable. The heavy lobbying to join the SDR currency basket has a favor of the previous effort to join the WTO.

The prestige of being a member of elite group of global reserve currencies apparently has softened resistance to the campaign to liberalize financial markets and promote the international use of the RMB. Indeed, we observed a flurry of liberalizing measures for interest rates, the exchange rate, and financial markets implemented in 2014 and 2015. Before liberalizing the domestic financial sector and opening up the capital account, China is leveraging on its size to seek an active role of the RMB in the global market. With the increase in the use of the RMB overseas,

---

[11] It was reported that China is considering the set up a centralized regulatory supervision agency (Tham and Lim, 2015). Back in August 2013, a conference system headed by the People's Bank of China was established to coordinate cross-sectoral financial regulations (Sun, 2013).

[12] In passing, we note that the IMF and the US have been encouraging, if not pressuring, China to liberalize its exchange rate and capital market.

financial liberalization measures are then introduced in designated domestic sectors.

The challenges of managing market volatility in the summer 2015 have rekindled the concern of whether the scope and scale of the domestic financial sector are commensurate with the levels of capital account convertibility and exchange rate flexibility. On the one hand, opening up the capital account, albeit on a measured pace, facilitates China's integration with the global market. China's success in increasing the use of its currency around the world has encouraged domestic reforms and extended its influences in the international financial system. On the other hand, these developments have brought market forces and capital flows that cause the volatility of a modern financial market. The 2015 summer instance attests the possibility that domestic financial markets have not yet reached the degrees of breadth and sophistication to accommodate market volatility. Thus, a decision has to be made on the relative pace of opening up the capital account and reforming domestic financial markets.[13]

A basic question that China has to address is how to reconcile the apparent difference underlying a modern price-based financial market and a stable economic structure with Chinese socialist characteristics. A modern financial market that relies on market forces to price the capital to gain allocation efficiency has to endure volatility and risk. Despite its will to reform, China emphasizes the mandate of stability and favors a stable political structure under the communist reign. It thus inherently distrusts volatility and dislikes challenge to its power. When the volatility and risk are heightened, the authorities do not hesitate to resort to controls and restrictions, and, if necessary, even retribution. A notable example is China reverted to a tightly managed exchange rate in the midst of global financial crisis.

Apparently, such a strategy has lost its potency; it becomes difficult for China, on the one hand, fosters its level of integration with the world and promotes the use of its currency overseas and, on the other hand, retains a strong control over its economy. Despite all its continuing efforts, the Chinese economy by 2015 remains quite heavily state-managed, with both explicit and implicit controls across a range of economic matters. By most,

---

[13] At the risk of repeating, China did intervene by (re)introducing a number of control measures and moral suasion during the turbulence period.

if not all measure, China is not yet a market economy. Nevertheless, the combination of a partially open capital account and limited flexibility has already made China feels the difficulty of setting its economic policy. A broad and deep financial sector will help. The challenge, moving forward, is for China to establish a creditable financial system with the related regulatory and governance frameworks that functions like a modern and efficient financial market and, at the same time, is subject to its direct control. A larger question is how to balance the economic freedom implied by economic and financial reforms and the degree of democracy permitted under a structure with Chinese socialist characteristics.[14]

7.3 International Dimensions

In the process of transitioning from a centrally planned economy toward a market-based one, China has opened up its economy. In the last three and half decades, China has actively established links with the rest of the world. Backed by its growing economic prowess, China has become a key member of the global trade community. The financial reform program in recent years has brought the discussion of China's roles in the international monetary system. The efforts of liberalizing the financial markets and the exchange rate have gained traction. In the past few years, China's integration with the world economy has gradually expanded beyond trade and into the global financial system. As China's financial links with the global economy increase, its impact on the rest of the world is likely to grow in the years to come.

Coupled with the growing trade and financial links, China is getting active in the international political arena. It is not a hyperbole to say that China is a serious contender for the title of a global power.

The increasing global prominence has presented China both opportunities and challenges to complete the huge task of liberalizing and strengthening its financial sector, in particular, and its economy, in general. For instance, benefited from its economic strength and extensive trade network, China has been quite successful in seeking the increase in the

---

[14] According to the 2015 Economist Intelligence Unit's Democracy Index, China ranks the136[th] among 167 countries included in the Index.

overseas use of its currency. The use of the RMB in settling cross-border trade has increased in terms of both volume and geographical coverage. The surge of global RMB business opportunities has attracted various financial centers around the world to join the RMB global network.

Understandably, China formulates financial reform agenda including the RMB policy to benefit and better domestic economic performance and stability. However, in view of increasing stakes, a broad spectrum of policy-makers and investors has scrutinized China's policies. Market responses are driven not only by the policies themselves but also the way they are perceived. Both the market reality and authorities' communication skills matter. The opacity of China's policy intentions and its inability to explain can stir up unstable market psychology. Again, a case in point is the 2015 summer experience — China's ineffective policy elaborations and clumsy policy responses to the stock price and exchange rate swings triggered volatile market responses and contagious effects throughout financial markets overseas.

One side effect of China's progressive policy to enhance the global acceptance of its currency is that it has turned the spotlight on developments in China. The global investors expect, if not demand, a transparent policy framework and communication protocol for them to infer what is underlying China's policymaking and policy objectives. Ambiguities and perceived to be disingenuous responses are detrimental to credibility, which is known to be hard to establish but easy to destroy. To broaden and deepen its financial reforms, China has to uphold its policy credibility and re-assure its commitments to reform. As a contender of global financial power, China has to take up its global responsibilities, which at times, can complicate its policymaking.

As China is gaining its weight in the global economy, it has gradually evolved from being a passive participant of existing international order to an active stakeholder. The rapid expansion China experienced in the last few decades has outgrown what the existing international institutional framework can offer. To meet and protect its interest at home and overseas, China has actively engaged in various international institutions and sought representation that is commensurate with its contributions. At the same time, it has launched new initiatives, including the Asian Infrastructure Investment Bank and the Belt and Road Initiative to meet its own needs.

Similar to its other policies, China's attempts to play an alternative role in the global community have been greeted with both praise and skepticism. While some countries consider these new initiatives provide additional means to enhance global welfare, some consider they are threats to the *status quo* and are a backdoor for China to assert its undue influences. Conceivably, China's global financial initiatives can change the rule of the global economic game and, thus, create tensions between the uprising power and incumbents as both are striving to have an international apparatus to promote their economic and political interests.

The territorial disputes that China are engaged in do not help to assuage China's skeptics. While the territorial disputes are regional, they vividly revive the worry about hegemony and China's communist/socialist identity. To further its reform agenda and the acceptance of the RMB overseas, China has to overcome not only economic matters — political factors at times can triumph over economic considerations.

7.4 China's Currency in the Global Financial System

China's economic and finance reform programs have assigned an increasing role to demand and supply factors in allocating resources and guiding economic activities. The reforms have fostered China's integration with the rest of the world. As the main price that connects the domestic economy and the global market, the RMB exchange rate and its formation mechanism are an important component of China's efforts to transform its economy to a modern global one.

The accomplishments of economic reforms in growth and trade provide a firm underpinning for China's efforts to advance the global status of its currency. Since the 2008 global financial crisis, the world has witnessed a brisk increase in the volume of cross-border trade settled in RMB. For instance, the RMB's ranking as an international payment currency advanced from the 30th position in January 2011 to the fifth rank in November 2014.[15] The use of the RMB overseas has an initial concentration around the Asian region and is then gradually spread to other parts of

---

[15] The top four currencies are Japanese yen, British pound, euro, and US dollar. See SWIFT (2012, 2015a).

the world. The rapid global penetration creates attractive business opportunities that are hard to ignore for financial centers around the global.

The overseas use of its currency offers China a few benefits. In addition to reduce its reliance on other currencies for its international transactions, the RMB's going global policy is a compliment, and possibly a stimulant of China's financial liberalization policy.[16] Financial reforms are introduced along with the increases in the scope and scale of cross-border RMB transactions. Despite these reform measures, China still has a tight command over its financial markets, and full convertibility is still a goal to be accomplished.

In the last few decades, the world's sentiment about China has been swayed by its reform efforts and the outcome. The metaphor "two steps forward, one step back" or "one step back, two steps forward" is used at times to describe the progress in China's reforms. Nevertheless, China's overall achievement has slowly lent its credibility of maintaining a steadfast, though not necessarily evenly paced, reform rhythm. Against this backdrop, the RMB is gaining its acceptance in the global system. In addition to Chinese concerted efforts, the RMB's ascendant benefits from the credibility test faced by the prominent global currency; the US dollar, during and after the 2008 global financial crisis, which has triggered the debate on the danger of building the international monetary system around a single currency. The euro and Japanese yen — two other main global currencies — are confronted by their own credibility challenges due to sovereign debts and prolonged economic stagnation.

China's credibility of liberalizing its economy was questioned after its abrupt responses to the wild gyrations of the Chinese equity prices and foreign exchange rate in the summer 2015. The heavy-handed intervention measures that are meant to arrest market volatility and support prices sent a chilling shock wave across markets overseas. The market turmoil, on the one hand, highlights the economic imbalances in China and, on the other hand, illustrates the authorities' ineptitude in managing the growing economy. The choices of strong administrative means have raised the concern about China's ability or commitment to

---

[16] Some argue that China is seeking the global status of the RMB that is commensurate with its mighty economic strength.

continue its efforts to transit towards the market-based economic system, and to implement further reforms. The loss of policy credibility can impair the RMB's global image.

Undoubtedly, the market interruptions experienced by China in 2015 have crystallized several problems in its reform program, and remind us the challenges faced by the Chinese economy ahead. Nevertheless, bar from unexpected fundamental changes in its development strategy, China is almost certainly going to continue its economic reform and financial liberalization process, which are reaffirmed repeatedly even after the market turmoil. Since 1978, China's reform has run into speed bump a few times and has demonstrated its ability to overcome them and move on. The 2015 summer event will not be the last glitch from the ongoing (and long) reform process. The China meltdown scenario that has been depicted in various forms in the last few decades, however, is quite unlikely to occur.

Anecdotal evidence revealed by, for example, economic data in 2010 are in accordance with the officially declared rebalancing efforts of steering growth away from fixed (inefficient) investment and manufacturing toward consumption and services. The progress is moderate so far. To be fair, the transformation to a market-based and consumption led economy takes time and can entail some unexpected challenges; it is especially true for China whose economic infrastructure is arguably dated and the reform is still work in progress. The switch in the growth engine is meant to advance China to a sustainable, though, lower growth path in the medium to long run. The rebalancing act and the accompanying structural changes can cause short-term economic slowdown and economic pains in exchange of a more stable economic environment ahead.

Against this backdrop, we expect the RMB's role in the global system will gradually expand alongside China's reform success and increasing financial strength. China is going to consolidate RMB's position in servicing international trade transactions, and to lay a firm groundwork for RMB to participate fully in the global financial system. Given the complex economic and political nexus underlying a global currency, the overseas acceptance of the RMB, after the initial burst, is likely to grow slowly instead of exhibiting another quantum jump. The RMB is (or will be) is a global currency that goes beyond regional uses. However, it is unlikely for the RMB to "dethrone" the US dollar in international monetary system in anytime soon.

The introduction of the RMB to the global monetary system presents challenges to the incumbent global currencies. At the same time, a global RMB offers countries around the world an alternative means to conduct international transactions, and to diversify their international portfolios. With a responsible Chinese monetary policy and peaceful growth model, a global RMB adds liquidity to the world and supports global economic growth.

References

Ahmed, Shaghil, (2009), "Are Chinese Exports Sensitive to Changes in the Exchange Rate?" International Finance Discussion. Washington, D.C.: Federal Reserve Board, December, Paper No. 987.

Aizenman, Joshua, (2004), "Endogenous Pricing to Market and Financing Costs." *Journal of Monetary Economics*, 51(4), 691–712.

Aizenman, Joshua, Yin-Wong Cheung and Hiro Ito, (2015), "International Reserves Before and After the Global Crisis: Is There No End to Hoarding?" *Journal of International Money and Finance*, 52 (April), 102–126.

Aizenman, Joshua, Yothin Jinjarak and Donghyun Park, (2011), "International Reserves and Swap Lines: Substitutes or Complements?" *International Review of Economics and Finance*, 20(1), 5–18.

Aizenman, Joshua and Jaewoo Lee, (2007), "International Reserves: Precautionary Versus Mercantilist Views, Theory and Evidence," *Open Economies Review*, 18, 191–214.

Aizenman, Joshua, Yeonho Lee and Youngseop Rhee, (2007), "International Reserves Management and Capital Mobility in a Volatile World: Policy Considerations and a Case Study of Korea." *Journal of the Japanese and International Economies*, 21, 1–15.

Aizenman, Joshua and Nancy Marion, (2003), "The High demand for International Reserves in the Far East: What's Going On?" *Journal of the Japanese and International Economies*, 17, 370–400.

Aizenman, Joshua and Nancy Marion, (2004), "International Reserve Holdings with Sovereign Risk and Costly Tax Collection." *The Economic Journal*, 114, 569–591.

231

Aizenman, Joshua and Gurnain Kaur Pasricha, (2010), "Selective Swap Arrangements and the Global Financial Crisis: Analysis and Interpretation." *International Review of Economics and Finance*, 19(3), 353–365.

Alquist, Ron and Menzie D. Chinn, (2008), "Conventional and Unconventional Approaches to Exchange Rate Modelling and Assessment." *International Journal of Finance and Economics*, 13, 2–13.

Apte, Prakash, Marian Kane and Piet Sercu, (1994), "Relative PPP in the Medium Run." *Journal of International Money and Finance*, 13(5), 602–622.

Asia Pacific Foundation of Canada, (2005), "China Goes Global: A Survey of Chinese Companies' Outward Direct Investment Intentions." Asia Pacific Foundation of Canada.

Asia Pacific Foundation of Canada, (2006), "China Goes Global — II, 2006 Survey of Chinese Companies' Outward Direct Investment Intentions." Asia Pacific Foundation of Canada.

Asian Development Bank, (2007), "Purchasing Power Parities and Real Expenditures." Manila, Philippines: Asian Development Bank, December.

Aziz, Jahangir and Christoph Duenwald, (2001), "China's Provincial Growth Dynamics." *IMF Working Paper* No. WP/01/3.

Aziz, Jahangir and Xiangming Li, (2008), "China's Changing Trade Elasticities." *China and the World Economy*, 16(3), 1–21.

Bacchetta, Philippe, Eric van Wincoop and Toni Beutler, (2010), "Can Parameter Instability Explain the Meese–Rogoff Puzzle?" in Lucrezia Reichlin and Kenneth D. West (eds.), *NBER International Seminar on Macroeconomics 2009*, Chicago and London: University of Chicago Press, pp. 125–173.

Bai, Jennie, Michael Fleming and Casidhe Horan, (2013), "The Microstructure of China's Government Bond Market." *Federal Reserve Bank of New York Staff Report*, No. 622.

Balassa, Bela, (1964), "The Purchasing Power Parity Doctrine: A Reappraisal." *Journal of Political Economy*, 72(6), 584–596.

Bank for International Settlements, (2013), "Triennial Central Bank Survey of Foreign Exchange and Derivatives Market Activity in 2013, Basel."

Bank for International Settlements, (2010), "Triennial Central Bank Survey: Foreign Exchange and Derivative Market Activity in 2010, Basel."

Bank for International Settlements, (2007), "Triennial Central Bank Survey of Foreign Exchange and Derivatives Market Activity in 2007, Basel."

Bank for International Settlements, (2004), "Triennial Central Bank Survey of Foreign Exchange and Derivatives Market Activity in 2004, Basel."

Bank for International Settlements, (1995), "Triennial Central Bank Survey of Foreign Exchange and Derivatives Market Activity, 1995, Basel."

Bank of China, (1980), "Provisional Regulations of the Bank of China of Foreign Exchange Certificate." Available at: http://www.boc.cn/en/aboutboc/ab7/200809/t20080926_1601850.html

Bayoumi, Tamim and Franziska Ohnsorge, (2013), "Do Inflows or Outflows Dominate? Global Implications of Capital Account Liberalization in China." *IMF Working Paper,* No. WP/13/189.

Benkovskis, Konstantins and Julia Wörz, (2015), "'Made in China' — How Does It Affect Our Understanding of Global Market Shares?" *ECB Working Paper* No. 1787.

Bergsten, C. Fred, (2007), "The Chinese Exchange Rate and the US Economy." *Testimony before the Senate Committee on Banking, Housing and Urban Affairs, January 31.*

Bergsten, C. Fred, (2010a), "Correcting the Chinese Exchange Rate." *Testimony before the Hearing on China's Exchange Rate Policy, Committee on Ways and Means, US House of Representatives.*

Bergsten, C. Fred, (2010b), "We Can Fight Fire with Fire on the Renminbi." *Financial Times,* p. 4.

Bergsten, C. Fred and Joseph E. Gagnon, (2012), "Currency Manipulation, the US Economy, and the Global Economic Order." *Policy Brief 12–25.* Washington, D.C.: Peterson Institute for International Economics.

Berkowitz, Jeremy and Lorenzo Giorgianni, (2001). "Long-Horizon Exchange Rate Predictability?" *Review of Economics and Statistics,* 83(1), 81–91.

Bhagwati, Jagdish, (1984), "Why Are Services Cheaper in the Poor Countries?" *Economic Journal,* 94(374), 279–286.

Bhaumik, Suman K. and Catherine Yap Co, (2011), "China's Economic Cooperation Related Investment: An Investigation of Its Direction and Some Implications for Outward Investment." *China Economic Review,* 22, 75–87.

Bradsher, Keith, (2004), "Is China the Next Bubble?" *New York Times.*

Bräutigam, Deborah (2009), *The Dragon's Gift: The Real Story of China in Africa,* Oxford: Oxford University Press.

Broadman, Harry, (2007), "Africa's Silk Road: China and India's New Economic Frontier." Washington, D.C.: The World Bank.

Brummer, Chris, (2015), "Renminbi Ascending: How China's Currency Impacts Global Markets, Foreign Policy, and Transatlantic Financial Regulation." Washington, D.C.: Atlantic Council.

Buckley, Peter. J., Jeremy Clegg, Adam Cross, Xin Liu, Hinrich Voss and Ping Zheng (2007), "The Determinants of Chinese Outward Foreign Direct Investment." *Journal of International Business Studies,* 38, 499–518.

Cabinet Office, Government of Japan, (2002), "Annual Report on the Japanese Economy and Public Finance, 2001–2002." Available at: http://www5.cao. go.jp/zenbun/wp-e/wp-je02/wp-je02-00301.html

Cairns, John, (2005a), "China: How Undervalued is the CNY?" *IDEA global Economic Research (June 27)*.

Carter, Ben, (2014), "Is China's Economy Really the Largest in the World?" *BBC News*, December 16. Available at: http://www.bbc.com/news/magazine-30483762.

Cerra, Valerie and Anuradha, Dayal-Gulati, (1999), "China's Trade Flows-Changing Price Sensitivities and the Reform Process." *IMF Working Paper* No. 99/01.

Cerra, Valerie and Sweta Chaman Saxena, (2010). "The Monetary Model Strikes Back: Evidence from the World." *Journal of International Economics*, 81(2), 184–196.

Cerra, Valerie and Sweta Chaman Saxena, (2002), "An Empirical Analysis of China's Export Behavior." *IMF Working Paper* No. 02/200.

Cevik, Serhan and Carolina Correa-Caro, (2015), "Growing (Un)equal: Fiscal Policy and Income Inequality in China and BRIC+." *IMF Working Paper*, No. WP/15/68.

Chan, Ray, (2014), "China's Renminbi Currency to Become 10 Per Cent of Global Reserves by 2025." Available at: http://www.scmp.com/business/money/money-news/article/1765304/chinas-renmimbi-currency-become-10-cent-global-reserves)

Chantasasawat, Busakorn, K.C. Fung, Hitomi Iizaka and Alan Siu, (2004), "The Giant Sucking Sound: Is China Diverting Foreign Direct Investment from Other Asian Economies?" *Asian Economic Papers*, 3(3), 122–140.

Chantasasawat, Busakorn, K.C. Fung, Hitomi Iizaka and Alan Siu, (2003), "International Competition for Foreign Direct Investment: The Case of China." *Paper presented at the Hitotsubashi Conference on International Trade and FDI*.

Chen, Hongyi, Wensheng Peng and Chang Shu, (2009), "Renminbi as an International Currency: Potential and Policy Considerations." *HKIMR Working Paper* No. 18/2009.

Chen, Hongyi and Wensheng Peng (2010), "The Potential of the Renminbi as an International Currency," in Wensheng Peng and Chang Shu (eds.), *Currency Internationalization: Global Experiences and Implications for the Renminbi*, Palgrave Macmillan, Chapter 5, pp. 115–138.

Chen, Jinzhao, (2013), "Crisis, Capital Controls and Covered Interest Parity: Evidence from China in Transformation," in Yin-Wong Cheung and Jakob De Haan (eds.), *The Evolving Role of China in the Global Economy*, MIT Press, Chapter 11, pp. 339–371.

Chen, Michelle, (2014), "Reserve Managers See Yuan Taking 12.5 pct of Global Reserves by 2030." *HSBC Survey.* Available at: http://www.reuters.com/article/2015/04/13/china-yuan-offshore-idUSL4N0XA1UT20150413

Chen, Shaohua and Martin Ravallion. (2010a), "China Is Poorer than We Thought, but No Less Successful in the Fight against Poverty," in Sudhir Anand, Paul Segal and Joseph E. Stiglitz (eds.), *Debates on the Measurement of Global Poverty,* New York: Oxford University Press, pp. 327–40.

Chen, Shaohua and Martin Ravallion, (2010b), "The Developing World is Poorer than We Thought, but No Less Successful in the Fight against Poverty." *Quarterly Journal of Economics,* 125, 1577–1625.

Chen, Xiaoli and Yin-Wong Cheung, (2011), "Renminbi Going Global." *China & World Economy,* 19, 1–18.

Chen, Yu-chin, Kenneth S. Rogoff and Barbara Rossi, (2010), "Can Exchange Rates Forecast Commodity Prices." *Quarterly Journal of Economics,* 125(3), 1145–1194.

Cheng, Leonard K. and Yum Kwan, (2000), "What Are the Determinants of the Location of Foreign Direct Investment? The Chinese Experience." *Journal of International Economics,* 51, 379–400.

Cheremukhin, Anton, Mikhail Golosov, Sergei Guriev and Aleh Tsyvinski, (2015),"The Economy of People's Republic of China from 1953." *National Bureau of Economic Research, Working Paper* No. 21397.

Cheung, Yin-Wong, (2012), "Exchange Rate Misalignment — The Case of the Chinese Renminbi," in Jessica James, Ian W. Marsh and Lucio Sarno (eds), *Handbook of Exchange Rates,* John Wiley & Sons, Inc, Chapter 27, 751–765.

Cheung, Yin-Wong, (2015), "The Role of Offshore Financial Centers in the Process of Renminbi Internationalization," in Barry Eichengreen and Masahiro Kawai (eds), *Renminbi Internationalization: Achievements, Prospects, and Challenges,* Brookings Institution Press and Asian Development Bank, Chapter 7, 207–235.

Cheung, Yin-Wong and Menzie D. Chinn, (1996), "Deterministic, Stochastic, and Segmented Trends in Aggregate Output: A Cross-Country Analysis." *Oxford Economic Papers,* 48, 134–162.

Cheung, Yin-Wong, Menzie D. Chinn and Eiji Fujii, (2007a), "The Economic Integration of Greater China: Real and Financial Linkages and the Prospects for Currency Union" *Hong Kong: Hong Kong University Press.*

Cheung, Yin-Wong, Menzie D. Chinn, and Eiji Fujii, (2007b), "The Overvaluation of Renminbi Undervaluation," *Journal of International Money and Finance,* 26(5) (September), 762–785.

Cheung, Yin-Wong, Menzie D. Chinn and Eiji Fujii, (2010a), "China's Current Account and Exchange Rate," in Robert Feenstra and Shing-Jin Wei, (eds),

China's Growing Role in World Trade, University of Chicago Press for NBER. Chapter 9, 231–271.

Cheung, Yin-Wong, Menzie D. Chinn and Eiji Fujii. (2010b.), "Measuring Misalignment: Latest Estimates for the Chinese Renminbi," in Simon Evenett (eds), *The US-Sino Currency Dispute: New Insights from Economics, Politics and Law*, A VoxEU.org Publication. Chapter 10, 79–90.

Cheung, Yin-Wong, Menzie D. Chinn and Eiji Fujii. (2010c), "Measuring Renminbi Misalignment: Where Do We Stand?" *Korea and the World Economy* 11, 263–296.

Cheung, Yin-Wong, Menzie D. Chinn, and Eiji Fujii, (2011), "A Note on the Debate over Renminbi Undervaluation," in Yin-Wong Cheung and Guonan Ma (eds), *Asia and China in the Global Economy*, World Scientific Publishing Co. Chapter 6, 155–187.

Cheung, Yin-Wong, Menzie D. Chinn and Xin Nong, (2016), "Estimating Currency Misalignment Using the Penn Effect: It's Not As Simple As It Looks," *National Bureau of Economic Research Working Paper Series* No. 22539.

Cheung, Yin-Wong, Menzie D. Chinn and Antonio Garcia Pascual, (2005), "Empirical Exchange Rate Models of the Nineties: Are Any Fit to Survive?" *Journal of International Money and Finance*, 24, 1150–1175.

Cheung, Yin-Wong, Menzie D. Chinn and XingWang Qian, (2012), "Are Chinese Trade Flows Different?", *Journal of International Money and Finance*, 31 (December), 2127–2146.

Cheung, Yin-Wong, Menzie D. Chinn, and Xingwang Qian, (2016), "China-US Trade Flow Behavior: The Implications of Alternative Exchange Rate Measures and Trade Classifications," *Review of World Economics*, 152, 43–67.

Cheung, Yin-Wong, and Ulf G. Erlandsson. (2005). "Exchange Rates and Markov Switching Dynamics."*Journal of Business and Economic Statistics*, 23(3), 314–320.

Cheung, Yin-Wong and Eiji Fujii, (2014), "Exchange Rate Misalignment Estimates — Sources of Differences," *International Journal of Finance and Economics*, 19(2) (March), 91–121.

Cheung, Yin-Wong, Jakob de Haan, XingWang Qian and Shu Yu (2012), "China's Outward Direct Investment in Africa," *Review of International Economics*, 20(2), 201–220.

Cheung, Yin-Wong, Jakob de Haan, XingWang Qian and Shu Yu (2013), "China's Investments in Africa," in Yin-Wong Cheung and Jakob de Haan (eds), *The Evolving Role of China in the World Economy*, MIT Press, 419–444.

Cheung, Yin-Wong, Jakob de Haan, XingWang Qian, and Shu Yu, (2014), "The Missing Link: China's Contracted Engineering Projects in Africa," *Review of Development Economics*, 18(3), 564–580.

Cheung, Yin-Wong and Risto Herrala, (2014), "China's Capital Controls — Through the Prism of Covered Interest Differentials," *Pacific Economic Review*, 19, 112–134.

Cheung, Yin-Wong, Cho-Hoi Hui and Andrew Tsang, (2016), The Renminbi Central Parity: An Empirical Investigation, *HKIMR Working Paper* 2016–10.

Cheung, Yin-Wong and Hiro Ito, (2008), "Hoarding of International Reserves: A Comparison of the Asian and Latin American Experiences," in Ramkishen S. Rajan, Shandre Thangavelu, and Rasyad A Parinduri (eds), *Exchange Rate, Monetary and Financial Issues and Policies in Asia*, World Scientific Press, 77–115.

Cheung, Yin-Wong and Hiro Ito, (2009), "A Cross-Country Empirical Analysis of International Reserves," *International Economic Journal*, 23, 447–481.

Cheung, Yin-Wong and Kon S. Lai, (2000), "On Cross-Country Differences in the Persistence of Real Exchange Rates," *Journal of International Economics*, 50(2), 375–397.

Cheung, Yin-Wong, Kon S. Lai, and Mike Bergman (2004), Dissecting the PPP puzzle: The unconventional roles of nominal exchange rate and price adjustments, *Journal of International Economics*, 64, 135–150.

Cheung, Yin-Wong, Guonan Ma and Robert N. McCauley, (2011a), "Renminbising China's foreign assets," *Pacific Economic Review*, 16 (February), 1–17.

Cheung, Yin-Wong, Guonan Ma and Robert N. McCauley, (2011b), "Why Does China Attempt to Internationalise the Renminbi?" in Jane Golley and Ligang Song (eds), *Rising China: Global Challenges and Opportunities* (June), the ANU E Press. Chapter 4, 45–68.

Cheung, Yin-Wong and Hui Miao, (2014), "The offshore RMB market in Hong Kong and RMB Internationalization," in Inderjit Kaur and Nirvikar Singh, (eds), *Oxford Handbook of the Economics of the Pacific Rim*, Oxford University Press, Chapter 26, 649–666.

Cheung, Yin-Wong and XingWang Qian (2009a), "Empirics of China's Outward Direct Investment," *Pacific Economic Review*, 14, 312–341.

Cheung, Yin-Wong and Xingwang Qian. (2009b), "Hoarding of International Reserves: Mrs Machlup's Wardrobe and the Joneses," *Review of International Economics*, 17(4), 824–843.

Cheung, Yin-Wong and Xingwang Qian, (2010), "Capital Flight: China's Experience," *Review of Development Economics*, 14(2), 227–247.

Cheung, Yin-Wong and XingWang Qian (2011), "Deviations from Covered Interest Parity: The Case of China," in Yin-Wong Cheung, Vikas Kakkar and Guonan Ma (eds), *The Evolving Role of Asia in Global Finance* — Frontiers of Economics and Globalization Volume 9, Emerald Group Publishing Limited, Chapter 15, 369–386.

Cheung, Yin-Wong and Rajeswari Sengupta, (2011), "Accumulation of Reserves and Keeping Up with the Joneses: The Case of LATAM Economies," *International Review of Economics and Finance*, 20 (January), 19–31.

Cheung, Yin-Wong, Sven Steinkamp, and Frank Westermann, (2016), "China's Capital Flight: Pre- and Post-Crisis Experiences," *Journal of International Money and Finance*, 66 (September), 88–112.

Cheung, Yin-Wong, Clement Yuk-Pang Wong, (2008), "Are All Measures of International Reserves Created Equal? An Empirical Comparison of International Reserve Ratios," Economics: The Open-Access, Open-Assessment E-Journal, Vol. 2, http://www.economics-ejournal.org/economics/journalarticles/2008-15.

Chinn, Menzie D., (2006), "A Primer on Real Effective Exchange Rates: Determinants, Overvaluation, Trade Flows and Competitive Devaluations." *Open Economies Review*, 17(1) (January), 115–143.

Chinn, Menzie D. and Jeffrey Frankel, (2007), "Will the Euro Eventually Surpass the Dollar as Leading International Reserve Currency?" in Richard Clarida (ed.), *G7 Current Account Imbalances: Sustainability and Adjustment*, University of Chicago Press, pp. 285–322.

Chinn, Menzie D. and Richard A. Meese, (1995), "Banking on Currency Forecasts: How Predictable Is Change in Money?" *Journal of International Economics*, 38(1–2), 161–178.

Ciccone, Antonio and Marek Jarocinksi, (2010), "Determinants of Economic Growth: Will Data Tell?" *American Economic Journal: Macroeconomics*, 2(4), 223–247.

Clark, Peter B., Leonardo Bartolini, Tamim Bayoumi and Steven Symansky, (1994)." Exchange Rates and Economic Fundamentals: A Framework for Analysis." *IMF Occasional Paper*, No. 115, Washington: International Monetary Fund.

Clark, Peter B. and Ronald MacDonald, (1998), "Exchange Rates and Economic Fundamentals: A Methodological Comparison of BEERs and FEERs." *IMF Working Paper* No. 98/67.

Cline William R. (2015), "Estimates of Fundamental Equilibrium Exchange Rates, May 2015." *Policy Brief 15-8.* Washington, D.C.: Peterson Institute for International Economics.

Cline, William R., John Williamson, (2008a), "New Estimates of Fundamental Equilibrium Exchange Rates." *Policy Brief 08-7.* Washington: Peterson Institute for International Economics.

Cline, William R. and John Williamson, (2008b), "Estimates of the Equilibrium Exchange Rate of the Renminbi: Is There a Consensus and, If Not, Why Not?" in M. Goldstein and Nicholas R. Lardy (eds.), *Debating China's Exchange Rate*

Policy, Nicholas Washington, D.C.: Peterson Institute for International Economics, pp. 131–168.

Cline, William R. and John Williamson, (2010), "Notes on Equilibrium Exchange Rates: January 2010." *Policy Brief PB10-2*. Washington, D.C.: Peterson Institute for International Economics.

Coakley, Jerry, Robert P. Flood, Ana M. Fuertes and Mark P. Taylor, (2005), "Purchasing Power Parity and the Theory of General Relativity: The First Tests." *Journal of International Money and Finance*, 24(2), 293–316.

Cohen, Benjamin J., (1971), *The Future of Sterling as an International Currency*, Macmillan.

Cohen, Benjamin J., (2009), "The Future of Reserve Currencies." *Finance & Development*, 46(3), 26–29.

Committee on the Global Financial System, (2010), "The Functioning and Resilience of Cross-Border Funding Markets." *CGFS Report* No. 37 (March).

Corkin, Lucy, Christopher Burke and Martyn Davies, (2008), "China's Role in the Development of Africa's Infrastructure." *SAIS Working Papers in African Studies 04-08*, John Hopkins University.

Coudert, Virginie and Cécile Couharde, (2007), "Real Equilibrium Exchange rate in China: Is the Renminbi Undervalued?" *Journal of Asian Economics* 18(4), 568–594.

CRS Report for Congress, (2012), "Pivot to the Pacific? The Obama Administration's 'Rebalancing' Toward Asia." Mark E. Manyin (Coordinator), Congressional Research Service. Available at: http://fas.org/sgp/crs/natsec/R42448.pdf.

Dawson, John W., Joseph P. DeJuan, John J. Seater and E. Frank Stephenson, (2001), "Economic Information versus Quality Variation in Cross-country Data." *Canadian Journal of Economics*, 34(4), 988–1009.

de Beaufort Wijnholds, J. Onno and Arie Kapteyn, (2001), "International Reserve Adequacy in Emerging Market Economies." *IMF Working Paper* No. 01/43.

Deaton, Angus and Alan Heston, (2010), "Understanding PPPs and PPP-based National Accounts." *American Economic Journal: Macroeconomics*, 2, 1–35.

Dekle, Robert and Murat Ungor, (2013), "The Real Exchange Rate and the Structural Transformation(s) of China and the U.S." *International Economic Journal*, 27(2), 303–319.

Démurger, Sylvie, Jeffrey D. Sachs, Wing Thye Woo, Shuming Bao, Gene Chang and Andrew Mellinger, (2002), "Geography, Economic Policy, and Regional Development in China." *Asian Economic Papers*, 1, 146–197.

Ding, David, Yiuman Tse and Michael Williams, (2014), "The Price Discovery Puzzle in Offshore Yuan Trading: Different Contributions for Different Contracts," *The Journal of Futures Markets*, 34(2), 103-123.

Dornbusch, Rudiger, (1976). "Expectations and Exchange Rate Dynamics." *Journal of Political Economy,* 84(6), 1161–1176.

Dorrucci, Ettore, Gabor Pula and Daniel Santabárbara, (2013), "China's Economic Growth and Rebalancing", *European Central Bank Occasional Paper Series* No. 142.

Dufey Gunter and Ian Giddy, (1994), *The International Money Market,* 2nd ed., Prentice Hall International Inc. New Jersey.

Dunaway, Steven, Lamin Leigh and Xiangming Li, (2009), "How Robust are Estimates of Equilibrium Real Exchange Rates: The Case of China." *Pacific Economic Review,* 14(3), 361–375.

Economist Intelligence Unit, (2014), "Renminbi rising: Onshore and Offshore Perspectives on Chinese Financial Liberalization." *The Economist.*

Eichengreen, Barry, (2011), *Exorbitant Privilege: The Rise and Fall of the Dollar and the Future of the International Monetary System,* Oxford University Press.

Eichengreen, Barry, (2013), "Renminbi Internationalization: Tempest in a Teapot?" *Asian Development Review,* 30, 148–164.

Eichengreen, Barry, (2014), "International Currencies Past, Present and Future: Two Views from Economic History." *Bank of Korea,* WP No. 2014–31.

Eichengreen, Barry and Marc Flandreau, (2012), "The Federal Reserve, the Bank of England, and the Rise of the Dollar as an International Currency, 1914–1939." *Open Economies Review,* 23(1), 57–87.

Eichengreen, Barry and Jeffrey A. Frankel, (1996), "On the SDR: Reserve Currencies and the Future of the International Monetary System." Manuscript, UCB.

Eichengreen, Barry, Yeongseop Rhee and Hui Tong, (2007), "China and the Exports of Other Asian Countries." *Review of World Economics,* 143(2), 201–226.

Eichengreen, Barry and Hui Tong, (2007), "Is China's FDI Coming at the Expense of Other Countries?" *Journal of the Japanese and International Economies,* 21, 153–172.

Elekdag, Selim and Subir Lall, (2008), "International Statistical Comparison: Global Growth Estimates Trimmed After PPP Revisions." *IMF Survey Magazine.* Washington, D.C.: IMF, January 8.

Engel, Charles, Nelson C. Mark and Kenneth D. West, (2008), "Exchange Rate Models are not as Bad as You Think," in Daron Acemoglu, Kenneth S. Rogoff and Michael Woodford (eds.), *NBER Macroeconomics Annual 2007,* Chicago and London: University of Chicago Press, pp. 381–444.

Engel, Charles, (2009), "Exchange Rate Policies." *Staff Papers,* Federal Reserve Bank of Dallas.

Ernst and Young, (2015), "European Attractiveness Survey 2015." Ernst & Young Global Limited.

European Central Bank, (2013), "The International Role of the Euro." European Central Bank.

Faust, Jon, John Rogers and Jonathan Wright, (2000), "News and Noise in G-7 GDP Announcements." Board of Governors of the Federal Reserve System, *International Finance and Discussion Papers* No. 690.

Fernald, John, Eric Hsu and Mark M. Spiegel, (2015), "Is China Fudging its Figures? Evidence from Trading Partner Data." *Federal Reserve Bank of San Francisco Working Paper Series, Working Paper* No. 2015-12.

Fernald, John, Hali Edison and Prakash Loungani, (1999), "Was China the First Domino? Assessing Links between China and Other Asian Economies." *Journal of International Money and Finance*, 18(4), 515–535.

Finance and Strategy, Policy and Review Departments, IMF, (2011), "Criteria for Broadening the SDR Currency Basket." International Monetary Fund.

Fischer, Christoph and Oliver Hossfeld, (2014), "A Consistent Set of Multilateral Productivity Approach-based Indicators of Price Competitiveness — Results for Pacific Rim Economies." *Journal of International Money and Finance*, 49, Part A, 152–169.

Flood, Robert P. and Nancy Marion, (2002), "Holding International Reserves in an Era of High Capital Mobility." *IMF Working Paper* No. 02/62.

Foster, Vivien, William Butterfield, Chuan Chen and Nataliya Pushak, (2008), "Building Bridges: China's Growing Role as Infrastructure Financier for Sub-Saharan Africa." Washington, D.C.: World Bank.

Franke, Günter, (1999), "The Bundesbank and the Markets," in Deutsche Bundesbank (eds.), *Fifty Years of the Deutsche Mark: Central Bank and the Currency in Germany since 1948*, Oxford: Oxford University Press, Chapter V, pp. 219–267.

Frankel, Jeffrey A., (2006), "On the Yuan: The Choice between Adjustment under a Fixed Exchange Rate and Adjustment under a Flexible Rate." *CESifo Economic Studies*, 52(2), 246–275.

Frankel, Jeffrey A., (2009), "New Estimation of China's Exchange Rate Regime." *Pacific Economic Review*, 14, 346–360.

Frankel, Jeffrey A., (2010), "Comment on 'China's Current Account and Exchange Rate'," in R. Feenstra and S.J. Wei (eds.), *China's Growing Role in World Trade*, University of Chicago Press for NBER.

Frankel, Jeffrey A., (2012), "Internationalization of the RMB and Historical Precedents." *Journal of Economic Integration*, 27, 329–365.

Frankel, Jeffery (2014), "China is not yet Number One." Available at: http://www. voxeu.org/article/china-not-yet-number-one.

Fu, Xiaolan, Raphael Kaplinsky and Jing Zhang, (2012). "The Impact of China on Low and Middle Income Countries, Export Prices in Industrial Country Markets." *World Development*, 40(8), 1483–1496.

Fujita, Masahisa and Dapeng Hu, (2001), "Regional Disparity in China 1985–94: The Effects of Globalization and Economic Liberalization." *Annals of Regional Science*, 35(1), 3–37.

Fung, K.C., Hitomi Iizaka and Alan Siu, (2003), "Japanese Direct Investment in China." *China Economic Review*, 14, 304–315.

Fung, K.C., Hitomi Iizaka and Stephen Parker, (2002), "Determinants of U.S. and Japanese Direct Investment in China." *Journal of Comparative Economics*, 30, 567–578.

Fung, K.C., Lawrence J. Lau and Joseph Lee, (2004), *U.S. Direct Investment in China*, AEI Press, American Enterprise Institute for Public Policy Research, Washington, D.C.

Fung, San-Saw, Marc Klau, Guonan Ma and Robert McCauley, (2009), "Implications of Refined Renminbi Effective Exchange Rates with Asian Entrepôt and Intra-regional Trade," in Yin-Wong Cheung and Kar-Yiu Wong (eds.), *China and Asia: Economic and Financial Interactions*, London: Routledge, pp. 178–193.

Funke, Michael and Marc Gronwald, (2008), "The Undisclosed Renminbi Basket: Are the Markets Telling Us Something about Where the Renminbi–US Dollar Exchange Rate is Going?" *The World Economy*, 31, 1581–1598.

Funke, Michael and Jörg Rahn, (2005), "Just How Undervalued is the Chinese Renminbi?" *World Economy*, 28, 465–489.

Gagnon, Joseph and Gary Hufbauer, (2011), "Taxing China's Assets: How to Increase U.S. Employment Without Launching a Trade War." *Foreign Affairs (online)*.

Garcia-Herrero, Alicia and Le Xia, (2015). "RMB Bilateral Swap Agreements: How China Chooses Its Partners?" *Asia-Pacific Journal of Accounting & Economics*, DOI: 10.1080/16081625.2014.960059

Garcia-Herrero, Alicia and Tuuli Koivu, (2007), "Can the Chinese Trade Surplus Be Reduced through Exchange Rate Policy?" *BOFIT Discussion Papers* No. 2007-6, Helsinki: Bank of Finland, March.

Gaulier, Guillaume, Françoise Lemoine and Deniz Ünal, (2006), "China's Emergence and the Reorganization of Trade Flows in Asia." *CEPII Working Paper* No. 2006-05. Paris: CEPII, March.

Gauthier-Villars, David, (2011), "France Proposes Way to Raise Yuan." *Wall Street Journal*, p. A.9.

Genberg, Hans, (2009), "Currency Internationalisation: Analytical and Policy Issues." *HKIMR Working Paper* No. 31.

Genberg, Hans, Robert McCauley, Avinash Persaud and Yung Chul Park (2005), "Official Reserves and Currency Management in Asia: Myth, Reality and the Future, Geneva Reports on the World Economy." Number 7. Geneva and London: International Centre for Monetary and Banking Studies and Centre for Economic Policy Research.

Goldberg, Linda S. and Cédric Tille, (2008), "Vehicle Currency Use in International Trade." *Journal of International Economics*, 76, 177–192.

Goldstein, Morris and Nicholas Lardy, (2009), "The Future of China's Exchange Rate Policy." *Policy Analyses in International Economics* 87, Washington, DC: Peterson Institute for International Economics (July).

Greenspan, A., (2001), "The Euro as an International Currency." Paper presented at the Euro 50 Group Roundtable, November 30.

Gunter, Frank R., (1996), "Capital Flight from the People's Republic of China: 1984–1994." *China Economic Review*, 7, 77–96.

Gunter, Frank R., (2004), "Capital Flight from China: 1984–2001." *China Economic Review*, 15, 63–85.

Hale, Galina and Cheryl Long, (2011), "Are There Productivity Spillovers from Foreign Direct Investment in China?" *Pacific Economic Review*, 16(2), 135–153.

Hanemann, Thilo and Mikko Huotari, (2015), "Chinese FDI in Europe and Germany: Preparing for a New Era of Chinese Capital." Mercator Institute for China Studies and Rhodium Group, LLC.

Hassan, Fadi, 2014. The Price of Development, *The Institute for International Integration Studies Discussion Paper Series* No. 446 (Dublin: Trinity College).

He, Dong and Robert N. McCauley, (2013), "Offshore Markets for the Domestic Currency: Monetary and Financial Stability Issues," in Yin-Wong Cheung and Jakob de Haan (eds.), *The Evolving Role of China in the Global Economy*, Cambridge, Mass: MIT Press, Chapter 10, pp. 301–337.

Henderson, J. Vernon, Adam Storeygard and David N. Weil, (2012), "Measuring Economic Growth from Outer Space." *American Economic Review*, 102(2), pp. 994–1028.

Hockenhull, Thomas (ed.), (2015), *Symbols of Power: Ten Coins that Change the World*, Columbia University Press.

Holmes, Mark J., (2000), "Does Purchasing Power Parity Hold in African Less Developed Countries? Evidence from a Panel Data Unit Root Test." *Journal of African Economies*, 9(1), 63–78.

Holz, Carsten A., (2004), "China's Statistical System in Transition: Challenges, Data Problems, and Institutional Innovations." *Review of Income and Wealth*, 50(3), 381–409.

Holz, Carsten A., (2014), "Can We Trust The Numbers?" *China Economic Quarterly,* 18(1), 43–50.

Hong Kong Monetary Authority, (2010), "Press Releases: Signing of Memorandum of Co-operation on Renminbi Business." Available at: http://www.hkma.gov.hk/eng/key-information/press-releases/2010/20100719-4.shtml.

Hong Kong Monetary Authority, (2015), "Hong Kong: The Premier Offshore Renminbi Business Centre."

Hong Kong Monetary Authority, (2016), "Hong Kong: The Global Offshore Renminbi Business Hub." Available at: http://www.hkma.gov.hk/eng/key-functions/international-financial-centre/renminbi-business-hong-kong.shtml

Hsu, Chen-Min and Wan-Chun Liu, (2004), "The Role of Taiwanese Foreign Direct Investment in China: Economic Integration or Hollowing-Out?" *The Journal of the Korean Economy,* 5, 207–231.

Hu, Albert Guangzhou and Robert F. Owen, (2005), "Gravitation at Home and Abroad: Regional Distribution of FDI in China." Manuscript, National University of Singapore.

Hu, Chuntian and Zhijun Chen, (2010), "Renminbi Already Overappreciated: Evidence from FEERs (1994–2008)." *China Economist,* 26, 64–78.

Hu, Fred, (2008), "The Role of the RMB in the World Economy." *Cato Journal,* 28, 219–224.

Hu, Fred, Jonathan Anderson, Dick Li, Rita Ng, Enoch Fung, (2002), "Myth 2: 'New Industrial China' Is Hollowing Out Manufacturing and Stifling Growth in the Rest of the World." Goldman Sachs Economic Research. Hong Kong: The Goldman Sachs, Group, Inc.

Huang, Haizhou and Shuilin Wang, (2004), "Exchange Rate Regimes: China's Experience and Choices." *China Economic Review,* 15, 336–342.

Huang, Jing and Andrew Billo, (2015), *Territorial Disputes in the South China Sea: Navigating Rough Waters,* Palgrave Macmillian.

Huang, Yiping and Bijun Wang, (2011), "Chinese Outward Direct Investment: Is There a China Model?" *China & World Economy,* 19(4), 1–21.

Hufbauer, Gary C. and Claire Brunel, (2008), "The US Congress and the Chinese Renminbi," in Morris Goldstein and Nicholas R. Lardy (eds.), *Debating China's Exchange Rate Policy,* Washington: Peterson Institute for International Economics.

Iikka Korhonen and Maria Ritola, (2011), "Renminbi Misaligned — Results from Meta-Regressions," in Yin-Wong Cheung and Guonan Ma (eds.), *Asia and China in the Global Economy,* World Scientific Publishing Company, Chapter 4, pp. 97–122.

International Comparison Program, (2004), *The ICP 2004 Handbook*, The World Bank Group, Available at: http://worldbank.org.

International Comparison Program, (2007), "Preliminary Results: Frequently Asked Questions." Mimeo. Available at: http://siteresources.worldbank.org/ICPINT/Resources/backgrounder-FAQ.pdf

International Monetary Fund, (2009), *Balance of Payments and International Investment Position Manual*, 6th ed.

International Monetary Fund, (2010a), "Reserve Accumulation and International Monetary Stability: Supplementary Information." International Monetary Fund, Strategy, Policy and Review Department. Available at: http://www.imf.org/external/np/pp/eng/2010/041310a.pdf

International Monetary Fund, (2010b), "IMF Determines New Currency Weights for SDR Valuation Basket." Press Release No. 10/434. Available at: http://www.imf.org/external/np/sec/pr/2010/pr10434.htm

International Monetary Fund, (2010c), "Review of the Method of Valuation of the SDR." October 26.

International Monetary Fund, (2013), "Outcome of the Quota Formula Review — Report of the Executive Board to the Board of Governors." Available at: http://www.imf.org/external/np/pp/eng/2013/013013.pdf.

International Monetary Fund, (2014), "World Economic Outlook: Legacies, Clouds, Uncertainties."

International Monetary Fund, (2015), "Factsheet: Special Drawing Rights (SDRs)." Available at: http://www.imf.org/external/np/exr/facts/sdr.htm

International Monetary Fund, (2016), Global Financial Stability Report, April 2016, International Monetary Fund: Washington.

International Monetary Fund Communications Department, (2015), "IMF Staff Completes the 2015 Article IV Consultation Mission to China." Press Release No. 15/237. Available at: http://www.imf.org/external/np/sec/pr/2015/pr15237.htm.

Ito, Takatoshi, Satoshi Koibuchi, Kiyotaka Sato and Junko Shimizu, (2010), "Why Has the Yen Failed to Become a Dominant Invoicing Currency in Asia? A Firm-Level Analysis of Japanese Exporters' Invoicing Behavior." *NBER Working Paper*, No. 16231.

Jian, Tianlun, Jeffrey D. Sachs and Andrew M. Warner, (1996), "Trends in Regional Inequality in China." *China Economic Review*, 7(1), 1–21.

Johnson, Simon, William Larson, Chris Papageorgiou and Arvind Subramanian, (2009), "Is Newer Better? The Penn World Table Revisions and the Cross-Country Growth Literature." *NBER Working Paper* No. 15455.

Jones, Derek C., Cheng Li and Ann L. Owen, (2003), "Growth and Regional Inequality in China during the Reform Era." *China Economic Review*, 14(2), 186–200.

Kar, Dev and Sarah Freitas, (2012), "Illicit Financial Flows from China and the Role of Trade Misinvoicing, Global Financial Integrity." Washington, D.C.

Kenen, Peter, B., (1983), "The Role of the Dollar as an International Currency." *Occasional Papers* No. 13, Group of Thirty, New York.

Klein, Lawrence and Suleyman Ozmucur, (2003), "The Estimation of China's Economic Growth Rate." Manuscript, University of Pennsylvania.

Koch-Weser and Iacob N., (2013), "The Reliability of China's Economic Data: An Analysis of National Output." U.S.-China Economic and Security Review Commission Staff Research Project.

Kolstad, Ivar and Arne Wiig, (2012), "What Determines Chinese Outward FDI?" *Journal of World Business*, 47(1), 26–34.

Kravis, Irving B., Alan Heston and Robert Summers, (1978), *International Comparisons of Real Product and Purchasing Power*, Baltimore, The Johns Hopkins University Press.

Kravis, Irving B. and Lipsey, Robert E., (1983), "Toward an Explanation of National Price Levels." *Princeton Studies in International Finance* No. 52, International Finance Centre, Princeton University.

Kravis, Irving B. and Lipsey, Robert E., (1987), "The Assessment of National Price Levels," in Sven W. Arndt and J. David Richardson (eds.), *Real Financial Linkages among Open Economies*, Cambridge, MA: MIT Press, pp. 97–134.

Krongkaew, Medhi, (1999), "Capital Flows and Economic Crisis in Thailand." *The Developing Economies*, 37, 395–416.

Krugman, Paul, (1984), "The International Role of the Dollar: Theory and Prospect," in John Bilson and Richard Marston (eds.), *Exchange Rate Theory and Practice*, University of Chicago Press, Chapter 8, pp. 261–278.

Kwack, Sung Yeung, Choong Y. Ahn, Young S. Lee and Doo Y. Yang, (2007), "Consistent Estimates of World Trade Elasticities and an Application to the Effects of Chinese Yuan (RMB) Appreciation." *Journal of Asian Economics*, 18, 314–330.

Lane, Philip R. and Dominic Burke, (2001), "The Empirics of Foreign International Reserves." *Open Economies Review*, 12, 423–434.

Lee, Jong-Wha, (2014), "Will the Renminbi Emerge as an International Reserve Currency?" *The World Economy*, 37(1), 42–62, (January).

Leigh, Daniel (team lead), Weicheng Lian, Marcos Poplawski-Ribeiro and Viktor Tsyrennikov, (2015), "Exchange Rates and Trade Flows: Disconnected?" *World Economic Outlook*, International Monetary Fund, Chapter 3. Available at: http://www.imf.org/external/pubs/ft/weo/2015/02/pdf/c3.pdf

Li, Cui, Shu Chang and Jian Chang, (2009), "Exchange Rate Pass-Through and Currency Involving in Exports," *HKMA China Economic Issues*, No. 2/09.

Li, Shi, Hiroshi Sato and Terry Sicular, (2013), *Rising Inequality in China: Challenges to a Harmonious Society*, Cambridge University Press.

Liao, Steven and Daniel McDowell, (2014), "Redback Rising: China's Bilateral Swap Agreements and Renminbi Internationalization." *International Studies Quarterly*, 59, 401–422.

Liew, Leong H. and Harry X. Wu, (2007). *The Making of China's Exchange Rate Policy*, Cheltenham: Edward Elgar Publishing Limited.

Lin, Guijuna and Ronald M. Schramm, (2003), "China's Foreign Exchange Policies since 1979: A Review of Developments and an Assessment." *China Economic Review*, 14, 246–280.

Lin, Zhitao, Wenjie Zhan and Yin-Wong Cheung, (2016), "China's Bilateral Currency Swap Lines." *China & World Economy*, 24, 1–24.

Liu, Xiaming, Chengang Wang and Yingqi Wei, (2001), "Causal Links between Foreign Direct Investment and Trade in China." *China Economic Review*, 12, 190–202.

Ma, Guonan and Haiwen Zhou, (2009). "China's Evolving External Wealth and Rising Creditor Position." *BIS Working Papers*, No. 286.

Ma, Guonan and Robert N. McCauley, (2011), "The Implications of Renminbi Basket Management for Asian Currency Stability," in Y.-W. Cheung, V. Kakkar and G. Ma (eds.), *The Evolving Role of Asia in Global Finance*, Emerald Publishing, Chapter 5, pp. 97–121.

Ma, Guonan and Wang Yao, (2015), "Can The Chinese Bond Market Facilitate A Globalizing Renminbi?" *FGI Working Paper*, Fung Global Institute.

Maddison, Angus, (1998), "Chinese Economic Performance in the Long Run." Paris: Organization for Economic Cooperation and Development.

Mann, Catherine and Katerina Plück, (2007), "The US Trade Deficit: A Disaggregated Perspective," in Richard Clarida (ed.), *G7 Current Account Imbalances: Sustainability and Adjustment*, University of Chicago Press.

Marquez, Jaime and John W. Schindler, (2007), "Exchange-Rate Effects on China's Trade." *Review of International Economics*, 15(5), 837–853.

Maziad, Samar and Joong Shik Kang, (2012), "RMB Internationalization: Onshore/Offshore Links." *IMF Working Paper* No. WP/12/133.

McCauley, Robert N., (2010), "Managing Recent Hot Money Inflows in Asia," in M. Kawai and M. Lamberte (eds.), *Managing Capital Flows in Asia: Search for a Framework*, Edward Elgar Publishing Ltd.

McCauley, Robert N., (2011), "Renminbi Internationalization and China's Financial Development Model." *CGS/IIGG Working Paper*.

McCauley, Robert and Patrick McGuire, (2009): "Dollar Appreciation in 2008: Safe Haven, Carry Trades, Dollar Shortage and Overhedging." *BIS Quarterly Review* (December), 85–93.

McGuire, Patrick and Goetz von Peter, (2009). "The US Dollar Shortage in Global Banking." *BIS Quarterly Review*, March, 47–63.

McMahon, Dinny, (2010), "China's Call for More Clout." *Wall Street Journal*, p. C.20.

Medina, Leandro, Jordi Prat and Alun Thomas, (2010), "Current Account Balance Estimates for Emerging Market Economies." *IMF Working Paper* No. 10/43.

Meese, Richard and Kenneth Rogoff, (1983a), "Empirical Exchange Rate Models of the Seventies: Do They Fit Out of Sample?" *Journal of International Economics*, 14, 3–24.

Meese, Richard A. and Kenneth S. Rogoff, (1983b), "The Out-of-Sample Failure of Empirical Exchange Rate Models: Sampling Error or Misspecification?" in Jacob A. Frenkel (ed.), *Exchange Rates and International Macroeconomics*, Chicago and London: University of Chicago Press, pp. 67–112.

Mercereau, Benoît, (2005), "FDI Flows to Asia: Did the Dragon Crowd Out the Tigers?" *IMF Working Paper* No. #WP/05/18.

Merson, John, (1990), *The Genius That Was China: East and West in the Making of the Modern World*, Overlook Press.

Milanovic, Branko, (2009), "Global Inequality Recalculated: The Effect of New 2005 PPP Estimates on Global Inequality." *World Bank Policy Research Working Paper* No. 5061.

Ministry of Finance, Japan, (2003), "Study Group for the Promotion of the Internationalization of the Yen." *Chairperson's Report*. Available at: http://www.mof.go.jp/english/international_policy/others/e20030123/e20030123g.htm

Miyashita, Tadeo, (1966), *The Currency and Financial System of Mainland China*, University of Washington Press.

Molodtsova, Tanya and David H. Papell, (2009), "Out-of-Sample Exchange Rate Predictability with Taylor Rule Fundamentals." *Journal of International Economics*, 77(2), 167–180.

Morck, Randall, Bernard Yeung and Minyuan Zhao, (2008), "Perspectives on China's Outward Foreign Direct investment", *Journal of International Business Studies*, 39(3), 337–350.

Mundell, Robert, (1993), "EMU and the International Monetary System: A Transatlantic Perspective." *Austrian National Bank Working Paper 13 (Vienna)*.

National Committee on US–China Relations and Rhodium Group, (2015), "New Neighbors: Chinese Investment in the United States by Congressional District." National Committee on US–China Relations and Rhodium Group.

Needham, Joseph, (2004), *1954 to 2004, Science and Civilisation in China,* Vols. 1 to 7, Cambridge University Press.

OECD, (2003), "Investment Policy Review of China: Progress and Reform Challenge." Paris: Organization for Economic Cooperation and Development.

OECD, (2005), "OECD Economic Surveys — China 2005." Paris: Organization for Economic Cooperation and Development.

OECD, (2010), "OECD Economic Surveys — China 2010." Paris: Organization for Economic Cooperation and Development.

OECD, (2013), "OECD Economic Surveys — China 2013." Paris: Organization for Economic Cooperation and Development.

OECD, (2015), "OECD Economic Surveys — China 2015." Paris: Organization for Economic Cooperation and Development.

Osugi, Kazuhito, (1990), "Japan's Experience of Financial Deregulation Since 1984 in an International Perspective." *BIS Economic Papers* No. 26.

People's Bank of China, (2014), "China Monetary Policy Report Quarter Two, 2014." People's Bank of China.

People's Bank of China, (2015), "Report on Renminbi Internationalization — 2015" (renminbi guojihua baogao-2015). Available at: http://upload.xh08.cn/2015/0611/1434018340443.pdf.

People's Bank of China, the Ministry of Finance, the National Development and Reform Commission, and the China Securities Regulatory Commission (2010), 公告 2010 第 10 号 《国际开发机构人民币债券发行管理暂行办法》. Available at: http://www.mof.gov.cn/mofhome/jinrongsi/zhengwuxinxi/zhengce-fabu/201009/t20100930_341568.html.

People's Bank of China (2013), "China Monetary Policy Report Quarter Four, 2013." People's Bank of China.

People's Bank of China and the International Monetary Fund, (2009), "Note Purchase Agreement between the People's Bank of China and the International Monetary Fund." Available at: http://www.imf.org/external/np/pp/eng/2009/090209.pdf

Pethokoukis, James, (2014), "Sorry, China, the US is Still the World's Leading Economic Power." *AEIdeas.* Available at: http://www.aei.org/publication/sorry-china-the-us-is-still-the-worlds-leading-economic-power/

Ponomareva, Natalia and Hajime Katayama, (2010), "Does the Version of the Penn World Tables Matter? An Analysis of the Relationship between Growth and Volatility." *Canadian Journal of Economics,* 43, 152–179.

Prasad, Eswar, (2014), *The Dollar Trap: How the US Dollar Tightened its Grip on Global Finance,* Princeton University Press.

Prasad, Eswar and Shang-Jin Wei, (2007), "China's Approach to Capital Inflows: Patterns and Possible Explanations," in Sebastian Edwards (ed.), *Capital*

Controls and Capital Flows in Emerging Economies: Policies, Practices and
Consequences, Chicago IL: University of Chicago Press, pp. 421–480.

Prasad, Eswar and Lei (Sandy) Ye, (2012), "The Renminbi's Role in the Global
Monetary System." Brooking Institute.

Prasad, Eswar and Lei (Sandy) Ye, (2013), "The Renminbi's Prospects as a Global
Reserve Currency." *Cato Journal*, 33(3), 563–570.

Pritchard, Simon, (2001), "Responses to the Recession." *South China Morning Post*.

Pula, Gabor and Daniel Santabárbara, (2011), "Is China Climbing Up the Quality
Ladder? — Estimating Cross Country Differences in Product Quality Using
Eurostat's Comext Trade Database." *European Central Bank Working Paper
Series* No. 1310.

PwC and the China Development Research Foundation, (2013), "Choosing
China: Improving the Investment Environment for Multinationals, 2013."
China Development Forum Survey Report.

Qian, Xingwang, (2013), "China's Outward Direct Investment and Its Oil Quest."
in Y.W. Cheung and J. de Haan (eds.), *The Evolving Role of China in the World
Economy*, MIT Press, pp. 375–417.

Ramasamy, Bala, Matthew Yeung and Sylvie Laforet, (2012), "China's Outward
Foreign Direct Investment: Location Choice and Firm Ownership." *Journal of
World Business*, 47(1), 17–25.

Rawski, Thomas, (2001), "What Is Happening to China's GDP Statistics?" *China
Economic Review*, 12(4), 347–354.

Rawski, Thomas, (2002), "Measuring China's Recent GDP Growth: Where Do We
Stand?" Manuscript, University of Pittsburgh.

Reinhart, Carmen M. and Kenneth S. Rogoff, (2004), "The Modern History of
Exchange Rate Arrangements: A Reinterpretation." *The Quarterly Journal of
Economics*, 119(1), 1–48.

Ren, Xiao (任晓) (2014), "央行 副行长: 人民币已成为第七大储备货币."
Available at: http://finance.ce.cn/rolling/201410/21/t20141021_3742517.shtml

Rogoff, Kenneth S., (1996), "The Purchasing Power Parity Puzzle." *Journal of
Economic Literature*, 34(2), 647–668.

Rogoff, Kenneth S. and Vania Stavrakeva, (2008), "The Continuing Puzzle of
Short Horizon Exchange Rate Forecasting." *NBER Working Papers* No. 14071,
National Bureau of Economic Research, Inc.

Rosen, Daniel, (1999), *Behind the Open Door: Foreign Enterprises in the Chinese
Marketplace*, Institute for International Economics.

Ross, Andrew S., (2013), "SF Seeks to be Hub for Chinese Currency." Available at:
http://www.sfgate.com/business/bottomline/article/SF-seeks-to-be-hub-for-
Chinese-currency-4284909.php.

Rossi, Barbara, (2013), "Exchange Rate Predictability." *Journal of Economic Literature*, 51(4), 1063–1119.

Ruoen, Ren and Chen Kai, (1995), "China's GDP in U.S. Dollars Based on Purchasing Power Parity." *Policy Research Working Paper* No. 1415, Washington, D.C.: World Bank.

Sakakibara, Eisuke and Sharon Yamakawa, (2003a), "Regional Integration in East Asia: Challenges and Opportunities, Part I: History and Institutions." *World Bank Policy Research Working Paper Series* No. 3078.

Sakakibara, Eisuke and Sharon Yamakawa, (2003b), "Regional Integration in East Asia: Challenges and Opportunities, Part II: Trade Finance and Integration." *World Bank Policy Research Working Paper Series* No. 3079.

Samuelson, Paul, (1964), "Theoretical Notes on Trade Problems." *Review of Economics and Statistics*, 46(2), 145–154.

Samuelson, Paul, (1994), "Facets of Balassa-Samuelson Thirty Years Later." *Review of International Economics*, 2(3), 201–226.

Sauvant, Karl P., (2011), "China: Inward and Outward Foreign Direct Investment." *Transnational Corporations Review*, 3(1), 1–4.

Schenk, Catherine R., (2009), "The Retirement of Sterling as a Reserve Currency after 1945: Lessons for the US Dollar?" Manuscript, University of Glasgow.

Schnatz, Bernd, (2011), "Global Imbalances and the Pretence of Knowing FEERs." *Pacific Economic Review*, 16, 604–615.

Sethi, Deepak, William Q. Judge and Qian Sun, (2011), "FDI Distribution within China: An Integrative Conceptual Framework for Analyzing Intra-Country FDI Variations." *Asia Pacific Journal of Management*, 28(2), 325–352.

Shi, Lei 石雷, (1998), Renminbi shi hua (人民币史话), Beijing: Zhongguo Jinroung Chubanshe (北京:中国金融出版社).

Sicular, Terry, (2013), "The Challenge of High Inequality in China." Inequality in Focus, World Bank, Vol. 2, No. 2, August. Available at: http://www.worldbank. org/content/dam/Worldbank/document/Poverty%20documents/Inequality-In-Focus-0813.pdf

Smith, Roy C., (2015), "Is China the Next Japan?" Manuscript, NYU Stern School of Business.

State Administration of Foreign Exchange, (2008), "2007 年中国国际收支报告" (China Annual Balance of Payments Report 2007).

State Administration of Foreign Exchange, (2003a), "Exchange Regulation for Border Trade" (bianjing maoyi waihui guanli banfa) [online; cited January 2016]. Available at: http://www.safe.gov.cn/wps/wcm/connect/f198a680481bf 83cb843bc70e36bc97c/%E8%BE%B9%E5%A2%83%E8%B4%B8%E6%98

%93%E5%A4%96%E6%B1%87%E7%AE%A1%E7%90%86%E5%8A%9E
%E6%B3%95.doc?MOD=AJPERES&CACHEID=f198a680481bf83cb843bc7
0e36bc97c.

State Administration of Foreign Exchange, (2003b), "Notice for Issues Relating to Domestic Institutions Using RMB as Denominated Currency in Foreign Trade" (guanyu jingneijigou duiwaimaoyi zhong yi renminbi zuowei jijia-huobi youguanwenti de tongzhi) [online; cited January 2016]. Available from: http://www.safe.gov.cn/wps/portal/!ut/p/c4/04_SB8K8xLLM9MSSzPy8xBz9CP0os3gPZxdnX293QwMLE09nA09Pr0BXLy8PQyNPI_2CbEdFAKLWUno!/?WCM_GLOBAL_CONTEXT=/wps/wcm/connect/safe_web_store/safe_web/zcfg/jcxmwhgl/jcxmzh/node_zcfg_jcxm_jcxmzh_store/8a4333004
81c779a984ad884909d05cd.

Stier, Olaf, Kerstin Bernoth, Alexander Fisher, (2010), "Internationalization of the Chinese Renminbi: An Opportunity for China." *Weekly Report* No. 17/2010, German Institute for Economic Research.

Stokes, Bruce, (2015), "How Asia-Pacific Publics See Each Other and Their National Leaders." Pew Research Center.

Stupnytska, Anna, Thomas Stolper and Malachy Meechan, (2009), "GSDEER On Track: Our Improved FX Fair Value Model." *Global Economics Weekly*, No. 09/38, Goldman Sachs Global Economics, October 28.

Subramanian, Arvind, (2010), "New PPP-Based Estimates of Renminbi Undervaluation and Policy Implications." *Policy Brief* PB10-18, Washington, D.C.: Peterson Institute for International Economics, April.

Subramanian, Arvind, (2011a), "Renminbi Rules: The Conditional Imminence of the Reserve Currency Transition." *Peterson Institute for International Economics Working Paper*, No. 11–14.

Subramanian, Arvind, (2011b), "Eclipse: Living in the Shadow of China's Economic Dominance." Institute of International Economics.

Summers, Robert and Alan Heston, (1991), "The Penn World Table (Mark5): An Expanded Set of International Comparisons." *Quarterly Journal of Economics*, 106(2), 327–368.

Sun, Jie, (2010), "Retrospect of the Chinese Exchange Rate Regime after Reform: Stylized Facts during the Period from 2005 to 2010." *China & World Economy*, 18(6), 19–35.

Sun, Celine, (2013), "Conference System to Link up China's Financial Watchdogs." Available at: http://www.scmp.com/business/banking-finance/article/1297999/china-create-agency-align-financial-supervision.

Sung, Yun-Wing, (1996), "Chinese Outward Investment in Hong Kong: Trends, Prospects and Policy Implications." *OECD Development Centre, Technical Papers* No. 113.

Sung, Yun-Wing, (1997), "Hong Kong and the Economic Integration of the China Circle," in Barry Naughton (ed.), *The China Circle: Economics and Electronics in the PRC, Taiwan, & Hong Kong*, Brookings Institution Press.

SWIFT, (2011), "Efficiency for Offshore Chinese Yuan (RMB) Settlement." Available at: http://www.swift.com/news/standards/chinese_Yuan_projects

SWIFT, (2012), "RMB Tracker — January 2012." SWIFT.

SWIFT, (2013), "RMB Tracker — April 2013." SWIFT.

SWIFT, (2015a), "RMB Tracker — January 2015." SWIFT.

SWIFT, (2015b), "Renminbi's Stellar Ascension: Are You on Top of It, RMB Tracker." Sibos 2015 edition, SWIFT.

Takagi, Shinji, (2011), "Internationalizing the Yen, 1984–2003: Unfinished Agenda or Mission Impossible?" in Yin-Wong Cheung and Gounan Ma (eds.), *Asia and China in the Global Economy*, The World Scientific Publishing Co. Pte. Ltd., Chapter 8, pp. 219–244.

Taylor, Alan M. and Mark P. Taylor, (2004), "The Purchasing Power Parity Debate." *Journal of Economic Perspectives*, 18(4), 135–158.

Tenengauzer, Daniel, (2010), "RMB: the People's Currency." EM FX and Debt Spotlight Bank of America, Merrill Lynch.

Tham, Engen and Benjamin K. Lim, (2015), "Exclusive: After Market Crash, China Mulls Single 'Super-Regulator' — Sources." Available at: http://www.reuters.com/article/us-china-regulators-idUSKCN0T60XH20151117

The Asian Development Bank, (2014), "ADB's Support for Inclusive Growth." Available at: http://www.adb.org/sites/default/files/evaluation-document/36217/files/tes-ig.pdf

The Economist, (2014), "Catching the Eagle." August 22, 2014. Available at: http://www.economist.com/blogs/graphicdetail/2014/08/chinese-and-american-gdp-forecasts

The Economist, (2015a), "Chinese Investment in Developed Markets: An Opportunity for Both Sides?" The Economist Intelligence Unit Limited.

The Economist, (2015b), "Whether to Believe China's GDP Figures." Available at: http://www.economist.com/blogs/freeexchange/2015/07/chinese-economy

The Economist, (2016), "The Big Mac Index." January 7, 2016. Available at: http://www.economist.com/content/big-mac-index/

The State Council, (1981), Circular of the State Council for Approving and Transmitting the Report Submitted by the State Planning Commission, the State Import and Export Commission and Other Departments on Improving Administration of Foreign Exchange Certificates. Available at: http://www.asianlii.org/cn/legis/cen/laws/cotscfaattrsbtspctsiaecaodoiaofec2249/.

Thorbecke, Willem, (2006), "How Would an Appreciation of the Renminbi Affect the US Trade Deficit with China?" *BE Press Macro Journal*, 6(3), Article 3.

Thorbecke, Willem, (2013), "Updated Estimates of the People's Republic of China's Export Elasticities: Using Panel Data and Integrated Exchange Rates." Manuscript, Research Institute of Economy, Trade and Industry.

Thorbecke, Willem, (2014), "China–US Trade: A Global Outlier." Manuscript, Research Institute of Economy, Trade and Industry.

Thorbecke, Willem and H. Zhang, (2009), "The Effect of Exchange Rate Changes on China's Labour-Intensive Manufacturing Exports." *Pacific Economic Review,* 14(3), 398–409.

Thorbecke, Willem and Gordon Smith, (2010), "How Would an Appreciation of the RMB and Other East Asian Currencies Affect China's Exports?" *Review of International Economics,* 18(1), 95–108.

Triffin, Robert, (1960), *Gold and the Dollar Crisis: The Future of Convertibility,* New Haven: Yale University Press.

Tseng, Wanda and Harm Zebregs, (2002), "Foreign Direct Investment in China: Some Lessons for Other Countries." *IMF Policy Discussion Paper* No. 02/03.

UNCTAD, (2003), "China: An Emerging FDI Outward Investor." *E-Brief,* Newyork and Gneva: United Nations.

UNCTAD, (2004), "Prospects for Foreign Direct Investment and the Strategies of Transnational Corporations, 2004–2007, The Global Investment Prospects Assessment (GIPA)," Newyork and Gneva: United Nations.

UNCTAD, (2005), "Prospects for Foreign Direct Investment and the Strategies of Transnational Corporations, 2005–2008 — The Global Investment Prospects Assessment (GIPA)," Newyork and Gneva: United Nations.

UNCTAD, (2007), "Asian Foreign Direct Investment in Africa: Towards a New Era of Cooperation among Developing Countries," Newyork and Gneva: United Nations.

UNCTAD, (2010a), "World Investment Prospects Survey 2010–2012," Newyork and Gneva: United Nations.

UNCTAD, (2010b), "Economic Development for Africa Report 2010: South–South Cooperation: Africa and the New Partnership for Development," United Nations.

UNCTAD, (2011), "World Investment Report," Newyork and Gneva: United Nations.

UNCTAD, (2012a), "World Investment Prospects Survey 2012–2014," Newyork and Gneva: United Nations.

UNCTAD, (2012b), "World Investment Report," Newyork and Gneva: United Nations.

UNCTAD, (2013a), "World Investment Prospects Survey 2013–2015," Newyork and Gneva: United Nations.

UNCTAD, (2013b), "World Investment Report," Newyork and Gneva: United Nations.

UNCTAD, (2014), "World Investment Report," Newyork and Gneva: United Nations.

UNCTAD, (2015), "World Investment Report," Newyork and Gneva: United Nations.

United Nations Economic and Social Commission for Asia and the Pacific, (2003), "Facts about the Bangkok Agreement." Available at: http://www.unescap.org/apta.

Wall, David, (1997), "Outflow of Capital from China." *Technical Papers* No. 123, OECD Development Centre.

Wang, Bijun, Rui Mao and Qin Gou, (2014), "Overseas Impacts of China's Outward Direct Investment." *Asian Economic Policy Review,* 9(2), 227–249.

Wang, Jiao and Andy G. Ji, (2006), "Exchange Rate Sensitivity of China's Bilateral Trade Flows." *BOFIT Discussion Papers* No. 2006-19, Helsinki: Bank of Finland, December.

Wang, Tao and Harrison Hu, (2010), "How Undervalued Is the RMB?" *Asian Economic Perspectives,* UBS Investment Research.

Wang, Xiaolu and Lian Meng, (2001), "A Reevaluation of China's Economic Growth." *China Economic Review,* 12(4), 338–346.

Wildau, Gabriel, (2015), "Shanghai Free Trade Zone Loosens Curbs on Offshore Borrowing." Available at: http://www.ft.com/intl/cms/s/0/3bd2056a-b339-11e4-b0d2-00144feab7de.html#axzz449PcyYsQ

Williamson, John (ed.), (1994), *Estimating Equilibrium Exchange Rates,* Washington, D.C.: Peterson Institute Press.

Williamson, J. and M. Mahar, (1998), "Current Account Targets," S. Wren-Lewis and R. Driver (eds.), *Real Exchange Rates for the Year 2000,* Policy Analyses in International Economics No. 54, Institute for International Economics, Washington, D.C.

Wolfowitz, Paul, (2005), Remarks at the Launch of China's Inaugural Panda Bond Issue. Available at: http://web.worldbank.org/WBSITE/EXTERNAL/NEWS/0,,contentMDK:20687464~pagePK:34370~piPK:42770~theSitePK:4607,00.html

Wong, Helen, (2015), "China's Free Trade Zones Will Accelerate Reform." Available at: http://www.businessspectator.com.au/article/2015/4/2/china/chinas-free-trade-zones-will-accelerate-reform.

Wong, John and Sarah Chan, (2003), "China's Outward Direct Investment: Expanding Worldwide." *China: An International Journal,* 1–2, 273–301.

World Bank, (2008a), "Global Purchasing Power Parities and Real Expenditures:" *2005 International Comparison Program,* International Comparison Program and International Bank for Reconstruction and Development. Washington, D.C.

World Bank, (2008b), "Comparison of New 2005 PPPs with Previous Estimates." *Appendix G Revised: Global Purchasing Power Parities and Real Expenditures,* Washington, D.C.

World Bank, (2008c), *ICP 2003–2006 Handbook*. Available at: http://go.world-bank.org/MW520NNFK0.

World Bank, (2015), "Purchasing Power Parities and the Real Size of World Economies:" *A Comprehensive Report of the 2011 International Comparison Program,* Washington, D.C.: World Bank.

World Bank, (2016), *Live Long and Prosper: Aging in East Asia and Pacific,* Washington, D.C.: World Bank.

Wu, Friedrich and Leslie Tang, (2000), "China's Capital Flight, 1990–1999: Estimates and Implications." *Review of Pacific Basin Financial Markets and Policies,* 3, 59–75.

Wu, Hsiu-Ling and Chien-Hsun Chen, (2001), "An Assessment of Outward Foreign Direct Investment from China's Transitional Economy." *Europe-Asia Studies,* 53, 1235–1254.

Wu, Nianlu 吴念鲁 and Chen, Quangeng 陈全庚, 2002. Renminbi huilü yanjiu — xiudingben (人民币汇率研究 — 修订本). Beijing: Zhongguo Jinroung Chubanshe (北京: 中国金融出版社).

Xie, Yu and Xiang Zhou, (2014), "Income Inequality in Today's China." *Proceedings of the National Academy of Sciences of the United States of America,* 111(19), 6928–6933.

Xu, Xinpeng and Sheng Yu, (2012), "Are FDI Spillovers Regional? Firm-level Evidence from China." *Journal of Asian Economics,* 23(3), 244–258 (June).

Xu, Yingfeng, (2000), "China's Exchange Rate Policy." *China Economic Review,* 11, 262–277.

Yang, Hu, (2010), "IMF May Replace Yen with Yuan in SDR Basket: Report." Available at: http://www.chinadaily.com.cn/bizchina/2010-12/31/content_11783355.htm

Yang, Yanlin and Shuchang Xu, (2012), "Analysis of Industrial Trends in China's Overseas Direct Investment." *China: An International Journal,* 10(2), 105–118.

Yu, Yongding, (2012), "Revisiting the Internationalization of the Yuan." *ADBI Working Paper 366.*

Yu, Yongding and Haihong Gao, (2011), "Internationalisation of the Renminbi," in Yin-Wong Cheung and Guonan Ma (eds.), *Asia and China in the Global Economy,* World Scientific Publishing, Chapter 7, pp. 191–217.

Zhang, Kevin Honglin, (2005), "Why Does Do Much FDI from Hong Kong and Taiwan Go To Mainland China?" *China Economic Review,* 16, 293–307.

Zhou, Xiaochuan, (2009), "Reform the International Monetary System." People's Bank of China, Available at: http://www.bis.org/review/r090402c.pdf

Index

Printed in the United States
by Bookmasters

Printed in the United States
By Bookmasters